THE SOUTH AS A CONSCIOUS MINORITY

THE SOUTH
AS A
CONSCIOUS MINORITY
1789–1861

A STUDY IN POLITICAL THOUGHT

By

JESSE T. CARPENTER, Ph.D.

Assistant Professor of Political Science
New York University

GLOUCESTER, MASS.

PETER SMITH

1963

TO

MY MOTHER AND FATHER

PREFACE

THIS is a study in the political thought of the Old South as a conscious minority seeking protection in the American Union from the political power of a Northern majority during the years 1789-1861. Only after considerable research did the thesis evolve into its present chapter headings, representing the major sources of Southern reliance for political protection throughout the Ante-Bellum Period. Further study disclosed a marked coincidence between sources of Southern protection and definite chronological data, so that the present work undertakes to treat the chief phases of Southern political thought in the order of their historical sequence. It is this analysis of a minority philosophy traced through its successive epochs of development that represents the possible contribution of this volume to the field of American political theory.

This study was originally prepared as a doctoral dissertation at Harvard University. It has been awarded the first Mrs. Simon Baruch University Prize offered biennially by the United Daughters of the Confederacy.

The book has been read in manuscript by Professor B. F. Wright, Jr., of Harvard University, Professor W. K. Boyd of Duke University, Professor E. C. Smith of New York University, and Dr. Matthew Page Andrews of Baltimore, Maryland. To these men the author is indebted for many valuable suggestions, and he wishes to acknowledge a special indebtedness to his colleague Professor Smith, who, in addition to his suggestions as to content, has painstakingly and most generously coöperated in the editing of the manuscript and in the reading of the page-proof. For courtesy, patience, and assistance in locating materials, further acknowledgments are extended to the library staffs at the Harvard University Library, the Duke University Library, and the New York Public Library, especially at the last-named where most of the final work of verification has been done.

J. T. C.

New York University,
  September 16, 1930.

TABLE OF CONTENTS

CHAPTER I

CHAPTER II

THE SOUTH AS A SECTIONAL MINORITY

CHAPTER III

THE PRINCIPLE OF LOCAL SELF-GOVERNMENT

CHAPTER IV

THE PRINCIPLE OF THE CONCURRENT VOICE

CHAPTER V

THE PRINCIPLE OF CONSTITUTIONAL GUARANTEES

TABLE OF CONTENTS

CHAPTER VI

THE PRINCIPLE OF SOUTHERN INDEPENDENCE

CHAPTER VII

APPLICATIONS IN THE CONFEDERATE CONSTITUTION

THE SOUTH AS A CONSCIOUS
MINORITY

CHAPTER I

INTRODUCTION

THE last decade of government in continental Europe has successfully demonstrated that no problem is more pressing in governments of the people and by the people than the problem of minorities. If in a democracy political power resides in numbers, what rights, if any, has a minority to impose restraints upon the will of a numerical majority? And if such rights exist, how are they to be exercised and by what means are they to be enforced? The quest for an answer to these questions has led to a study of the Ante-bellum South; for the South of pre-Civil War days was itself a conscious minority struggling with the problem of political control by numerical majorities from the formation of the Constitution in 1787 to the stroke for independence in 1861.

Though the story of the Ante-bellum South has been told and retold a thousand times, yet in one respect at least the subject is still new: for no one has yet conceived of the Old South as a sectional minority consciously striving for seventy odd years to evolve an adequate philosophy of protection to its interests in the American Union. Here in the first great experiment in democracy is found the first thorough treatment of democracy's greatest problem: the relation of numerical majority rule to effective minority protection. To this problem as then and there developed in the minds and opinions of Southern men everywhere, this study is exclusively devoted.

As a premise to this study, it is deemed necessary to establish the existence of the Southern States as a common sec-

3

tion, united by economic and social bonds, which tended to develop a distinct Southern nationality, even from the earliest days of the Union. That the inhabitants of those states below the Mason and Dixon line always considered themselves a separate and distinct people cannot be denied by those who read their literature or seek to explain their actions. And it was this consciousness of unity — however justified — that obliterated state boundaries and consolidated a geographic section of the Union into a single people.

At the same time, this *united* people was a *minority* people, ever subjected in all branches of the national government to the potential control of those who lived north of the Mason and Dixon line. In every decade of the Union, the sectional distribution of population and of states consigned to the South a minority rôle in the central government. But here again, it was primarily the consciousness of a minority position, together with the presumed results attendant upon that position, that crystallized Southern opinion and led to the development of a minority philosophy. For it was assumed — and, indeed, often supported by facts which appear to be conclusive — that the South as the minority section was bearing an excessive portion of the burdens of the national government, while the North as the majority was receiving an equally disproportionate share of the benefits. In seeking protection against this sectional discrimination, the South evolved a political philosophy of effective minority control in government.

Needless to say, political philosophy does not develop deliberately according to preconceived plans. Certainly it was true that Southern political thought was a creature of circumstance, devised solely to meet the exigencies of practical situations and pressing conditions. Of no people may it more truthfully be said that, in their political thinking, they were groping in the dark for the way. "Glimmering as the light may be which directs our path," once wrote Thomas

4

Ritchie to the editors of the *Richmond Enquirer,* "we are prepared to tread it for ourselves." [1]

Yet the existence of a unified Southern minority consciously striving for so long a time towards a common goal, was most conducive to the discovery and exhaustion of all sources of protection upon which minorities in government might conceivably rely. In the seven decades of union that preceded the Civil War, there evolved in the South four major sources of minority protection which succeeded each other in general chronological order. The first source was that of the principle of local self-government, advanced and defended in the Union from the establishment of the government on April 30, 1789, to the enactment of the Missouri Compromise on March 6, 1820. The second was the principle of the concurrent voice, chiefly relied upon by the South during the middle decades — the twenties, the thirties, and the forties. The third source of protection was the principle of constitutional guarantees, in which the South placed its confidence from the admission of California into the Union on September 9, 1850, to the election of Abraham Lincoln to the presidency on November 6, 1860. And finally there came the principle of independence intensively advanced from the election of Lincoln until the outbreak of the Civil War on April 12, 1861. In the closing months of the Antebellum Period, Southern political philosophy found adequate opportunity of expression in the provisions of the Confederate Constitution drafted at Montgomery, Alabama.

Of course, epochs of political thought cannot be entirely confined within definite chronological dates; nor will all the people think alike on political issues even in the most homogeneous populations. There were numerous discrepancies — men who relied upon local self-government until the out-

[1] Letter of September 6, 1852, expressing the sentiments of the South in 1850 as quoted in a Washington paper. Reprinted in *Thomas Ritchie's Letter Containing Reminiscences of Henry Clay and the Compromise,* pamphlet, 12.

break of the Civil War, and others who preferred Southern independence from the formation of the Union. Some men were in advance of the general trend of Southern thought; others lagged behind; but there is still sufficient justification for a study in chronological order of these four major possibilities of minority protection advanced by the South during the Ante-bellum Period.

In advancing these Southern theories, the author makes no apologies for lengthy and numerous quotations. He has merely attempted to play the part of a compiler and organizer, helping those who then saw as through a glass darkly, to place their ideas in a form more readily available for anyone who may wish to understand the peculiar political theory of the Old South.

CHAPTER II

THE SOUTH AS A SECTIONAL MINORITY

BELOW the Mason and Dixon line lie the states of the American Union which are to-day collectively termed the *South*. But the peculiarities which gave those states a common name cannot accurately be confined to definite geographical boundaries; for sectional influences overlap each other, and regional boundary-lines become broad areas of vague characteristics impossible of accurate demarcation. So was it with the South. That there was a South, how there came to be a South, and why there continued to be a South throughout the Ante-bellum Period of the American Union, we shall undertake to establish; but the exact limitations of the term need not concern us here. The present Atlantic and Gulf States from the Potomac to the Mississippi — Virginia, the Carolinas, Georgia, Florida, Alabama, Mississippi, and Louisiana — were peculiarly *Southern* states; the states of Arkansas, Tennessee, and Texas were less so; and the present border states below the Mason and Dixon line — Maryland, West Virginia, Kentucky, and Missouri — were *Southern* least of all. In any event, delimitation is secondary to existence: first to be established is the premise that there existed among these Southern states peculiarities justifying a common sectional designation which implies something more than mere geographic affinity.

THE SOUTH AS A SECTION

The roots of Southern unity are grounded in the laws of nature; for soil, climate, and topography had created a South of agriculture as opposed to a North of manufacturing and

7

commerce even before the formation of the present Union. Indeed, outcroppings of sectional differences based upon occupations left their imprint upon the compromises of the Constitution itself, and upon the objections north and south to its ratification. In the Federal Convention of 1787, for example, Charles Pinckney of South Carolina repeatedly observed that there was a real distinction between the Northern and the Southern interests arising from the character of their means of livelihood; while his colleague Pierce Butler considered the interests of the Southern and of the Eastern states in this respect "to be as different as the interests of Russia and Turkey." [1] In the Virginia ratifying convention, Patrick Henry and John Tyler reiterated these distinctions in arguing for a rejection of the Constitution. "There is a striking difference, and great contrariety of interests, between the states," declared Henry. "They are naturally divided into carrying and productive states. This is an actual, existing distinction, which cannot be altered." And it was with a prophetic eye to the future that John Tyler expressed the conviction that "so long as climate will have effect on men, so long will the different climates of the United States render us different." [2]

In spite of all efforts to diversify the industry of the South,[3] these occupational distinctions continued unabated until the Civil War. In 1830, P. P. Barbour of Virginia explained before Congress that "the natural pursuits of the North, for example, are those of commerce and navigation; that of the South is agriculture" [4] — a distinction which A. B. Longstreet of Georgia, writing in 1837 to his friend

---

[1] Max Farrand, ed., *Records*, I, 510; II, 449.
[2] Jonathan Elliot, ed., *Debates*, (2 ed.) III, 328, 639. For a similar Northern viewpoint, see Alexander Hamilton, speech in the New York Convention, II, 235-236, 237.
[3] See particularly the efforts of the South-

ern Commercial Conventions in William W. Davis, "Ante-Bellum Southern Commercial Conventions," *Transactions* of the Alabama Historical Society, 1904, V, 153-202.
[4] Speech in the House, March 23, 1830. *Register of Debates in Congress*, 21 Cong., 1 sess., 651.

M. B. Lamar of Texas, found to be inevitable; for he asserted that the "North & N. West, must be a commercial, and manufacturing people," whereas the "South & S. West must be an agricultural people."[5] In 1850, Benjamin F. Perry reiterated before the South Carolina Legislature the sentiment that the South had remained a land of farmers and planters; the North, a land of manufacturers and traders.[6]

The system of slave-labor strengthened this occupational distinction between the two sections. This difference, too, was as old as the Union; for, while twelve of the thirteen original states still sanctioned slavery within their borders, James Madison was proclaiming in the Federal Convention that the great division of interest in the United States lay not between the large and small states but between the Northern and Southern states — a difference arising "principally from the effects of their having or not having slaves."[7] Though continental in scope, slavery was at that time local in concentration, so that the final disestablishment of slavery north of the Mason and Dixon line by 1804 marks a date of minor significance in the development of Southern sectionalism.

As time advanced, this slave-labor system employed in the large-scale production of agricultural staples increasingly became the source of Southern economic prosperity. "It is, in

[5] C. A. Gulick, Jr., ed., *Papers of Mirabeau Buonaparte Lamar,* II, 2.
[6] *Speech of Hon. B. F. Perry . . . ,* pamphlet, 13. For further references to this occupational distinction, see Robert J. Turnbull, *The Crisis,* no. 23, p. 112; J. F. Jameson, ed., *Correspondence of Calhoun,* American Historical Association, *Annual Report,* 1899, II, 1134; J. W. DuBose, *Life and Times of Yancey,* 301; and "Cecil" [Sidney G. Fisher], *Kansas and the Constitution,* pamphlet, 3.
In 1860, the South had only 16.2% of the capital employed in manufacturing, engaged only 13.9% of the persons so employed, and

produced only 15% of the manufacturing output of the country. R. P. Brooks, "Industrialization of the South," in University of Georgia, School of Commerce, *Bureau of Business Research, Study no. 1,* April, 1929, p. 8.
[7] Remarks on June 30. *Documents Illustrative of the Formation of the Union,* 310. "In the Northern States," asserted Edmund Rutledge before the South Carolina Convention in 1788, "the labor is performed by white people, in the Southern by black." Jonathan Elliott, ed., *Debates,* (2 ed.) IV, 277. See also his statement in the Federal Convention, *Ibid.,* V, 457.

truth, the slave labor in Virginia," wrote Thomas R. Dew in the early thirties, "which gives value to her soil and her habitations; take away this, and you pull down the Atlas that upholds the whole system." [8] And from the newer South of the Mississippi basin into which slaves were pouring in never-ending streams throughout the decades of the forties and fifties, there came a similar note from a great plantation owner. "Ours presents a new problem," said Jefferson Davis in the United States Senate, February 8, 1858, ". . . it is the problem of a semi-tropical climate, the problem of malarial districts, of staple products. . . . A race suited to our labor exists there." [9]

To defend slave-labor was to defend not only the prosperity of the Southern slave-owner, but also the prosperity of the independent farmer as well. Writing on "The Interest in Slavery of the Southern Non-Slaveholder" in 1860, J. D. B. DeBow, long editor of *DeBow's Review,* thus stated the case: *"The non-slaveholder knows that as soon as his savings will admit, he can become a slaveholder, and thus relieve his wife from the necessities of the kitchen and the laundry, and his children from the labors of the field."* [10] It was this prospect of a more general ownership of slaves that superimposed one Southern sectional interest upon an-

[8] William Harper, *Pro Slavery Arguments,* 358. "I said the [Southern] States would never have entered into the Confederation, unless their property had been guarantied to them, for such is the state of agriculture in that country, that without slaves it must be abandoned." William L. Smith of South Carolina, speech in the House, February 12, 1790. *Annals of Congress,* 1 Cong., 2 sess., 1202. Slavery, so Wilson of Perquimons County contended in the North Carolina Convention of 1835, is a great blessing in the South: "Our system of Agriculture could not be carried on, in the Southern States, without it—might as well attempt to build a railroad to the moon, as to cultivate our swamp lands without slaves." *Proceedings and Debates of the Convention of North Carolina, 1835,* 80.

[9] *Congressional Globe,* 35 Cong., 1 sess., 619. For further statements on the economic advantages of slavery, see the speeches of James S. Green in the House on April 4, 1850, of Alexander H. Stephens in the House on April 27, 1852, and of Thomas L. Clingman in the Senate on February 4, 1861. *Appendix to the Congressional Globe,* 31 Cong., 1 sess., 426, and 32 Cong., 1 sess., 463; *Congressional Globe,* 36 Cong., 2 sess., 723. Also William Harper, "Memoir on Slavery," *Pro Slavery Arguments,* 87; *Free Negroism,* pamphlet; and U. B. Phillips, "Economic Views of Slavery," *American Negro Slavery,* ch. 18.

[10] *The Interest in Slavery of the Southern Non-Slaveholder,* 1860. Association Tract no. 5, pamphlet, 9.

other, giving the South of slave-labor a common boundary with the South of agricultural occupation. And the reaction of these two interests upon each other served only to solidify the various elements of the Southern states into a common section.[11]

With the coming of the slave to fasten a peculiar agricultural labor-system upon the South, there came at the same time, unfortunately, a far more significant factor in the creation of a common South. For the slave was something more than an economic machine: he was a human being, endowed with all the faculties of other human beings, but "black" and "inferior." As such, living in a "superior" society of opposite color, he presented a social, political, and criminal menace, ever to be watched and always to be feared. William Cabell Rives, a Virginia delegate to the Peace Convention of 1861 called to prevent the impending war between the states, was not far wrong, when, in reflecting upon the historic slavery-issue between the sections, he said: "In fact, it is not a question of slavery at all. It is a question of race." [12]

The presumption of negro inferiority as a basis for this common racial menace was well-nigh universal in the South; but its most insistent champion, oddly enough, was one of the poorest physical specimens of white "superiority" ever to receive public recognition. Perhaps the ailing midget of Georgia, Alexander H. Stephens, was somewhat self-conscious when he limited his distinctions between the African and the Anglo-Saxon to those which were mental, moral, and social.[13] Representative of Stephens' general attitude are the following words from one of his speeches in Con-

[11] For interesting comments on this inter-action of agriculture with slave-labor, see the words of George Mason in the Federal Convention of 1787, Max Farrand, ed., *Records* II, 370; Sidney G. Fisher, *The Trial of the Constitution*, (1862), 177-182; J. E. Cairnes, *The Slave Power*, (1862) *passim.*

[12] L. E. Chittenden, *Proceedings of the [Peace] Conference*, 139.

[13] Speech in the House of Representatives, April 27, 1852. *Appendix to the Congressional Globe*, 32 Congress, 1 sess., 464.

gress: "The negro is inferior to the white man; nature has made him so; observation and history, from the remotest times, establish the fact; and all attempts to make the inferior equal to the superior is but an effort to reverse the decrees of the Creator. . . . The Ethiopian can no more change his nature or his skin than the leopard his spots. Do what you will, a negro is a negro, and he will remain a negro still." [14]

To many, the negro presented a menace to white supremacy in the affairs of government. By the middle of the thirties, the franchise had been denied to all negroes in the South; and, had the laws been otherwise, William Harper predicted that the negroes would have been "used by unprincipled politicians, of irregular ambition, for the advancement of their schemes," until, gaining control of the government and avenging themselves upon the white race, they would have established "universal anarchy, or kakistocracy, the government of the worst." [15] And that well-known address of 1849 from the Southern delegates in Congress to their constituents reveals the fear that the negro, as the fast political associate of the North, might be able to hold "the

---

[14] Speech in the House, June 28, 1856. *Appendix to the Congressional Globe*, 34 Cong., 1 sess., 728. "Of all the races of man, the negro race is the most inferior," declared R. B. Rhett in 1850. *Death and Funeral Services of John Caldwell Calhoun*, pamphlet, 151. See also the interesting mudsill doctrine of society as developed by ex-Governor James H. Hammond of South Carolina, in a speech before the Senate on March 4, 1858. *Congressional Globe*, 35 Cong., 1 sess., 962. The same idea was expressed by Robert Toombs of Georgia in an address at Tremont Temple, Boston, on January 24, 1856. A. H. Stephens, *War between the States*, Vol. I, Appendix G, 625. Compare Abraham Lincoln, speeches at Charleston, Illinois, September 18, 1858, and at Quincy, Illinois, October 13, 1858.

J. G. Nicolay and J. Hay, *Complete Works of Abraham Lincoln*, I, 369, 458.
[15] William Harper, *Pro Slavery Arguments*, 90, 91. "The white portion of the population of this country constitutes the proper depository of political power." Hugh McQueens in the North Carolina Convention of 1835. *Proceedings and Debates of the Convention of North Carolina, 1835*, 78. The debates of this convention are interesting, for North Carolina was the last state south of the Mason and Dixon line to deny free negroes the right to vote. The motion for prohibition was carried, 66-61. W. K. Boyd et. al., *History of North Carolina*, II, 162-163. See also the resolutions of Habersham County, Georgia, in 1860. A. D. Candler, ed., *Confederate Records of Georgia*, I, 120.

white race at the South in complete subjection." [16] Against this possibility, the Ante-bellum South drafted a number of "indispensable" amendments to the Federal Constitution, providing that "the elective franchise and the right to hold office, whether Federal, State, territorial, or municipal, shall not be exercised by persons who are, in whole or in part, of the African race." [17]

More to be feared was the torch of crime as wielded in the hands of a Nat Turner or a John Brown.[18] The tragic escapades of these two fanatics had sent men hurrying to the records of the past, only to discover that criminal instincts were common to the entire negro race. Thus, Robert Toombs of Georgia found that in the West Indies "revolutions, tumults and disorders have been the ordinary pastimes of the emancipated blacks"; while, in our own Northern states, the negro, he discovered, had cherished a career of freedom "most usually found recorded in criminal courts, jails, poor-houses, and penitentiaries." [19]

Robert J. Walker of Mississippi garnered from the census of 1840 the information that there are twenty-two times as many negroes "who are deaf and dumb, blind, idiots, and insane, paupers, and in prison" in the non-slaveholding states proportionate to the negro population as in the slaveholding

[16] R. K. Crallé ed., *Works of Calhoun*, VI, 310-311.
[17] This amendment was twice submitted to the peace conference in Washington as a substitute for the Crittenden Resolutions. L. E. Chittenden, *Proceedings of the [Peace] Conference*, 419, 423. For a similar amendment submitted by H. V. Johnson to the State Convention of Georgia on January 18, 1861, see the *Journal of the Georgia Convention of 1861*, 18.
[18] See the letter of Governor John Floyd of Virginia in reply to an inquiry from Governor Hamilton of South Carolina concerning the Nat Turner Insurrection (1831). C. H. Ambler, "Life of John Floyd," *John P. Branch Historical Papers*, June, 1918, V, nos. 1 and 2, 85-87.
[19] Address at Emory College, Georgia, July 20, 1853. U. B. Phillips, *Life of Toombs*, 158-160. For other analogies, see Thomas L. Clingman, speech in the House, January 22, 1850. *Congressional Globe*, 31 Cong., 1 sess., 200 *et seq.*; Jefferson Davis, speech in the Senate, February 14, 1850. *Appendix to the Congressional Globe*, 31 Cong., 1 sess., 154 *et seq.*; Edmund Ruffin, *The Political Economy of Slavery*, pamphlet, 17-18; *Free Negroism*, pamphlet, 7-24.

states;[20] Governor Giles of Virginia gleaned from the penitentiary records of his own state the evidence that crimes among the free blacks are more than three times as numerous as among the whites, and four and a half times more numerous than among the slaves.[21] Robert J. Turnbull and Josiah J. Evans, both of South Carolina, and Jefferson Davis of Mississippi were among others who found the free negro in the North "covering the records of the criminal courts, and filling the penitentiaries."[22]

The alarming feature of these disclosures lay in the large percentage of negroes in relation to the total population in the Southern states. For the peculiarly *Southern* problem of the negro was a problem of numbers — a factor most emphatically revealed in the following tables:[23]

SECTIONAL DISTRIBUTION OF THE NEGRO POPULATION BY DECADES

Year	Negroes in North	Negroes in South	Percentage of all Negroes in the U. S. in the South
1790	67,424	689,784	91.1
1800	83,701	914,309	91.6
1810	105,691	1,264,173	92.3
1820	118,415	1,642,816	93.2
1830	141,091	2,175,274	93.9
1840	171,857	2,688,736	94.0
1850	196,570	3,428,492	94.6
1860	226,216	4,201,298	94.9

[20] *Letter of Mr. Walker, of Mississippi, Relative to the Annexation of Texas,* pamphlet, 12.

[21] As quoted by Thomas R. Dew in William Harper, *Pro Slavery Arguments,* 434-435.

[22] The quotation is from Jefferson Davis, Speech in the Senate, July 12, 1848. *Appendix to the Congressional Globe,* 30 Cong., 1 sess., 913. Other references are to R. J. Turnbull, *The Crisis,* no. 27, p. 134; and Josiah J. Evans, speech in the Senate, June 23, 1856. *Appendix to the Congressional Globe,* 34 Cong., 1 sess., 704. See further, William Harper, "M'emoir on Slavery," *Pro Slavery Arguments,* 89-90; James S. Green, Speech in the House, April 4, 1850. *Appendix to the Congressional Globe,* 31 Cong., 1 sess., 426; and the Virginia Constitution of 1851, Art. 4,

sec., 19, 20. The most striking compilation of extracts, largely from pamphlet material, dealing with the criminal menace of the negro in the South is found in William Jay, *A Letter to the Right Rev. L. Silliman Ives,* pamphlet (3 ed.) (1848), especially pp. 7, 9. For a general treatment see the chapter on "Slave Crime" in U. B. Phillips, *American Negro Slavery,* 454-488; and also J. H. Russell, *The Free Negro in Virginia* (1619-1865).

[23] Bureau of the Census, *Negro population in the United States, 1790-1915.* Compiled from a table of population by states, negro and white, at each census, pp. 44-45. Delaware, Maryland, Kentucky, and Missouri are considered Southern; California, as Northern. Territories are included.

THE SOUTH AS A SECTIONAL MINORITY

PERCENTAGE OF TOTAL SECTIONAL POPULATION IN NEGROES

Year	Northern %	Southern %
1790	3.4	35.2
1800	3.1	35.1
1810	2.8	36.6
1820	2.3	36.9
1830	2.0	37.4
1840	1.8	36.9
1850	1.4	36.7
1860	1.2	34.3

Keen students of the racial problem saw in this factor of numbers the crux of every racial conflict, and observed it even then at work among their Northern neighbors. "In southern Ohio, for example," asserted Thomas L. Clingman of North Carolina in 1860, "where free negroes are quite common, there is little or no Abolitionism; while in the northern part, in which the negro is seldom seen, anti-slavery carries everything before it." [24]   Even more elaborately the author of an article entitled "Free Negroes in the Northern United States" presented his thesis that negroes "are commonly esteemed just in proportion to their scarcity." [25]

So it was this presence of the negro in large numbers that hung like a veritable sword of Damocles over the heads of the Southern people, rallying them to a man, whether they would or would not, to the support of the institution of negro slavery. Thomas Jefferson, that great expounder of the equality of man, who would gladly have released his slaves,

[24] Speech in the Senate, January 16, 1860. *Congressional Globe*, 36 Cong., 1 sess., 452. Also his speech in the House January 22, 1850. 31 Cong., 1 sess., 203.
[25] W. W. Wright of New Orleans, *DeBow's Review*, May, 1860, XXVIII, 574. "Wherever they have been found in any considerable numbers among Anglo-Saxons in northern countries, their laziness, their viciousness, their licentiousness and improvidence, have soon disgusted their best friends, and made the several communities in which they dwelt, anxious to be rid of them." *Ibid.*, 573. Other interesting comments upon this problem of numbers may be found in the words of Sterling Ruffin in 1804, J. G. R. Hamilton, ed., *Papers of Thomas Ruffin*, I, 55; in the sentiments of a South Carolina Statesman, as quoted in the *Richmond Enquirer*, January 7, 1832, and cited in C. H. Ambler, *Sectionalism in Virginia, 1776-1861*, 190; in the opinions of S. F. Hale in W. R. Smith, *Debates of the Alabama Convention of 1861*, 380; and in the speech of James A. Bayard of Delaware before the Senate, March 21, 1861. *Congressional Globe*, 36 Cong., 2 sess., 1487.

"if, in that way, a general emancipation and *expatriation* could be effected," was using a different figure to illustrate this dilemma when he wrote in 1820: "We have the wolf by the ears, and we can neither hold him, nor safely let him go. Justice is in one scale, and self-preservation in the other." [26]

These economic and social distinctions between the two sections, so well exemplified in the institution of negro slavery,[27] soon left their imprint upon the character of the two peoples. At least such was the opinion of a number of Southerners who expressed their ideas upon this subject. Thomas L. Clingman, for example, found the Southern people "less sensitive to immediate popular impressions" and "more accustomed to take a large and philosophic view of a subject";[28] John A. Quitman of Mississippi pointed out "that strong Southern characteristic [of] individual independence of thought and action";[29] while William L. Yancey of Alabama found the Southerner "ardent, brave and magnanimous, more disposed to give than to accumulate, to enjoy ease rather than to labor." [30] These peculiar personal traits, like the separation of the churches,[31] which was also a product of negro slavery, served further to unify the South by distinguishing it as a section from the "cool, calculating, en-

[26] P. L. Ford, ed., *Writings of Jefferson,* X, 157-158.

[27] For an explanation of why negro slavery as a social institution was not confined to the regions of negro concentration in the South, see the illuminating address of Jefferson Davis at Aberdeen, Mississippi, on May 26, 1851, Dunbar Rowland, ed., *Davis, Constitutionalist,* II, 73-74; and the equally suggestive remarks of Governor J. E. Brown in his address to the Georgia Legislature, November 7, 1860: A. D. Candler, ed., *Confederate Records of Georgia,* I, 55-56.

[28] Speech in the House, February 15, 1851. *Appendix to the Congressional Globe,* 31 Cong., 2 sess., 211.

[29] Letter to Col. John S. Preston, dated March 29, 1851: J. F. H. Claiborne, *Life*

and Correspondence of Quitman, II, 123.

[30] Address at Columbus, Georgia, in 1855. J. W. DuBose, *Life and Times of Yancey,* 301. See also, Charles Pinckney, speech in the South Carolina Convention, May 14, 1788. Jonathan Elliot, ed., *Debates,* (2 ed.) IV, 324.

[31] "The strong ties which held each denomination together formed a strong cord to hold the whole Union together; but, as powerful as they were, they have not been able to resist the explosive effect of slavery agitation." John C. Calhoun, farewell address to the Senate, March 4, 1850. *Congressional Globe,* 31 Cong., 1 sess., 453. See also James F. Dowdell, speech in the House, July 28, 1856. *Appendix to the Congressional Globe,* 34 Cong., 1 sess., 1057.

terprising, selfish, and grasping" inhabitants of the Northern states.[32]

The greatest contribution of Southern conditions to the development of sectional unity came through the creation of a Southern mind — a common consciousness of common interests, common traditions, common aspirations, common problems, and common dangers. Such was the essence of a distinct Southern nationality that led the people to think of themselves first as a part of the South, and only then, if at all, as a part of the Union.

It is not surprising to find the South on the verge of a stroke for independence "united by a common devotion to Southern rights, to Southern institutions, to Southern manners and Southern chivalry"[33] with its magazines featuring articles on "How the South Should Meet the Present Exigencies"[34] and its statesmen imploring that federal coercion "unite every Southern State and every Southern man in the most determined and energetic resistance."[35] Nor might Alfred Iverson's portrayal of sectional animosity in the Senate be questioned when it is understood that he was speaking of conditions as he observed them there on December 6, 1860, when he said: "Look at the spectacle exhibited on this floor. How is it? There are the Republican northern Senators upon that side. Here are the southern Senators on this side. . . . Here are two hostile bodies on this floor; . . . We are enemies as much as if we were hostile States. I believe that the northern people hate the South worse than ever the English people hated France; and I can tell my

---

[32] J. W. Dubose, *Life and Times of Yancey*, 301.

[33] C. H. Ambler, *Sectionalism in Virginia, 1776-1861*, 280, quoting the *Kanawha Valley Star* for July 12, 1859, in reference to the students at the University of Virginia.

[34] This was the title of an article in *DeBow's Review*, August, 1860. Other articles in the same issue carried the titles: "Wants

of the South"; "Southern Wealth and Northern Profits"; "Southern Patronage to Southern Imports and Domestic Industry." Vol. XXIX.

[35] Governor Richard K. Call of Florida, in a letter dated February 12, 1861, to John S. Little of Germantown, Pennsylvania. The letter was printed as a pamphlet, and the quotation is found on page 27.

brethren over there that there is no love lost upon the part of the South." [36]

It is not surprising to find those scattering radicals who sought independence as an end in itself, consciously soliciting a mental attitude of mind common to the Southern states, many years before the crisis of 1860-61 precipitated a stroke for Southern independence.[37] Somewhat striking, however, is the revelation that this consciousness of Southern unity was not confined to a single decade or to a single question, or to an interest, or a class, or a state. For while the decade of the fifties protested "the sacrifice of Southern interests; the abandonment of Southern principles, the surrender of Southern rights and concessions to Northern rapacity," [38] that of the thirties lifted a toast to *"The Cause of the South"*; [39] and that of the twenties found that "the People of the South might almost be considered as strangers in the land of their fathers." [40] The early nineties revealed the "North & South" hanging by a thread upon the shoulders of their common president, George Washington.[41] And even

[36] *Congressional Globe*, 36 Cong., 2 sess., 12. For an amusing account of a fight between Northern and Southern members of the House on February 5-6, 1858, see an extract from the *New Orleans Picayune* in Edward Mayes, *L. Q. C. Lamar: His Life, Times, and Speeches*, 74-75. Of John Brown's raid, Lamar said: "Southern citizens . . . are shot down like dogs in the streets of a Southern town; Southern soil is polluted. . . ." 621.

[37] See, for example, the letter of Duff Green to Judge N. B. Tucker, November 9, 1833. "Correspondence of Judge Tucker," *William and Mary College Quarterly Historical Magazine*, October, 1903, XII, 88.

[38] From a letter by John A. Campbell published on December 11, 1850, in the *Advertizer and State Gazette* and reproduced as Appendix D in G. W. Duncan, "John Archibald Campbell," Alabama Historical Society, *Transactions*, 1904, V, 142.

[39] Robert J. Turnbull delivered this toast on July 1, 1830. *Proceedings of the State Rights Celebration at Charleston, S. C.*, pamphlet, 45.

[40] Robert Y. Hayne, speech in the Senate, February 10, 1829. *Register of Debates in Congress*, 20 Cong., 2 sess., 56. For a first-hand impression of the animosity that developed between the North and the South during the debates in Congress over the Missouri question in 1820, see E. S. Brown, ed., *The Missouri Compromises and Presidential Politics, 1820-1825, From the Letters of William Plumer, Junior, passim*. Plumer was a representative from New Hampshire.

[41] Thomas Jefferson, letter to Washington, dated May 23, 1792. P. L. Ford, ed., *Writings of Jefferson*, VI, 5. On February 8, 1792, William B. Giles of Virginia observed in the House "that it is not unfrequent at this time to hear of an Eastern and Southern interest, and he had for some time silently and indignantly seen, or thought he saw, attempts by this means to influence the deliberations of this House upon almost every important question." *Annals of Congress*, 2 Cong., 1 sess., 400. See also Gaillard Hunt, ed., *Disunion Sentiment in Congress in 1794. A Confidential Memorandum Hitherto Unpublished*. A pamphlet written by John Taylor of Virginia.

the eighties wherein the Union was born, found a contest between the Northern and Southern states over the formation and ratification of many clauses in the Federal Constitution.[42]

He was not a radical who pleaded that, in considering the sectional controversy, every "Southern man should remember that every other Southern man is as much interested as himself; and every Southern State should remember that every other Southern State must be, more or less, involved by her action." [43] And it was long before 1860 that George Washington "observed that the vote [in Congress] for & against the bill was perfectly geographical, a northern agt a southern vote." [44] In the eyes of the South, the tariff was "a bill to rob and plunder nearly one half of the Union, for the benefit of the residue"; [45] the national bank would "disturb and break up forever the quiet, the peace, and the repose of the Southern people"; [46] internal improvements were "a great southern question, in which South Carolina is no more interested than the rest of the southern states"; [47] and the assault upon slavery would "and must, if continued, *make two people of one,* by destroying every sympathy between the two great sections." [48]

[42] "The true question at present is, whether the Southern States shall or shall not be parties to the Union." John Rutledge of South Carolina in the Federal Convention on August 21, 1787. Jonathan Elliot, ed., *Debates,* (2 ed.) V, 457. Extracts from the sectional debates in the Federal Convention may be conveniently found in B. F. Wright, Jr., ed., *A Source Book of American Political Theory,* 198-206. Extracts on sectionalism in the Southern ratifying conventions are found in *The Constitution a Pro Slavery Compact,* pamphlet, 64-66. See also p. 44.

[43] B. H. Hill in his letter of acceptance as a delegate to the Georgia session convention. B. H. Hill, Jr., *Senator B. H. Hill of Georgia, His Life, Speeches and Writings,* 39.

[44] An interview with Thomas Jefferson, April 6, 1792. P. L. Ford, ed., *Writings of Jefferson,* I, 192.

[45] John Randolph, speech in the House, April 22, 1828, *Register of Debates in Congress,* 20 Cong., 1 sess., 2472.

[46] R. M. Saunders of North Carolina, speech in the House, August 2, 1841. *Appendix to the Congressional Globe,* 27 Cong., 1 sess., 295.

[47] Langdon Cheves in a state rights celebration at Charleston, South Carolina, July 1, 1830. *Proceedings of the State Rights Celebration,* pamphlet, 26-27. He was referring to the tariff as well as internal improvements.

[48] John C. Calhoun, speech in the Senate, January 5, 1838. *Appendix to the Congressional Globe,* 25 Cong., 2 sess., 29.

Moreover, throughout the Ante-bellum Period, there ran a current of thought that Southern youths must be bred upon Southern principles. "Upon what ground," asked an alumnus of the University of North Carolina, "can a Southern instructor relying for his support upon Southern money, selected to impart healthy instruction to the *sons of Southern slave owners,* and indebted for his situation to a Southern State, *excuse* his support of Fremont?" [49] After a prolonged dispute, such an instructor was forced to resign from the staff of the University. Better had the students remain at home where they might find copies of the *Southern Review* or the *Southern Literary Messenger,* the latter dedicated "especially to the people of the Southern States."

Finally, to enter the realm of the emotional, there arose a voice out of Alabama in 1839 that "the South is 'my own, my native land' — my home, and the birthplace of my children. Her people are my people; her hopes are my hopes; her interests are my interests." [50] This voice brought a response — indeed, almost an echo — in 1845 from the heart of Georgia: the "South is my home — my fatherland. There sleep the ashes of my sire and grandsires; there are my hopes and prospects; with her my fortunes are cast; her fate is my fate, and her destiny my destiny." [51] Meanwhile, a son of the Old Dominion resolves "that while my little bark keeps afloat it shall bear the flag of the South & of constitutional liberty nailed to the mast." [52] To those who lived in this sectional atmosphere, the South was something more than a

---

[49] From a letter written by John A. Engelhard and published on September 29, 1856, in the *North Carolina Standard.* Here taken from an article, "Benjamin Sherwood Hedrick," *The James Sprunt Historical Publications,* Vol. 10, no. 1, p. 10. For another interesting article on Southern education, see George Fitzhugh, "Southern Thought— Its New and Important Manifestations," *DeBow's Review,* October, 1857, XXIII, 337-349.

[50] Henry W. Hilliard, speech in the Alabama State Legislature, 1839. H. W. Hilliard, *Speeches and Addresses,* 48.
[51] Alexander H. Stephens, speech in the House, January 25, 1845. *Appendix to the Congressional Globe,* 28 Cong., 2 sess., 314.
[52] Duff Green, letter to N. B. Tucker, September 9, 1837. "Correspondence of Judge Tucker," *William and Mary College Quarterly Historical Magazine,* October, 1903, XII, 95.

geographic designation: it was, even from the formation of the Union, a distinct nationality — a nation in the making.

THE SOUTH AS A MINORITY

The sectional South was also a minority South, for at no time during the Ante-bellum Period did the Southern states, by reason of their sectional strength, possess the potential power of controlling the central government of the American Union. The source of this minority position lay in the sectional distribution of the two elements that constitute the national government: states and population estimated in federal numbers. "Whatever section concentrates the two in itself," said John C. Calhoun, "possesses the control of the entire Government." [53]

When the national government was first organized, the population of the United States could only be estimated; but, beginning in 1790, the federal census compiled by decades reveals the sectional distribution of population north and south of the Mason and Dixon line. This distribution is shown in the following tables: [54]

TOTAL SECTIONAL POPULATION BY DECADES

Year	North	South	Southern % of total
1790	1,968,040	1,961,174	49.9
1800	2,686,582	2,607,808	49.3
1810	3,758,999	3,456,859	47.9
1820	5,152,635	4,452,779	46.7
1830	7,012,399	5,808,469	45.3
1840	9,728,922	7,290,719	42.8
1850	13,527,220	9,612,929	41.5
1860	19,051,291	12,237,997	39.1

[53] Speech in the Senate, March 4, 1850. *Congressional Globe*, 31 Cong., 1 sess., 451.
[54] Bureau of the Census, *Negro Population in the United States 1790-1915*. Compiled from a table of population by states in blacks and whites, pp. 44-45. Delaware, Kentucky, Maryland, and Missouri are Southern; California, Northern. Territorial populations are included where given.

THE SOUTH AS A CONSCIOUS MINORITY

TOTAL WHITE POPULATION BY DECADES

Year	North	South	Southern % of total
1790	1,900,616	1,271,390	40.1
1800	2,602,881	1,693,449	39.4
1810	3,653,308	2,192,686	37.5
1820	5,034,220	2,809,963	35.8
1830	6,871,302	3,633,195	34.6
1840	9,557,063	4,601,893	32.5
1850	13,330,650	6,184,477	31.7
1860	18,825,075	8,036,699	29.9

The minority position of the South in the House of Representatives lay between the strength of the Southern states as shown in these two tables, for the negro slave-population in the Southern states was given only partial representation. Under the terms of the three-fifths compromise, five slaves were equivalent to only three whites in ascertaining the number of representatives to which each state was entitled. The effect of this clause upon Southern strength in the House is revealed in the following table: [55]

SECTIONAL DISTRIBUTION OF MEMBERSHIP IN THE HOUSE OF REPRESENTATIVES BY DECADES

Year	North	South	Southern % of total
1789	35	30	46
1790	59	47	44
1800	77	65	46
1810	105	81	43
1820	123	90	42
1830	142	100	41
1840	141	91	39
1850	147	90	38
1860	163	85	35

In the Senate, representation based upon states gave the South a stronger position but not a dominating one. Seven of the thirteen original states in the Union were north of

[55] *Biographical Directory of the American Congress, 1774-1927.* House Document no. 783, 69 Cong., 2 sess. Compiled from a table of representatives by states under each apportionment, p. 39. Delaware, Maryland, Kentucky, and Missouri are considered Southern states.

the Mason and Dixon line. Within a decade, the sectional ratio was brought to a position of equality about which it oscillated continually until 1850. Thereafter, the original Northern predominance was definitely restored until, in 1860, the sectional distribution of states stood at the ratio of eighteen to fifteen. This distribution gave to the North thirty-six senators and to the South only thirty.

The control of the presidency was based both upon states and upon population, for the number of presidential electors from each state was determined by the total number of senators and representatives in the national Congress to which that state was entitled. Accordingly, the South again found itself in the minority, and to what extent the following table discloses: [56]

SECTIONAL DISTRIBUTION OF PRESIDENTIAL ELECTORS BY DECADES

Year	North	South	Southern % of total
1790	61	49	45
1800	79	67	46
1810	107	83	44
1820	125	92	42
1830	145	102	41
1840	143	93	39
1850	149	92	38
1860	165	87	35

Nor did the South ever gain potential control of the national judiciary, for the personnel of this branch of the central government depended upon the combined action of the executive and of the legislative departments. The President with the approval of the Senate had the power to appoint the judges, who were subject to impeachment by the House and to trial before the Senate, sitting as a court.[57] In all three

[56] *Ibid.* Compiled from a table of representatives by states under each apportionment, with the addition of two electors to represent the senators from each state. Delaware, Maryland, Kentucky, and Missouri are considered Southern states.

[57] U. S. Constitution, Art. II, sec. 2, cl. 2; Art. I, sec. 2, cl. 5; Art. I, sec. 3, cl. 6. Congress had final control over the structure and jurisdiction of the inferior federal courts. Art. III, sec. 1.

of the major departments of the national government, therefore, the South throughout the Ante-bellum Period was always potentially in the minority.

This problem of the South as a minority section was the most vital issue confronting the Southern political mind. As in the growth of a sectional consciousness, so here again it might naturally be presumed that the South became aware of its weak position in the Union only during the late fifties and early sixties. The multitude of references to this weakness which flood the period, 1855-1861, would seemingly indicate a great awakening upon which the stroke for Southern independence was based. At that time, the two elements of strength in the Union, population and territory, both received unusual attention. It once fell to the lot of C. C. Clay, Jr., of Alabama to present the case of Southern territorial weakness in an elaborate historical discourse before the Senate on April 21, 1856. He said in part:

"At the conclusion of peace, in 1783, the States then north of Mason and Dixon's line had 164,081 square miles; and the States then south of that line had 647,202 square miles. . . . The South has grown from 647,202 to 882,245 square miles; having added but 235,043 square miles to her area since 1783. In the same time, the North, from 164,081, has grown to 1,903,204 square miles; having added in the same time, 1,738,123 square miles to her limits. The South has increased less than fifty percent., the North near 1,100 per cent. in territorial area since the Revolution. The South commenced with more than four times the territory of the North; the North now has near two and a half times the territory of the South." [58]

The case of population as an element of Southern weakness was, to cite a single instance, presented to the Southern Commercial Convention of 1857 which convened at Knoxville, Tennessee. The discussion there centered around the

[58] *Appendix to the Congressional Globe*, 34 Cong., 1 sess., 482, 483.

effect of reopening the slave-trade upon Southern strength in the Union. L. W. Spratt thought it wise "to introduce African labor on a large scale into the Southern States, to enable them the better to resist the encroachments of their Northern brethren"; but O. P. Temple objected because slavery, he thought, had been responsible for the fact that only about one-fourth of the hundreds of thousands of foreigners annually coming to the United States had settled in the South. These immigrants were "swelling the population of the Northern States and thus rendering them too powerful for us"; whereas, said he, "instead of increasing in population we were decreasing, and, as a consequence, were losing one or two members of Congress every year." [59]

Upon such wide-spread information, James M. Mason of Virginia could well observe in 1856: "we are in a minority in the Senate where the States are represented; we are in a minority in the other branch where the people are represented numerically; and we are in a minority in the electoral college." [60] And a South Carolina pamphleteer of the sixties could follow up with these words: "Let the South, then, face the reality, with such feelings as she may; that she is now in a MINORITY, in the Federal Government; in a *minority* which will be *largely increased* with the result of the approaching Federal elections . . . a minority which will be *permanent*, and increasing year by year." [61]

But any impression that this minority consciousness was solely the product of those last six years before the Civil

---

[59] "The Southern Convention at Knoxville," *DeBow's Review*, September, 1857. XXXII, 319. The entire quotation is from Temple's speech. He was restating Spratt's position, which is found on p. 317.
[60] Remarks in the Senate, May 20, 1856. *Appendix to the Congressional Globe*, 34 Cong., 1 sess., 546.
[61] John Townsend, "An Address to the Edisto Island Vigilant Association," *Doom of Slavery*, pamphlet, 7. More elaborately does C. G. Memminger of South Carolina

present the Southern minority position during an address to the Virginia Legislature in January, 1860. H. D. Capers, *Life and Times of Memminger*, 270. And with equal detail does William L. Yancey stress the minority rôle of the South in all departments of the government, during an address in New York City on October 10, 1860. E. D. Fite, *Presidential Campaign of 1860*, Appendix D, 321, citing the *New York Herald*, October 11, 1860.

War certainly is far from the truth; for throughout the Ante-bellum Period the thought of a minority was always indelibly associated with the thought of the South. It was the mental atmosphere of a *minority* section that permeated every decade of the Union and found expression in every walk of life. Southern minority reflections in the last six years may easily be duplicated from the records of the first six years following the call of the Federal Convention in 1787. In this Convention, James Madison saw that the difficulty with any method of *electing* the President "arose from the disproportion of qualified voters in the N. & S. States, and the disadvantages which this mode would throw on the latter." [62] There also his colleague George Mason held out for more favorable commercial provisions, since the "Southern States are the *minority* in both Houses." Hence he wonders if it is to be expected "that they will deliver themselves, bound hand & foot to the Eastern States." [63]

Even more outspoken was Patrick Henry in the Virginia Convention, 1788: "This government subjects every thing to the northern majority. Is there not, then, a settled purpose to check the southern interest? . . . How can the Southern members prevent the adoption of the most oppressive mode of taxation in the Southern States, as there is a majority in favor of the Northern States?" [64] And scarcely had the new government been established when in 1790 Governor Henry Lee of Virginia wrote that he had rather see the Union dissolved than submit to "the rule of a fixed and insolent majority." [65] Furthermore, as if the North

[62] Max Farrand, ed., *Records,* II, 111.
[63] *Documents Illustrative of the Formation of the Union,* House Document no. 398, 69 Cong., 1 sess., p. 635.
[64] Jonathan Elliott, ed., *Debates,* (2 ed.) III, 328. And in the South Carolina Convention Rawlins Lowndes wondered "what reason was there for expectancy that, in Congress, the interest of five Southern States would be considered in a preferable point of view to the nine Eastern ones." Speech on January 18, 1788. IV, 309. See further, George Mason, "Objections to the Proposed Federal Constitution" in P. L. Ford, ed., *Pamphlets on the Constitution,* 331.

in itself did not create sufficient concern, John Taylor, Virginian, in 1794 foresaw a probable alliance between Great Britain and the Eastern States so that "Britain & the east united, could operate powerfully in various ways to bring the south to their terms." [66]

The middle decades reveal the same story of a Southern minority consciousness. Maria Pinckney, doubtless of the South Carolina family, in an interesting political catechism, considered the greatest anomaly in the Union to be that the South "is now in vassalage to the North, East and West"; [67] while in the same year, 1830, William Harper found that "it is useless and impracticable to disguise the fact, that the South is in a permanent minority, and that there is a *sectional* majority against it — a majority of different views and interests and little common sympathy." [68] A. B. Longstreet of Georgia established the principle in 1837 that "the North and Northwest must in the very nature of things rule the South & South West"; [69] while Thomas L. Clingman proceeded to explain to the House of Representatives the application of this principle to conditions in 1847: "The free States are in the ascendency in all branches of the Government, and their majority of more than fifty votes on this floor and in the electoral colleges, is greater than they ever had in former times. This excess must be increased too hereafter — nine-tenths of the territory in the northwest being intended to be carved into free States, and being more than can be filled up for centuries to come, and those States in-

---

[65] Here taken from the Introduction (p. 10) by Gaillard Hunt, ed., *Disunion Sentiment in Congress in 1794.* A pamphlet written by John Taylor.
[66] Gaillard Hunt, ed., *Disunion Sentiment in Congress in 1794,* p. 23. A pamphlet written by John Taylor.
[67] Maria Pinckney, *The Quintessence of Long Speeches Arranged as a Political Catechism,* pamphlet, 20.

[68] Chancellor William Harper, *The Remedy by State Interposition or Nullification.* Political Tract, no. 5, pamphlet, 15. See further, George McDuffie, representative from South Carolina, speech in the House, April 18, 1828. *Register of Debates in Congress,* 20 Cong., 1 sess., 2404.
[69] C. A. Gulick, Jr., ed., *Papers of Mirabeau Buonaparte Lamar,* II, 2.

creasing as they do, faster in population than the slave States." [70]

To impart an element of personal unity to these fragments of the decades, we need only examine the works of John C. Calhoun. Born in McCormick County, South Carolina, on March 18, 1782, graduated from Yale College in 1804, and from the Litchfield (Connecticut) Law School in 1806, John C. Calhoun, two years later, at the age of twenty-six, began his political career as a representative in the South Carolina Legislature; and before he was thirty, he had entered the halls of Congress, to which, either as a representative or as a senator, he was to devote twenty-two years of his active life. In further preparation for his great contributions to Southern political thought, Calhoun interspersed his life in Congress with approximately eight years as Secretary of War (1817-1825), eight years as Vice-President of the United States (1825-1832), and one year as Secretary of State (1844-1845). He resigned his last executive office to return to the Senate, where he remained in active service until the month of his death, March 31, 1850. [71]

Let it be impressed here that no man was more conscious of the minority rôle that the South was playing in the American Union than he, who of all men was most deserving of the title, "Leader of Southern Political Thought." In 1833, Calhoun believed that the South as the *weaker* section of the Union would necessarily advocate limitations on the powers of the central government; in 1836, he said of the Southern members in Congress: "We are here but a handful in the midst of an overwhelming majority"; in 1838, he referred to the South as "the weak and exposed portion of the Union"; and in 1848, he wrote that the Southern people

[70] Speech in the House, December 22, 1847. *Appendix to the Congressional Globe*, 30 Cong., 1 sess., 44-45. See also the Jefferson Davis letter to S. Cobun and others, November 7, 1850. Dunbar Rowland, ed., *Davis, Constitutionalist*, I, 594.

[71] For biographical material frequent use has been made of the convenient *Biographical Directory of the American Congress, 1774-1927*. House Document no. 783. 69 Cong., 2 sess.

composing the weaker section of the Union "are in a minority, both of the States and of population; and, of consequence, in every department of the government." Finally in his farewell address to the Senate on March 4, 1850, a few weeks before his death, Calhoun examined the strength of the sections in an elaborate historical review and concluded that "the North has acquired a decided ascendency over every department of this Government, and through it a control over all the powers of the system. A single section, governed by the will of the numerical majority, has now, in fact, the control of the Government and the entire powers of the system." [72]

OPPRESSION: FOUNTAIN OF POLITICAL THOUGHT

Scarcely had the new national government begun to function before those who opposed the adoption of the Federal Constitution because it subjected the South to the control of a Northern majority were finding their predictions of oppression under this majority well fulfilled. On June 12, 1789, William Grayson thus wrote Patrick Henry concerning the first tariff act: "Inclosed you have the bill for the imposts, by which you will see there is a great disposition here for the advancement of commerce and manufactures in preference to agriculture. . . . You will easily perceive the ascendency of the Eastern interests by looking at the molasses, which is reduced to two-and-a-half cents, while salt continues at six cents, and with an allowance of a drawback to their fish, etc." To this, Grayson shortly thereafter added, with more satisfaction than comfort, that "gentlemen now begin to feel the observations of the Antis, when they informed them of the different interest in the Union, and the probable consequences that would result therefrom to the Southern

[72] *Register of Debates in Congress,* 22 Cong., 2 sess., 552; 24 Cong., 1 sess., 482. J. F. Jameson, ed., *Correspondence of Calhoun,* American Historical Association, *Annual Report,* 1899, II, 408. R. K. Crallé, ed., *Works of Calhoun,* I, 396. *Congressional Globe,* 31 Cong., 1 sess., 452.

States, who would be the milch cow out of whom the substance would be extracted." [73] Thus, before the Union was yet two months old, there began the policy of obliging the Southern states periodically to fill the pail of the national treasury with the milk of sectional revenues and taxes.

Southern explanations of this process are so numerous and varied as to defy classification. Almost everyone in political life presented at some time a case for the disproportionate financial burdens imposed upon the South by the operation of the protective tariff laws. Suffice it here to give a single example of this sentiment — that of a comparatively unknown citizen of Virginia writing in 1850 in a pamphlet entitled *The Union, Past and Future: How It Works and How to Save It:* "The whole amount of duties collected from the year 1791, to June 30, 1845, after deducting the drawbacks on foreign merchandize exported, was $927,050,097. Of this sum the slaveholding States paid $711,200,000, and the free States only $215,850,097. Had the same amount been paid by the two sections in the constitutional ratio of their federal population, the South would have paid only $394,707,917, and the North $532,342,180. Therefore, the slaveholding States paid $316,492,083 more than their just share, and the free States as much less." And of the income from public lands, the author, M. R. H. Garnett, showed that the South had contributed an even larger disproportionate share. [74]

[73] Grayson's letters are copied from manuscript in L. G. Tyler, *Letters and Times of the Tylers*, I, 167-168; Letter to Henry, September 29, 1789, 170. Compare this early statement with one at the close of the Ante-bellum Period: "From 1789 to this day," asserted Robert Toombs before the Senate, March 7, 1860, "a continual, incessant cry has come up to the Capital from them [the North] for protection, prohibition, and bounties. Give, give, give, has been the steady cry of New England; the middle States of the North have been equally urgent." *Appendix to the Congressional Globe*, 36 Cong., 1 sess., 156-157.
[74] Pp. 11, 12. Other interesting estimates

of the excessive financial burdens imposed upon the South were made by John Taylor, "Curtius," *A Defence of the Measures of the Administration of Thomas Jefferson*, pamphlet, 31; John Tyler, Letter to Dr. Henry Curtis, March 18, 1828, L. G. Tyler, *Letters and Times of the Tylers*, I, 385; Report of the Committee of 21 to the South Carolina Convention of 1832 and the address to the People of the United States by this Convention. *Reports, Ordinances and Addresses of the South Carolina Convention of 1832*, 2, 6-7; Thomas L. Clingman, speech in the House, January 22, 1850. *Congressional Globe*, 31 Cong., 1 sess., 203-204.

But if, as Garnett estimated, the South had been forced to provide seven-ninths of the national revenue, no injustice would have been done if she, in return, had received seven-ninths of the national disbursements. For what did it matter if the fruits of Southern industry had been "flowing to the North, in a current as steady and undeviating as the waters of the great Gulf," [75] if those fruits were returned in other forms?

Adequate return from this outlay, however, was, in the opinion of the South, far from a realized fact. South Carolina, for instance, finds that "her soil bears no imprint of the nation's hand"; [76] North Carolina, though burdened by Federal taxes to the extent of three millions a year, "does not get back one hundred thousand dollars in any way from the Government"; [77] and Georgia thus presents its case: "Who is it that is constantly appealing here for legislative aid and legislative patronage? . . . Why, it is the industrial interests of the North. We of the South, it is true, sometimes grumble and complain; . . . But when did we ever come up and ask any aid from the Government of the United States? The constant prayer of the South to you has been to stay your hands. All that we ask of you is, keep your hands out of our pockets." [78] And yet, during the five-year period from 1833 to 1837 inclusive, ninety millions of dollars in duties alone were taken from the Southern people, while only thirty-seven millions were returned in the form of federal disbursements. [79]

[75] Robert Y. Hayne, speech in the Senate, February 10, 1829, *Register of Debates in Congress*, 20 Cong., 2 sess., 56.

[76] *Speech of the Honorable Daniel E. Huger, in the House of Representatives of South Carolina, December, 1830*, pamphlet, 26.

[77] Thomas L. Clingman, speech in the House, January 22, 1850. *Congressional Globe*, 31 Cong., 1 sess., 204. "We have often paid into the coffers of the United States within the space of six months, more money than has been expended for our security in twenty-three years." Archibald

D. Murphy, "Circular Letter to Freemen of Orange County," December 25, 1813. Murphy recounts how in the absence of adequate national defense, North Carolina had to defend itself against the British during the war of 1812. W. H. Hoyt, ed., *Papers of Archibald D. Murphy*, II, 8, 10. Also, 31-32.

[78] Alexander H. Stephens, speech in the House, December 14, 1854. *Congressional Globe*, 33 Cong., 2 sess., 56.

[79] [M. R. H. Garnett], *The Union, Past and Future: How It Works and How to Save It*, pamphlet, 12.

THE SOUTH AS A CONSCIOUS MINORITY

C. C. Clay, Jr., who succeeded his father in the Senate from the state of Alabama, essayed to present the facts on April 21, 1856: "Of $15,201,223 expended up to 1845, upon roads, rivers, and harbors (excluding the Mississippi and Ohio, which are common to both sections), $12,743,-407 were expended in the North; $2,757,816 in the South: being $2,805 for every ten miles square of the northern States, and $451 for each ten miles square of the southern States. . . . Up to 1850, there had been granted to the new non-slaveholding States for internal improvements 18.5 acres for each square mile of their surface; to the new *slave*-holding States 9.3 acres to the square mile. Louisiana had received 29.6, and Indiana 47.6 acres. . . . The bounties on pickled fish, and allowances to fishing vessels have exceeded $10,000,000, of which nearly every cent has been paid to the North, and chiefly to New England. About $300,000 is annually paid at the North for catching codfish."

Turning to the subject of national pensions, Clay made even more unanswerable exposures; for though "the South has furnished more soldiers for all our wars than the North," pensions have been distributed largely in the Northern states. "Of $35,598,964 paid in revolutionary pensions from 1791 to 1838, inclusive," so Clay explained, "$28,262,597 were paid to the North and $7,336,367 to the South; being $127.29 for every soldier which the North had in the war, and $40.89 for every soldier the South had in the war; . . . Of invalid pensions, there was paid during the year ending 30th June, 1854, to the North $303,652.81; to the South, $132,087.35. . . . Of pensions of all kinds, there was paid in the same year, to the South, $459,965.84; to the North, $1,068,010.30 — New York alone receiving $292,209.55." [80]

[80] *Appendix to the Congressional Globe*, 34 Cong., 1 sess., 484. For striking arguments to the contrary, showing that the South had received more than it contributed, see Henry C. Carey, *The North and the South*, (1854), pamphlet, 6, 18. See also p. 31. Another contention to the same effect is found in *Notes on Thomas Prentice Kettell's 'Southern Wealth and Northern Profits,'* March 28, 1861, pamphlet, 15.

THE SOUTH AS A SECTIONAL MINORITY

Throughout the Ante-bellum Period, this disparity between sectional income and sectional disbursements was thought to be "gradually converting the South into a desert, and the north into a garden." [81] And what was worse, to attack the "system" was to arouse the ghost of a political death. Calhoun had visions of this ghost, when, in closing one of his great speeches in the Senate, he asserted that every "Southern man, true to the interests of his section, and faithful to the duties which Providence has allotted him, will be forever excluded 'from the honors and emoluments of this Government." [82] But come what might, an attack through the development of a minority philosophy of political control was never to be lacking.

Geography made of the South a section; population relegated that section to a minority rôle in the American Union. The influence of geographical conditions found expression in the institution of American negro slavery; the influence of numbers, in the constitutional structure of the national government. Both factors in the development of a conscious sectional minority are as old as the Union itself, and together they constitute the *raison d'être* of Southern political thought.

[81] "Aristides," *The Prospect before Us,* February, 1832. Political Tract, no. 6, Letter I, p. 4. John C. Calhoun, in propounding an abstract theory to fit concrete conditions, declared that "some one portion of the community must pay in taxes more that it receives back in disbursements; while another receives in disbursements more that it pays in taxes . . . the greater the taxes and disbursements, the greater the gain of the one and the loss of the other—and *vice versa." Disquisition on Government,* R. K. Crallé, ed., *Works of Calhoun,* I, 19, 21.

[82] Speech in the Senate, February 15, 1833. *Register of Debates in Congress,* 22 Cong., 2 sess., 553. "If we of the North will not vote for a southern man merely because he *is* a southern man," remarked Robert C. Schenck of Ohio in the House on December 27, 1849, during the long contest over the election of the speaker, "and men of the South will not vote for a northern man because he *is* a northern man, and if that principle is to be carried out from here into all our national politics and elections, what must be the result?" *Appendix to the Congressional Globe,* 31 Cong., 1 sess., 42. For a very early statement on sectionalism in appointments, see General Sullivan, letter to Washington, March 6, 1781. Jared Sparks, *Correspondence of the American Revolution,* III, 253.

CHAPTER III

THE PRINCIPLE OF LOCAL SELF-GOVERNMENT

"I AM persuaded that no constitution was ever before so well calculated as ours for . . . self government."[1] These words, written in 1809, are those of the leading exponent of a principle predominantly supported as the chief bulwark of Southern minority protection within the Union during the first three decades of its existence. The leader is Thomas Jefferson, and the principle is that of local self-government. In defense of this principle, Jefferson was ably supported not only by the person to whom he was writing — James Madison, then occupying the President's chair — but also by thousands of lesser lights scattered throughout the South, though concentrated chiefly within the bounds of the Old Dominion. The leadership of Virginia is indicative of the necessity for defending the sectional South through the medium of its artificial units, the states; and in this defense it was only fitting that the oldest and ablest of these units should assume the leading rôle.

THE CONCEPT OF A DIVISION OF POWERS

From the letters of Jefferson it would appear that he was partly responsible for the provisions of the Constitution dividing governmental powers between the central unit and the component units of the Federal System; for though unable to participate in the work of the Constitutional Convention, Jefferson, from his diplomatic post in Paris, repeatedly insisted in his letters to his friends back home upon a division of powers in the new Constitution most favorable

[1] As quoted in A. M. Harvey, "Hamilton and Jefferson and the American Constitu- tion," *Collections of the Kansas State Historical Society, 1926-1928*, XVII, 771.

to the principle of local autonomy. When Madison wrote him concerning the plans for calling a general convention to revise the Articles of Confederation, Jefferson replied, in a letter dated December 16, 1786, that "to make us one nation as to foreign concerns, & keep us distinct in Domestic ones, gives the outline of the proper division of power between the general & particular governments."[2] At least twice he reiterated these distinctions while the Convention was in session the following summer. To Edward Carrington he wrote on August 4, 1787: "My general plan would be, to make the states one as to every thing connected with foreign nations, & several as to everything purely domestic"; and nine days later he repeated the substance of these words in a letter to Blair.[3]

Jefferson's was the characteristic Southern concept of a division of powers; but the application of this concept in the Federal Constitution was not so much the work of one man as of the general opposition at the time both north and south to a strong central government. For localism was not peculiarly Southern in the Federal Convention, though it was predominantly so.

In the control over external affairs delegated to the national government, the South found its justification for the adoption of the Federal Constitution. During the debates over ratification, Hugh Williamson of North Carolina insisted that his state needed the help of the Union to repel invasions. "You are not in a condition to resist the most contemptuous enemy," he said. "What is there to prevent an Algerine pirate from landing on your coast, and carrying your citizens into slavery? You have not a single sloop of war."[4]

[2] P. L. Ford, ed., *Writings of Jefferson*, IV, 333.
[3] *Ibid.*, 424. His letter to Blair appears in part in A. M. Harvey, "Jefferson and Hamilton and the American Constitution," *Collections of the Kansas State Historical Society, 1926-1928*, XVII, 776.
[4] P. L. Ford, ed., *Essays on the Constitution*, 403.

Protection from external aggression was likewise the lever with which C. C. Pinckney, defended the adoption of the Constitution in the South Carolina Convention. On January 17, 1788, he spoke to this effect in answering the critics of adoption: "The honorable gentleman alleges that the Southern States are weak. I sincerely agree with him. We are so weak that by ourselves we could not form a union strong enough for the purpose of effectually protecting each other. Without union with the other states, South Carolina must soon fall. Is there any one among us so much a Quixote as to suppose that this state could long maintain her independence if she stood alone, or was only connected with the Southern States?" [5] James Madison, defending the Constitution in the Virginia Convention, explained that "the powers in the general government are those which will be exercised mostly in time of war"; and their object, according to Francis Corbin, "is to protect, defend, and strengthen the United States." [6]

Throughout the early decades of Union, the defenders of local self-government were continually reverting to this fundamental principle of the "fathers" that the Union was formed for protection. In 1803, Judge St. George Tucker, one of the ablest lawyers among Virginia's many exponents of the cause of localism, and the father of two influential sons who were to follow in his footsteps, found the national government "to be the organ through which the united republics communicate with foreign nations, and with each other." [7] Twenty years later, another noted Virginian, John Randolph of Roanoke, well expressed his indomitable state-rights philosophy in attacking the proposals of the House of Representatives to legislate beyond its authority. "The Constitution," he said, "was formed for external purposes,

[5] Jonathan Elliot, ed., *Debates,* (2 ed.) IV, 283-284.
[6] *Ibid.,* III, pp. 259, 107.

[7] St. George Tucker, ed., *Blackstone's Commentaries,* I. Appendix, 187.

to raise armies and navies, and to lay uniform duties on imports, to raise a revenue to defray the expenditure for such objects." [8]

In seeking to limit national activities to a purely protective sphere, the South adopted, consciously or unconsciously, an abstract theory of the negative character of government. James Iredell, soon to become North Carolina's first contribution to the bench of the United States Supreme Court, wrote in 1787 that "in a republican Government (as I conceive) *individual liberty* is a matter of the utmost moment." [9] George McDuffie, representative of the old South and of South Carolina in particular, with more than half of his thirteen continuous years in the halls of Congress already behind him, condemned the idea that "national prosperity and individual wealth are to be derived, not from individual industry and economy, but from government bounties"; [10] and a few years later, John A. Quitman, an adopted son of Mississippi and a devoted spokesman of the new Southwest, began a checkered political career that was to carry him to the highest legislative, judicial, and executive offices of his state, with the contention in 1832 that "a state should not control its citizens in their opinions, their conduct, their labor, their property, any farther than is necessary to preserve the social tie, to punish offenses against society, and to sustain the powers of government." [11]

This individualistic laissez-faire philosophy disclosed its

---

[8] Speech in the House, April 15, 1824. *Annals of Congress,* 18 Cong., 1 sess., 2366. For later sentiment, see R. J. Turnbull, *The Crisis,* no. 11, p. 43; T. L. Clingman, *Selections from His Speeches and Writings,* 105; H. A. Wise, *Seven Decades of the Union,* 13; A. H. Stephens, *History of the United States,* appendix, 930-931. Jefferson reiterated his earlier statements in his letter to Gideon Granger, August 13, 1800, and in his letter to William Johnson, June 12, 1823. P. L. Ford, ed., *Writings of Jefferson,* VII, 451-452; X, 232, note.

[9] G. J. McRee, *Life and Correspondence of Iredell,* II, 173.

[10] Speech in the House, April 18, 1828. *Register of Debates in Congress,* 20 Cong., 1 sess., 2404.

[11] Address to the electors of Adams County. J. F. H. Claiborne, *Life and Correspondence of Quitman,* I, 126. Quitman later wrote John O. Knox of Virginia that "capital, industry, enterprise, and intellect should be left as free as the air we breathe." II, 13.

true colors when subjected to the spectroscope of Southern state governmental activities. While the leading sons of Virginia were supporting the abstract doctrine of "a wise and frugal Government, which shall restrain men from injuring one another, [and] shall leave them otherwise free to regulate their own pursuits of industry and improvement," [12] Virginia herself was engaging in paternalistic enterprises of the first importance. In 1810 her governor, John Tyler, recommended "the opening of our rivers, and improving and extending their navigation to the remotest corners of our State"; [13] and in 1816 her legislature created a fund for internal improvement "to be applied exclusively to the purpose of rendering navigable and uniting (by canals) the principal rivers, and of more intimately connecting, by public highways, the different parts of the commonwealth." To administer this fund, a Board of Public Works was created, and among its members was Thomas Jefferson himself, who publicly preached that government was only a sort of glorified policeman to maintain peace and order. Within a month this board had at its disposal a fund estimated at a million dollars. [14]

Almost simultaneously, the Senate of the State of North Carolina was unanimously agreeing that "it is the duty of the government to aid the enterprise of its citizens, and to afford to them facilities of disposing, to advantage, of the products of their industry." Under the tireless leadership of Archibald D. Murphy, leading champion of this cause,

---

[12] Thomas Jefferson, First Inaugural Address, March 4, 1801. J. D. Richardson, ed., *Messages and Papers*, I, 323. "Agriculture, manufactures, commerce, and navigation, the four pillars of our prosperity, are then most thriving when left most free to individual enterprise." First Annual Message to Congress, December 8, 1801. *Ibid.*, I, 330.

[13] Address before the House of Delegates, December 3, 1810. L. G. Tyler, *Letters and Times of the Tylers*, I, 253.

[14] *Niles Weekly Register*, February 17 and 24, 1816. IX, 429, 451-452. "Next to the enjoyment of civil liberty itself, it may be questioned whether the best organized government can assure to those, for whose happiness all governments are instituted, a greater blessing than an open, free and easy intercourse with one another, by good roads, navigable rivers, and canals." Report of the Committee on Roads and Inland Navigation, December 27, 1816. *Ibid.*, IX, Supplement, 149.

North Carolina from 1815 to 1823 assumed a pace-setting rôle in its programme of paternalistic state legislation.[15]

In a remarkable summary of the Southern ante-bellum practice, with such perspective as the year 1858 could offer, there appeared in the December issue of *DeBow's Review* an article containing this statement: "For twenty years past, the South has been busy in *protecting,* encouraging, and diversifying, Southern industrial pursuits, Southern skill, commerce, education, etc. . . . The South has not only adopted the protective policy, but, strange to-say, the editors, legislators, and statesmen, who are loudest in professing free-trade doctrines, are, invariably, the warmest advocates of exclusive and protective State legislation."[16]

These extensive governmental activities by the states were not inconsistent with the Southern concept of a division of powers. Did not Jefferson concede to the states "everything purely domestic"; and had not Madison explained in *The Federalist* that the "powers reserved to the several States will extend to all the objects which, in the ordinary course of affairs, concern the lives, liberties, and properties of the people, and the internal order, improvement, and prosperity of the State"?[17]

Relying upon this concept, Governor Giles of Virginia contended that "the peculiar character of the power to make internal improvements is LOCALITY — locality in its MOST LIMITED form, and therefore *peculiarly unsuited* to the jurisdiction of the General Government, which is GENERAL in its

[15] W. H. Hoyt, ed., *Papers of Archibald D. Murphy,* II, 21, quoting the North Carolina *Senate Journal* for December 6, 1815, pp. 22-25. See also Hoyt, II, 30 note, and 19 note; and I, xxvi. Despite all that he did for the state, Murphy opposed internal improvements by the national government. I, 359. By 1860, Georgia, according to A. H. Stephens, had spent $25,000,000.00 on its railroads. Henry Cleveland, ed., *Stephens in Public and Private with Letters and Speeches,* 719. The funded debt of North Carolina to its railroads was in 1860 estimated at $8,883,305.00. *DeBow's Review,* XXIX, 245. And Tennessee was in 1857 under obligations to its railroads to the extent of $16,000,000.00. R. R. Russel, "Economic Aspects of Southern Sectionalism," *Illinois University Studies,* XI, 172, note.

[16] "State Rights and State Remedies," *DeBow's Review,* XXV, 699, 701.

[17] H. C. Lodge, ed., *The Federalist,* no. 45, p. 290.

character, and *peculiarly suited* to the jurisdiction of the State Governments, whose jurisdiction is intended for LOCAL objects." [18] Again, Robert J. Turnbull, a South Carolina journalist of the twenties, in opposing the national protective tariff acts, believed that "Congress cannot promote, the great Cotton Planting interest of South-Carolina, nor can it encourage the manufacturing interest of the North. And why? — Because these are *local* interests of the States, and not the *general* interests of the Union." [19] Then there was John Taylor, an outstanding political theorist, who applied the principle to that vital problem of negro slavery when he wrote in 1821: "A southern majority in congress has no right to compel the northern states to permit slavery, nor a northern majority to compel the southern states to abolish it, because it is a subject of internal state regulation prohibited to congress, and reserved to the states." [20] In these representative opinions, the Southern philosophy of individualism revealed its true character as a minority tool for furthering the cause of local self-government.

The original Constitution, as is well known, provided for such a distribution of powers as would permit the central government to exercise certain enumerated functions of common concern to the Union as a whole, and as would reserve, with certain prohibitions, all other powers to the separate states. But the Southern ratifying conventions were still dissatisfied with the uncertainty of this distribution,[21] and it was

[18] As quoted in R. J. Turnbull, *The Crisis*, no. 19, p. 84. "I do not wish to be understood as opposing the improvement of rivers and harbors, nor the making of canals and roads," asserted Jefferson Davis. "I am opposed to such works by the Federal Government, save where required for the use of the Army or the Navy. . . . " Speech in the Senate, March 1, 1851. *Appendix to the Congressional Globe*, 31 Cong., 2 sess., 340.
[19] R. J. Turnbull, *The Crisis*, no. 15, p. 63. In 1850 the North Carolina House of Commons resolved that its industries could be better protected "by State than by Congressional Legislation." R. R. Russel, "Economic Aspects of Southern Sectionalism," *Illinois University Studies*, XI, 161.
[20] John Taylor *Construction Construed and Constitutions Vindicated*, 300. See also the resolutions of the Senate adopted on January 12, 1838, *Congressional Globe*, 25 Cong., 2 sess., 98.
[21] See the Virginia Act of Ratification of the Constitution. Jonathan Elliot, ed., *Debates* (2 ed.), III, 656.

largely at their insistence that the tenth amendment was added to the Constitution, providing that "the powers not delegated to the United States by the Constitution, nor prohibited by it to the States, are reserved to the States respectively, or to the people." In this amendment, the South, led by Jefferson, who believed that "the foundation of the constitution was based on this ground," [22] found a source of protection for a minority interest within the Union.

The Sweeping Clauses of the Constitution

When the tenth amendment to the Constitution was brought before the first Congress for consideration, Thomas H. Tucker of South Carolina moved to insert the word *expressly,* so that the amendment might read: "the powers not *expressly* delegated to the United States . . . are reserved to the States, or to the people." James Madison objected. He recounted how this issue had been threshed out in the Virginia convention where the amendment had first been suggested, and he told how the convention after a full and fair discussion had rejected the use of the word. Madison himself thought that "it was impossible to confine a Government to the exercise of express powers" and that "there must necessarily be admitted powers by implication, unless the constitution descended to recount every minutiae." Tucker replied that after the insertion of the word *expressly* the amendment would still permit the national government to exercise every power "that could be clearly comprehended within any accurate definition of the general power." [23]

This clash between two Southern members of Congress clearly indicated that the principle of implied powers was universally recognized as a necessary concomitant of delegated powers. The real issue, as they so well recognized,

[22] Opinion on the constitutionality of the national bank, February 15, 1791. P. L. Ford, ed., *Writings of Jefferson,* V, 285.

[23] Debate in the House, August 18, 1789. *Annals of Congress,* 1 Cong., 1 sess., 761.

was the degree of extension to be granted the implications of the delegated powers. In this controversy, the advocates of national expansion naturally focused attention upon those constitutional provisions most favorable to their cause. On account of their generally indefinite character, these provisions were commonly denounced by Southern advocates of strict construction as the "sweeping clauses" of the Constitution.[24]

In the order of their appearance in the Constitution, the first of the sweeping clauses is found in the preamble: "We the People of the United States, in Order to . . . promote the general Welfare . . . do ordain and establish this Constitution." Of a like character is the first clause of the eighth section of the first Article: "The Congress shall have Power to lay and collect Taxes, Duties, Imposts and Excises, to pay the Debts and provide for the common Defence and general Welfare of the United States. . . ." The meaning of these two welfare clauses provided a bone of contention within the Union for more than forty years.

Scarcely had the new government been established before

[24] General expressions found their way into the adopted Constitution over the opposition of many leading statesmen from the South. Shortly after the "fathers" had completed their work in 1787, Edmund Randolph in a "Letter on the Federal Constitution" expressed the hope that the other states would join with Virginia in proposing an amendment "causing all ambiguities of expression to be precisely explained." P. L. Ford, ed., *Pamphlets on the Constitution*, 275.

In the following year when Virginia was debating the adoption of the Constitution, John Tyler stated his opposition in part as follows: "But when I find that the Constitution is expressed in indefinite terms, in terms which the gentlemen who composed it do not all concur in the meaning of,—I say that, when it is thus liable to objections and different constructions, I find no rest in my mind. Those clauses which answer different constructions will be used to serve particular purposes." Jonathan Elliot, ed., *Debates* (2 ed.), III, 637-638. The most frequent use of the term "sweeping clauses" is found in the debates of this convention.

For the South, the tenth amendment was a compensating factor, but in 1792, Joseph Jones wrote James Madison of a cause for common lament in the assertion that "general words give open field for those cavillers, [the nationalists] where they may range at large and say and do what they please, under the ambiguity of language." W. C. Ford, ed., *Letters of Joseph Jones to James Madison*, pamphlet, 24. Reprinted from the *Proceedings of the Massachusetts Historical Society*, June, 1901.

For a strong latter attack upon constitutional ambiguities, see R. M. Saunders, Representative from North Carolina, speech in the House, August 2, 1841. *Appendix to the Congressional Globe*, 27 Cong., 1 sess., 294.

there were attempts at national expansion through a *"general indefinite* power of providing for the general welfare." Alexander Hamilton, the first Secretary of the Treasury, relied upon this doctrine in his official report upon manufacturing in 1791. Therein he contended that it belonged "to the discretion of the National Legislature to pronounce upon the objects which concern the *general welfare,* and for which, under that description, an appropriation of money is requisite and proper. And there seems to be no room for a doubt that whatever concerns the general interests of LEARNING, of AGRICULTURE, of MANUFACTURES, and of COMMERCE, are within the sphere of the National Councils, *as far as regards an application of money."* [25] While neither this report nor a similar argument advanced in 1797 by a Committee of Congress on the promotion of agriculture led to immediate action by Congress, the Virginia Assembly in 1800 found grounds for alarm because "the extraordinary doctrine contained in both, has passed without the slightest positive mark of disapprobation from the authority to which it was addressed." [26]

In this attack upon the welfare clauses, the Virginia Assembly had first acted two years earlier by denouncing the Alien and Sedition Acts as unconstitutional expansions of national power. At that time, James Barbour had essayed to answer the supposition that "the preamble gave powers not given in the Constitution." Speaking on December 17, 1798, he thus stated his position: "The Preamble, to be sure, explains the end of the Constitution. It was to secure the liberties and welfare of the American people, but upon what terms? Why, upon the terms designated in the Constitution. . . . For what mind could hesitate to pronounce that the object of enumerating the powers must have been to fix barriers against the exercise of other powers. . . .

[25] As quoted in Madison's Report on the Resolutions, Gaillard Hunt, ed., *Writings* *of Madison,* VI, 355.
[26] *Ibid.,* 356.

what was the use of a specific enumeration of powers if it was intended to invest the General Government with sweeping powers?" [27]

After much debate, the first Virginia Resolutions were adopted lamenting "that indications have appeared of a design to expound certain general phrases . . . so as to destroy the meaning and effect of the particular enumeration" in the Constitution.[28] Copies were sent out to other states for an expression of their sentiment. The replies from the states, unfavorable on other grounds, led to further action by the Virginia Assembly, and finally to the adoption of a comprehensive committee report that became a handbook of Southern constitutional interpretation until the Civil War. Concerning the welfare clause in the preamble, the report, drafted by James Madison, substantiated the position taken by James Barbour in the debates before the Assembly. "A preamble," it stated, "usually contains the general motives or reasons for the particular regulations or measures which follow it, and is always understood to be explained and limited by them. In the present instance, a contrary interpretation would have the inadmissible effect of rendering nugatory or improper every part of the constitution which succeeds the preamble." [29]

It was more difficult to confine the general welfare provision of the taxing clause within the limits of its context. Here again the report did not break new ground, for in the Virginia ratifying convention, Edmund Randolph had defended the clause against the attacks of Patrick Henry and George Mason in these words: "You must violate every rule of construction and common sense, if you sever it from the power of raising money, and annex it to any thing else, in order to make it that formidable power which it is represented to

[27] *Alien and Sedition Laws*, Senate Document, 873, 62 Cong., 2 sess., 39.
[28] William MacDonald, ed., *Documentary Source Book*, (3 ed.) p. 275. The Resolu-

tions were adopted on December 24, 1798.
[29] Gaillard Hunt, ed., *Writings of Madison*, VI, 382.

be." [30] In like manner Thomas Jefferson, in attacking the constitutionality of the national bank in 1791, had explained that "the laying of taxes is the *power*, and the general welfare the *purpose* for which the power is to be exercised." [31] But the most elaborate prior explanation of the meaning of this clause had come from the pen of Madison himself in the forty-first issue of *The Federalist*. There Madison had explained at length that the term *general welfare* had been brought over from the Articles of Confederation, where it had been incorporated in three different places, yet in no instance had the term been used to justify an indefinite expansion of national power.[32]

So when Madison came to draft the famous report of 1800, he needed only to restate his historical explanations, and to point out, as he had earlier done, that the power granted in the clause was the power of taxation. This power, he said, was limited in purpose by the general welfare provision, and restricted in scope by the "recital of particulars" that followed the clause in Article I, section 8 of the Constitution. In the words of the report: "Money cannot be applied to the *general welfare*, otherwise than by an application of it to some *particular* measure conducive to the general welfare. Whenever, therefore, money has been raised by the general authority, and is to be applied to a particular measure, a question arises whether the particular measure be within the enumerated authorities vested in Congress. If it be, the money requisite for it may be applied to it; if it be not, no such application can be made." [33]

[30] Jonathan Elliot, ed., *Debates*, (2 ed.), III, 599-600.

[31] P. L. Ford, ed., *Writings of Jefferson*, V, 286.

[32] H. C. Lodge, ed., *The Federalist*, 257-258. In opposing the use of this general welfare clause to support the constitutionality of national bounties on cod-fisheries, Hugh Williamson of North Carolina declared in the House on February 3, 1792, that the "common defence and general welfare, in the hands of a good politician, may supercede every part of our Constitution, and leave us in the hands of time and chance." *Annals of Congress*, 2 Cong., 1 sess., 380. See farther, Madison's speech on this proposition, February 6, at pp. 386-388, and that of William B. Giles of Virginia, February 8, at pp. 398-399.

[33] Gaillard Hunt, ed., *Writings of Madison*,

These early explanations of the welfare clauses, however conclusive to the Southern mind, were not to be accepted by a national government bent upon expansion. For many years yet, the controversy over the proper interpretation of these clauses was to be continued. Looking backward over the intervening period from 1787 to 1819, Judge Spencer Roane, of whom more is to be said, wrote in the *Richmond Enquirer*: "Notwithstanding the opinion of the Federalist, the prophecy of the opponents of the Constitution turned out to be true. It was contended by some that Congress had a right to pass any law by which they might 'provide for the general welfare,' and they brought in the preamble to their aid; whilst others only claimed the privilege of providing for the general welfare in ALL cases in which there might be an application of the money to be raised by taxes. . . . The effect of either of these constructions is to render nugatory the particular enumeration of powers. There was no necessity for a specific enumeration of authorities, the execution of which required the raising of money by taxes, and the expenditure thereof if the general clause authorized the Congress to pass laws in all cases in which the expenditure of money might promote the general welfare." [34]

Again in 1825, Jefferson, perceiving that the welfare clauses had long been a means of national consolidation, sought to have the Virginia Legislature adopt another reso-

VI, 357. It should be noted that the limitation of appropriations under the second welfare clause to a "recital of particulars" in the Constitution — that is, to the objects over which Congress has been granted power of legislation — was a more extreme position than some Southern leaders were willing to take. James Monroe, for example, expressed a more liberal attitude in his "Views of the President of the United States on the Subject of Internal Improvements." Indeed, Monroe's interpretation of the clause is a classic statement of the position subsequently taken by the Supreme Court. By way of summary, Monroe wrote: "My idea is that Congress have an unlimited power to raise money, and that in its appropriation they have a discretionary power, restricted only by the duty to appropriate it to the purpose of common defense and of general, not local, national, not State, benefit." Paper submitted to the House of Representatives on May 4, 1822. J. D. Richardson, ed., *Messages and Papers*, II, 173.

[34] *Richmond Enquirer*, April 2, 1819, as quoted in *John P. Branch Historical Papers*, June, 1905, II, no. 1, pp. 73-74.

lution declaring "to be most false and unfounded, the doctrine, that the compact, in authorising it's federal branch to lay and collect taxes, duties, imposts and excises to pay the debts and provide for the common defence and general welfare of the U S. has given them thereby a power to do whatever *they* may think, or pretend, would promote the general welfare, which construction would make that, of itself, a complete government, without limitation of powers." [35]

James Madison felt obliged to restate his position again in his veto message of March 3, 1817, on the internal improvements bill; and in 1830, after further research, he discovered additional historical information that he should have included in his earlier studies of the welfare clauses. By following the development of the taxing clause through the Constitutional Convention, Madison concluded in his last and best study that "but for the old [revolutionary] debts, and their association with the terms 'common defence & general welfare,' the clause would have remained as reported in the first Draft of a Constitution, expressing generally a 'power in Congress to lay and collect taxes duties imposts & excises'; without any addition of the phrase 'to provide for the common defence & general welfare.' " [36]

[35] P. L. Ford, ed., *Writings of Jefferson,* X, 350-351, note.

[36] Veto Message: J. D. Richardson, ed., *Messages and Papers,* I, 584-585. Letter to Andrew Stevenson, November 17, 1830. Max Farrand, ed., *Records,* III, 486. Another leader in the opposition to the welfare clauses was Thomas Cooper of South Carolina, called by his recent biographer, "The Schoolmaster of State Rights." Few men were more active or more severe in their denunciations of national consolidation than was Cooper in his numerous writings scattered throughout the period, 1787-1830. In the second edition of his *Lectures on the Elements of Political Economy* (1829), p. 218, Cooper wrote: "I know of no pretence, no motive that can be set up, so well calculated to cover and protect every possible fraud on the people's rights, as the GENERAL WELFARE. It has no limitation; it extends to all things, to all times, persons, places, and proposals. . . . It is the assumption of legislative power, in a degree not conceded by any expressions in the constitution. . . ." For a comprehensive and critical bibliography of Cooper's writings, together with an excellent summary of his contributions to the cause of localism, see Dumas Malone, *The Public Life of Thomas Cooper,* 281-306 and bibliography. Robert J. Turnbull devoted several issues of *The Crisis* to an elaborate exposition of the welfare clauses. See especially, no. 16. A later attack is found in the "Address of the People of South Carolina . . . to the People of the Slaveholding States," *Journal of the South Caro-*

THE SOUTH AS A CONSCIOUS MINORITY

The last and most important of the three sweeping clauses in the Constitution is that giving Congress power "to make all Laws which shall be necessary and proper for carrying into Execution the foregoing Powers, and all other Powers vested by this Constitution in the Government of the United States, or in any officer or department thereof." [37] This clause follows an enumeration of the powers of Congress, and it logically became the constitutional justification for all implications arising from powers expressly delegated to the national government. For that reason, the crux of the sectional controversy involving the proper interpretation of the Constitution was for several decades concerned with the meaning of the words *necessary and proper* as they appear in this clause.

This conflict was not long in making itself felt. In fact, the clause in question became a major issue in the formation of the first two political parties. The *Federalists,* recruited chiefly from the North, advocated a strong central government through a liberal interpretation of this provision; and the *Anti-Federalists,* or *Republicans,* largely concentrated in the South, favored a weak national government through a strict interpretation of this clause. The opposing doctrines were never brought into higher relief than in the long controversy over the constitutionality of the national bank.

In the early stages of the bank controversy, Alexander

lina Convention, 1860-1-2, 468, 470.
The controversy over the welfare clauses has recently been reopened in the Congressional debates over the constitutionality of the national subsidy laws. It is interesting that a leader in the current controversy is Henry St. George Tucker, whose grandfather, Henry St. George Tucker, and whose great-grandfather, St. George Tucker, both contributed so ably to the Southern cause during the Antebellum Period. See Tucker's speech on the Maternity Act delivered in the House on March 3, 1926. *Congressional Record,* 69 Cong., 1 sess., 4931-4939; and especially his address before the Georgia Bar Association, June 2, 1927. This address was first published under the caption, "Judge Story's Position on the So-Called Welfare Clause" in *American Bar Association Journal,* July and August, 1927, XIII, 363-370, 465-469. It was reprinted as Senate Document 17, 70 Cong., 1 sess.; and again in the *Constitutional Review* for January, 1929, and discussed in the subsequent issues of April and July, 1929, XIII, 13-35, 98-100, 163-164.
[37] Art. I, sec., 8, cl. 18.

Hamilton led the advocates of liberal construction, and later his opinions received the authoritative judicial sanction of the Chief Justice of the Supreme Court, John Marshall. For when Hamilton wrote President Washington on February 23, 1791, that "necessary often means no more than *needful, requisite, incidental, useful, or conducive to,*" and that "the *relation* between the *measure* and the *end*" rather than "the *degree* to which a measure is necessary" must be the criterion of constitutionality,[38] he was contributing the substance of Marshall's classic statement twenty-eight years later in his opinion in *McCulloch* v. *Maryland.*

The defenders of strict construction lost no time in aligning their constitutional arguments. Indeed, Thomas Jefferson, Edmund Randolph, and James Madison, from their respective seats of authority within the national government, had already expressed their views when Alexander Hamilton labored through the night of February 23, 1791, preparing an answer for the President to the arguments of the three Virginians, who were seeking to have the President veto the pending bank bill. Thomas Jefferson, then secretary of state, in urging a veto made his most memorable contribution in these words: "It has been urged that a bank will give great facility or convenience in the collection of taxes. Suppose this were true: yet the Constitution allows only the means which are '*necessary,*' not those which are merely 'convenient' for effecting the enumerated powers. If such a latitude of construction be allowed to this phrase as to give any non-enumerated power, it will go to every one, for there is not one which ingenuity may not torture into a *convenience* in some instance *or other,* to *some one* of so long a list of enumerated powers. It would swallow up all the delegated powers, and reduce the whole to one power, as before observed. Therefore it was that the Constitution restrained

---

[38] H. C. Lodge, ed., *Works of Hamilton,* Constitutional edition, III, 452-453, 454.

them to the *necessary* means, that is to say, to those means without which the grant of power would be nugatory." [39]

Equally positive was the official opinion of the Attorney General, Edmund Randolph. Having shown that the power of creating a national bank was not expressly granted to Congress, Randolph set out at great length to prove that this power cannot be considered a "necessary and proper" implication from any of the enumerated powers.[40] In this respect, his methods were not unlike those of Madison who had been fighting the bank bill on the floor of Congress. On February 2, 1791, in a celebrated speech, Madison found the latitude of interpretation required to support the bank bill condemned by the Constitution itself; for, said he, "Congress have power 'to regulate the value of money'; yet it is expressly added, not left to be implied, that counterfeiters may be punished. They have the power 'to declare war,' to which armies are more incident than incorporated banks to borrowing; yet the power 'to raise and support armies' is expressly added. . . . The regulation and calling out of the militia are more appertinent to war than the proposed Bank to borrowing; yet the former is not left to construction." As contrasted with this logic, said Madison, "Mark the reasoning on which the validity of the bill depends ! To borrow money is made the end, and the accumulation of capitals implied as the means. The accumulation of capitals is then the end, and a Bank implied as the means. The Bank is then the end, and a charter of incorporation, a monopoly, capital punishments, &c. implied as the means." From this reasoning Madison concluded that "if implications, thus remote and thus multiplied, can be linked together, a chain may be formed that will reach every object of legisla-

[39] Opinion on the constitutionality of the national bank, February 15, 1791. P. L. Ford, ed., *Writings of Jefferson*, V, 287.
[40] Randolph's arguments are summarized and quoted in Hamilton's message. H. C. Lodge, ed., *Works of Hamilton*, Constitutional edition, III, 463-480.

tion, every object within the whole compass of political economy."[41]

When President Washington, with all the evidence before him, rendered a decision for the Federalists by signing the bank bill, he diverted for a time the dispute over implied powers to other subjects of legislation; but no sooner had the charter for the first bank expired in 1811 than the movement for a second national bank reopened the controversy in all its ramifications. Again the question was raised: Is a national bank a necessary and proper implication from any of the enumerated powers of Congress? This time, after the creation of a second bank, the question was answered authoritatively by Chief Justice Marshall in the opinion to which reference has been made. "Let the end be legitimate," asserted Marshall in the key sentence to this opinion, "let it be within the scope of the constitution, and all means which are appropriate, which are plainly adapted to that end, which are not prohibited, but consist with the letter and spirit of the constitution, are constitutional."[42]

But not even the weight of John Marshall's epoch-making opinion, backed by a unanimous court, could dismay the defenders of local autonomy. From the bench of the highest state court of Virginia, Judge Spencer Roane wrote the dissenting opinion that might, but for his misfortune, have been the majority opinion of the Supreme Court. Since 1801, Roane had spent his active but disappointed years on the Virginia Bench to which he had been relegated, as it were, by the inability of Thomas Jefferson to appoint him Chief Justice of the Supreme Court. It was unfortunate for Roane that the appointment which Jefferson was holding in store for him never materialized because the aging Oliver Ells-

[41] *Annals of Congress*, 1 Cong., 3 sess., 1899. In 1830 this speech by Madison was called "A GRAMMAR OF CONSTITUTIONAL LAW—A TEXT BOOK & KEY TO THE CONSTITUTION."

"Hampden," *Genuine Book of Nullification*, pamphlet, 110.
[42] U. S. Supreme Court Reports, 4 Wheaton 420.

worth, to whose position Roane was to have succeeded, re-signed in time for the retiring Federalist President, John Adams, to thwart Jefferson's plans by appointing a Federalist, John Marshall, to this important post.[43]

In addition to this personal grudge against Marshall, Roane found the way for his legal arguments paved by an aroused public opinion, crystallized against nationalism through the burning criticisms of Hezekiah Niles in the *Weekly Register,* at that time the most widely read and influential publication in the country. To this critical public, now sufficiently bestirred and enlightened to devour the most technical treatises supporting localism, Roane presented his logical refutation to Marshall's opinion through the columns of the *Richmond Enquirer,* the most influential of Southern newspapers.

Roane lost little time in attacking the interpretation of the necessary and proper clause as the vital issue in Marshall's opinion. "Why did the framers of the Constitution use the word 'necessary'?" Roane asked. "They had other words at their command which they might have used, if those other words had conveyed the ideas which they had in their minds. Would they not have said, if they so intended it, that Congress shall have power to make all laws which may be *useful* or *convenient,* or *conducive to* the effectual execution of the foregoing powers? Will any man assert that the word 'necessary' is synonymous with these other words?"

Adopting as a definition of *necessary* "those means *without which* the end *could not* be attained," Roane rejected the validity of Marshall's distinction between the use of the word *necessary* in the clause under consideration, and the term *absolutely necessary* in the clause prohibiting states from taxing imports and exports. Roane took no stock in this refinement of the term into its various degrees. "What

---

[43] William E. Dodd, "Chief Justice Marshall and Virginia," *American Historical* *Review,* July, 1907, XII, 776, citing *Virginia Law Register,* II, 480.

is *absolutely* necessary, is only *positively* necessary, that is, necessary," said he.

And upon the association of the word *necessary* with its counterpart, the word *proper,* Roane had this to say: "The word 'proper' has the larger meaning, and the word 'necessary' restricts that meaning. Suppose the word necessary had been omitted. Then Congress might have made all laws which might be 'proper,' that is *suitable,* or *fit,* for carrying into execution the other powers; in that case they would have had a wider field of discretion: they would then have only been obliged to enquire what were the suitable means to attain the desired end. But then comes the more important restriction. After you have ascertained the means which are suitable, or proper, you must go further and ascertain whether they are necessary. . . . But if you say that *'necessary'* means *convenient,* or *useful,* or *conducive* to, then it might have been totally omitted, because the word *proper* would have conveyed the whole meaning." [44]

In such fashion did Roane match logic with logic, neglecting as unwisely as Marshall had judiciously, the important historical support for his position on the necessary and proper clause. Could Roane only have used that belated but convincing treatise on the development of the necessary and proper clause in the Constitutional Convention, which appeared in the ninth issue of *The Crisis* some eight years later, how much more effectively might he have presented the cause of localism in one of its last concerted stands against centralization! But as it was, the principle of local self-government had become a forlorn hope when the brilliant South Carolina editor, Robert J. Turnbull, showed by historical review that the disputed clause in the Convention had originally stood "to make ALL laws for carrying the foregoing powers into execution"; and that John Marshall to the contrary

[44] "Amphictyon" letter, *Richmond Enquirer,* April 2, 1810, as quoted in *John P. Branch* *Historical Papers,* June, 1905, II, no. 1, pp. 64, 69, 65.

notwithstanding, "the plain unequivocal intention of the Convention by their alteration of the clause, was to *narrow the discretion* of Congress, as to the selection of its means in exercising its enumerated powers." [45]

STRICT CONSTRUCTION: APPLIED AND MISAPPLIED

The dispute over the national bank, which so well brought to light the dangers inherent in the sweeping clauses of the Constitution, was only one manifestation of the attempts of Southern political thinkers to apply a theory of minority protection to the activities of the national government. Whatever the power to be exercised — whether legislative, executive, or judicial — the defenders of local autonomy sought to confine that power to a sphere least likely to impair the efficacy of their cherished principle of protection. Most interesting in the defense of local self-government is the important rôle played by Southern state legislatures — a rôle justified, as the Virginia Assembly once asserted, by these words of Hamilton in the twenty-eighth issue of *The Federalist:* "Projects of usurpation cannot be masked under pretences so likely to escape the penetration of select bodies of men, as of the people at large. The legislatures will have better means of information. They can discover the danger at a distance; and possessing all the organs of civil power, and the confidence of the people, they can at once adopt a regular plan of opposition, in which they can combine all the resources of the community." [46]

The legislatures lost no time in accepting the position to which Hamilton had assigned them. In the first four decades of union the number and variety of their official utterances

[45] R. J. Turnbull, *The Crisis,* no. 9, p. 29. For other Southern ideas on the interpretation of the 'necessary and proper' clause. see Madison's Report of 1800. Gaillard Hunt, ed., *Writings of Madison,* VI, 384; T. R. Mitchell, Fourth-of-July Address to the Union State Rights Party at Charleston, South Carolina, in 1832. H. D. Capers, *Life and Times of Memminger,* 50; Abel P. Upshur, *Inquiry into the Character of the Federal Government* (1840), 102 et seq.

[46] H. C. Lodge, ed., *The Federalist,* 167.

is in itself a barometer of their activities on questions of federal relations. To arrive at the importance of these resolutions, it is not necessary to follow the dramatic events in each state leading up to their adoption; the documents, as conveniently compiled by Prof. H. V. Ames, speak for themselves.[47]

As early as 1790, the Virginia Legislature, considering themselves as sentinels placed by their constituents over the national government to prevent encroachments upon reserved powers, could "find no clause in the Constitution authorizing Congress to assume the debts of the states." Upon the distant horizon, these sentinels perceived in the Acts of Congress assuming state debts the creation of a large moneyed interest which would eventually lead to "the prostration of agriculture at the feet of commerce, or a change in the present form of fœderal government, fatal to the existence of American liberty." [48] So opposed was the lower branch of the North Carolina Legislature, at this time, to the assumption of state debts that its members refused to take the oath prescribed by Congress to support the Constitution.[49]

Again, as an outcome of the Alien and Sedition Laws, passed in 1798, the Kentucky Legislature, on November 16, 1798, resolved "that alien friends are under the jurisdiction and protection of the laws of the State wherein they are; that no power over them has been delegated to the United States, nor prohibited to the individual States distinct from their power over citizens," and that "no power over the freedom of religion, freedom of speech, or freedom of the press being delegated to the United States by the Constitution, nor prohibited by it to the States, all lawful powers

[47] H. V. Ames, ed., *State Documents on Federal Relations.*
[48] *Ibid.,* 6.
[49] W. K. Boyd, "North Carolina on the Eve of Secession," American Historical Association, *Annual Report,* 1910, 168. A fuller discussion is found in H. M. Wagstaff, "State Rights and Political Parties in North Carolina," *Johns Hopkins University Studies,* series 24, nos. 7-8, pp. 32-33.

respecting the same did of right remain, and were reserved to the States, or to the people." These ideas were repeated in the Virginia Resolutions which followed on the twenty-fourth of December.[50]

The formal remonstrances of state legislatures against national expansion reached their climax in the decade of the twenties with a flood of resolutions attacking the constitutionality of the protective tariff. Between the report adopted by the House of Representatives of South Carolina in December, 1820, and the Resolutions of the Virginia Legislature on February 24, 1829, Professor Ames in his *State Documents on Federal Relations* includes excerpts from a dozen different anti-tariff manifestoes of Southern state legislatures, nor does he pretend to exhaust the list.[51]

These legislatures sought to render their protests more effective by advancing another principle of local autonomy: the power of instructing their senators in Congress. The debate over this issue, which began in earnest in the very first session of the first Congress,[52] led back to a consideration of the nature of representation itself. The fundamental concept most generally supported in the South as in keeping with the principle of local self-government, is thus stated by the Virginia Legislature in its important resolutions upon this subject in 1811: "It cannot be pretended, that a representative is to be the organ of his own will alone; for then, he would be so far despotic. *He must be the organ of others* — of whom? not of the nation, for the nation deputes him not; but of his constituents, who alone know, alone have trusted, and can alone displace, him. And if it be his province and his duty, in general, to express the will of his constituents, to the best of his knowledge, without being particularly informed thereof; it seems impossible to contend, that he is

---

[50] William MacDonald, ed., *Documentary Source Book*, (3 ed.), 270, 269, 275.
[51] Pp. 134-157.

[52] Debate in the House, August 15, 1789. *Annals of Congress*, 1 Cong., 1 sess., 729-749.

not bound to do so, when he is so specifically informed and instructed." Legislatures, moreover, were acting within their constitutional sphere in instructing their senators, since, so the resolutions assert, "instructions from the constituent legislatures to their senators in Congress, are public acts within the sphere of that portion of the state sovereignty, not retained by the people, nor delegated by the constitution of the United States to the general government, but represented and possessed by the state legislatures." [53]

The instruction of Congressmen was more than once a paramount issue in North Carolina politics during the early years of the Union; but here, as elsewhere in the South, the state-rights parties favoring the power of instruction, usually carried the day. In 1792, for example, Senator Samuel Johnston, a Federalist, was defeated for re-election because he refused to be guided by the votes of the Assembly; and, in the Congressional elections of 1801, four other members met a similar fate upon the same issue.[54] Such experiences led Congressmen to institute the general custom of following their instructions or of tendering their resignations.

Through the exercise of the power of instruction, another channel was opened for the expression of a philosophy of localism upon a broad and official scale. Virginia used this avenue for propounding strictly Republican principles when it instructed its senators and requested its representatives on January 11, 1800, "to procure a reduction of the army, within the narrowest limits compatible with the protection of the forts and the preservation of the arsenals maintained by the United States; . . . to prevent any augmentation of the navy, and to promote any proposition for reducing it; . . . to oppose the passing of any law founded on, or recognizing the principle lately advanced, 'that the common law

[53] *Preamble & Resolutions Adopted by the General Assembly of Virginia on the Subject of the Right of the State Legislatures to Instruct Their Senators in Congress,* (1811), pamphlet, 12-13, 21.
[54] W. H. Hoyt, ed., *Papers of Archibald D. Murphy,* II, 3-5, notes.

of England is in force under the government of the United States'; . . . [and] to procure a repeal of the acts of Congress commonly called the alien and sedition-acts." [55]

Scarcely more than a year later, the probability of applying these principles, and others like them, received a new lease of life when the first Republican President, Thomas Jefferson, on March 4, 1801, stepped into his high office, fired, as he proclaimed in his inaugural address, with the determination to maintain "the support of the State governments in all their rights, as the most competent administrations for our domestic concerns and the surest bulwarks against antirepublican tendencies." [56] For twenty-four consecutive years thereafter, the highest executive office in the land was to be filled by a native Virginian engaged in promoting the Southern cause of local self-government.

At the end of Jefferson's first term, a contemporary chronicler of events could fill an eighty-eight page pamphlet largely with the accomplishments of the Republican Party in the interest of localism during its four years of office. The author, who signed the pen name "Curtius" (perhaps John Taylor), was furthermore optimistic about the future, for he commended Jefferson's proposals to Congress for

A retrenchment of unnecessary expence,
An abolition of useless offices,

[55] From an 1850 publication of *The Virginia Report of 1779-1800* . . . , 243-244. Typical Southern reactions towards other projects of national legislation are found in the speeches of James Madison, Hugh Williamson, and William B. Giles against national bounties, February 3-9, 1792. *Annals of Congress*, 2 Cong., 1 sess., 362-400, *passim;* Thomas Jefferson's constitutional objections to a national agricultural society, Letter to Robert Livingston, February 16, 1801, P. L. Ford, ed., *Writings of Jefferson*, VII, 493; Charles Pinckney's opposition to the constitutionality of a grand congressional committee to settle disputed election returns. Speech in the Senate, March 28, 1800. *Annals of Congress*, 6 Cong., 1 sess., 126 *et seq.;* Spencer Roane's opposition to a national seminary of education. Fragment of a letter to James Monroe, December, 1815. "Letters of Spencer Roane 1788-1822," *Bulletin of the New York Public Library*, March, 1906. X, no. 3, p. 168; James M. Mason's interpretation of the constitutional provision "to establish Post Offices and post Roads." Address to the Freeholders of Frederick County, Virginia, 1827. Virginia Mason, *Life and Correspondence of George Mason*, 24-25.
[56] J. D. Richardson, ed., *Messages and Papers*, I, 323.

> An adherence to specific appropriations,
> A reduction of the army,
> A faithful payment of the interest, and a
> prompt discharge of the principal of the
> public debt.[57]

Particularly to be commended, according to this pamphlet, was the work of Jefferson in the "abolition of useless offices"; for at that time the number of offices in a given unit of government was considered the best criterion of the power and influence of that government. Even during the fight for the adoption of the Constitution, James Madison found it necessary to convince the opponents of that instrument that the local governments had nothing to fear from the encroachments of national patronage. "Is it supposed that it [the national government] will preponderate against that of the state governments?" asked Madison in the Virginia Convention. "The means of influence consist in having the disposal of gifts and emoluments, and in the number of persons employed by and dependent upon a government. . . . The number of dependents upon the state governments will be infinitely greater than those on the general government. . . . Let us compare the members composing the legislative, executive, and judicial powers, in the general government, with these in the states, and let us take into view the vast number of persons employed in the states: from the chief officers to the lowest, we shall find the scale preponderating so much in favor of the states, that, while so many persons are attached to them, it will be impossible to turn the balance against them. There will be an irresistible bias toward the state governments." [58] In the forty-fifth number of *The Federalist,* Madison added: "If the federal government is to have collectors of revenue, the State governments will have theirs also. . . . Within every district to which a Federal collector would be allotted, there would be not less than thirty or forty, or even more, officers of different descriptions, and many of them persons of character and weight, whose influence would lie on the side of the State." [59]

Nothing more pleasing, therefore, could have reached the ears of the Southern supporters of local autonomy than these words of Jefferson in his first message to Congress on December 8, 1801: "Among those who are dependent on Executive discretion I have begun the reduction of what was deemed unnecessary. The expenses of diplomatic agency have been considerably diminished. The inspectors of internal revenue who were found to obstruct the accountability of the institution have been discontinued. Several agencies created by Executive authority, on salaries fixed by that also, have been suppressed. . . . But the great mass of public offices is established by law, and therefore by law alone can be abolished. Should the Legislature think it expedient to pass this roll in review and try all its parts by the test of public utility, they may be assured of every aid and light which Executive information can yield." [60] So anxious was Jefferson to further the reduction of public offices, that he was willing to repeal the internal revenue laws, despite the subsequent necessity for relying more heavily for revenues upon the import duties, which operated to the detriment of the South. The internal revenue system Jefferson feared would fasten on the South a system of extensive patronage dangerous to a republican government. [61]

Whether Jefferson, Madison, or Monroe was occupying the President's chair, the same yardstick of strict construction was used to measure the constitutionality of laws of Congress, enacted or proposed. To the subject of internal im-

[59] H. C. Lodge, ed., *The Federalist*, 289, 290.

[60] J. D. Richardson, ed., *Messages and Papers*, I, 328.

[61] "Curtius" [John Taylor], *A Defence of the Measures of the Administration of Thomas Jefferson*, pamphlet, 28.

provements — "public education, roads, rivers, canals," —
Jefferson applied the yardstick, and on December 2, 1806,
declared "an amendment to the Constitution, by consent of
the States, necessary, because the objects now recommended
are not among those enumerated in the Constitution, and to
which it permits the public moneys to be applied." [62]
Madison applied the yardstick after eight years as President,
and sent to Congress on the last full day of his second term,
March 3, 1817, a veto of an internal improvement bill, contending in his veto message that the " 'power to regulate commerce among the several States' can not include a power to
construct roads and canals, and to improve the navigation
of water courses in order to facilitate, promote, and secure
such a commerce without a latitude of construction departing from the ordinary import of the terms." [63] Monroe was
the third successive Southern president to apply the yardstick of strict construction to internal improvements. "If the
power exist," he stated in his veto message of May 4, 1822,
"it must be either because it has been specifically granted to
the United States or that it is incidental to some power which
has been specifically granted. If we examine the specific
grants of power we do not find it among them, nor is it incidental to any power which has been specifically granted." [64]

This influence which the South was exerting through the
executive department in support of localism, it gladly would
have wielded in the national judiciary. Jefferson, as we have
seen, had planned that it should be so, in selecting Spencer

[62] J. D. Richardson, ed., *Messages and Papers*, I, 409, 410. In purchasing the Louisiana territory, Jefferson declared that the Executive had done "an act beyond the Constitution"; but he hoped that a sub-sequent "appeal to *the nation* for an ad-ditional article to the Constitution, approv-ing & confirming the act which the nation had not previously authorized" would re-sult in a popular confirmation of the acts of the government "for doing for them [the people] what we know they would have done for themselves had they been in a situation to do it." Letter to John C. Breckinridge, August 12, 1803. P. L. Ford, ed., *Writings of Jefferson*, VIII, 244, note.
[63] J. D. Richardson, ed., *Messages and Papers*, I, 584.
[64] *Ibid.*, II, 143.

Roane to succeed Oliver Ellsworth as Chief Justice of the Supreme Court. Thwarted here, Jefferson and his Republican colleagues held out hopes that Marshall's decision in the case of *Marbury* v. *Madison* (1804) would be so politically biased as to justify impeachment of the Chief Justice.[65] Here again Jefferson was thwarted, so that he had to be content with exercising a good Republican influence over the lower branches of the judiciary and with the appointment of "sound" Republicans to other positions on the Supreme Court Bench as those posts fell vacant. Yet, in the latter instance, Jefferson lived to see, to his chagrin, both of his appointees, Joseph Story and William Johnson, become pliant tools in the hands of their leader, the Chief Justice. Although a majority of the Supreme Court was from the Southern states, it was not a majority representative of Southern interests in advancing the cause of local self-government.

Like other phases of the movement for local autonomy, the dispute over the structure and powers of the federal courts began in the formative period of the Union; but unlike other phases of the fight for localism, the position of the South was far from united on the most appropriate means of insuring protection against the consolidating tendencies of a national judiciary. In the earlier decades of the Union, it would appear that the South generally was advocating the use of the state courts as inferior national courts of the first instance for the adjudication of all questions of federal jurisdiction, thus restricting the national judiciary to a single Supreme Court, with the possible addition of inferior courts of admiralty. In the Federal Convention, John Rutledge of South Carolina argued "that the State Tribunals might and ought to be left in all cases to decide in the first instance"; and his colleague, Pierce Butler, could see no necessity for

[65] A. J. Beveridge, *Life of John Marshall*, III, 20-22, 51-53, 143-145, 154-222. Re-   publican activities against the judiciary are excellently treated in these pages.

inferior federal tribunals so long as "the State Tribunals might do the business." [66]

When the decision of the Constitutional Convention to leave this question of inferior tribunals to future legislation came before the Virginia ratifying convention, it was in part responsible for the massed attack there directed against the entire judiciary article of the Constitution. George Mason foresaw the creation of a system of national inferior courts "as numerous as Congress may think proper," which, together with an unlimited jurisdiction, would lead "slowly and imperceptibly rather than all at once" to the establishment of "one great, national, consolidated government." [67] James Madison and Edmund Randolph sought to allay such fears by popularizing the idea that the state courts would be used as the sole inferior federal courts; but the Convention was not to be satisfied short of an official recommendation for a constitutional amendment limiting Congress to the creation of inferior courts of admiralty.[68] The North Carolina Convention adopted the same proposal,[69] and it was several times submitted as an amendment during the first session of Congress.[70]

On one occasion the issue came before the first Congress during the debates over the judiciary act; and at that time a most interesting divergence of opinion developed within the ranks of the Southern members. James Jackson, representative from Georgia, in keeping with previous Southern sentiment, objected to a separate system of inferior federal courts, holding instead "that the harmony of the people, their liberties and properties, would be more secure under the legal paths of their ancestors; under their modes of trial,

---

[66] *Documents Illustrative of the Formation of the Union,* House Document no. 398, 69 Cong., 1 sess., 157-405.
[67] Jonathan Elliot, ed., *Debates,* (2 ed.) III, 521-522.

[68] *Ibid.,* 533-538, 570-573, 660.
[69] *Ibid.,* II, 246.
[70] *Annals of Congress,* 1 Cong., 1 sess., 762, 778.

and known methods of decision." But William L. Smith of
South Carolina saw that wherever the state courts were used
as inferior federal courts, an appeal must lie from them to
the national Supreme Court or "otherwise the judicial authority of the union might be altogether eluded." The dangers to local autonomy involved in such appeals, Smith described as follows: "It is, however, much to be apprehended
that this constant control of the Supreme Federal Court over
the adjudication of the State courts, would dissatisfy the
people, and weaken the importance and authority of the State
judges. Nay, more, it would lessen their respectability in the
eyes of the people, even in causes which properly appertain
to the State jurisdictions; because the people, being accustomed to see their decrees overhauled and annulled by a
superior tribunal, would soon learn to form an irreverent
opinion of their importance and abilities." Smith's conclusion was that the state and federal jurisdictions should be
kept entirely separate, and he brought to his support the
constitutional provision requiring all judges of inferior courts
to hold their commissions during good behavior. Since the
judges of the state courts do not hold their office during good
behavior, he contended, the state courts cannot become inferior federal courts. "Does not, then, the constitution," he
asked, "in the plainest and most unequivocal language, preclude us from alloting any part of the Judicial authority of
the Union to the State judicature?" [71]

The Judiciary Act of September 24, 1789, did not satisfy
the supporters of either viewpoint. On the one hand, the act
did create separate inferior federal courts, but it did not give
them exclusive jurisdiction over federal questions; on the
other hand, the act did make use of the state courts for disposing of federal questions, but it also expressly provided

[71] Debate in the House, August 29, 1789. *Annals of Congress*, 1 Cong., 1 sess., 802, 798, 818-819. See also, Alexander Hamilton, *The Federalist*, nos. 81, 82. H. C. Lodge, ed., *The Federalist*, 506-508; 513-516.

in the famous twenty-fifth section for appeal in such cases from the highest state court to the national Supreme Court.[72]

The Southern dilemma was most depressing! To demand for state courts a large concurring jurisdiction over federal questions was to impair the efficacy of these courts in the eyes of the people through more numerous appeals to the national Supreme Court; but to insist upon a separation of federal and state jurisdiction through the use of separate inferior federal tribunals was to forego the opportunity of exercising a strong retarding influence upon national expansion through extensive judicial interpretation by the state courts.

For many years the South was content to evade this dilemma by directing a general attack against the expansion of judicial power as delegated in the Constitution. One striking example of this attack was ushered in by the decision of the Supreme Court in *Chisholm* v. *Georgia* holding that, under the Constitutional provision extending judicial power to cases "between a State and citizens of another State," any state might be made a party defendant as well as a party plaintiff in a case brought before the courts. This decision led to the first official emanation from the Supreme Court of the doctrine of state rights through the able separate opinion of James Iredell, who rather conclusively demonstrated, in an opinion filling twenty pages of the Supreme Court Reports, that it was never the intention of the framers of the Constitution to have a "sovereign" state dragged into court at the behest of an individual.[73] It is well known that the strong movement against this decision culminated in 1798 with the adoption of the eleventh amendment designed to prohibit the recurrence of another such case without the consent of the state involved.[74]

---

[72] 1 Statutes at Large, 73-93.

[73] 2 Dallas 419. The decision was contrary to the opinion of Alexander Hamilton, *The Federalist*, no. 81. H. C. Lodge, ed., *The Federalist*, 508-509.

[74] "The Judicial power of the United States shall not be construed to extend to any suit in law or equity, commenced or prosecuted against one of the United States by Citizens of another State, or by Citizens or Subjects of any Foreign State." Amendment XI.

THE SOUTH AS A CONSCIOUS MINORITY

Still another early application of the state-rights doctrine came in the opposition to the use of a federal common law as a lever of national expansion. Beginning immediately after the government was established, the national courts assumed jurisdiction over persons charged with offenses based solely upon the common law of England; and during the first decade many indictments were permitted and punishments inflicted without the aid of the Constitution or of the Federal Statutes for a definition of the crime involved.[75] There were even assumptions, as in the case of the Alien and Sedition Laws, that Congress might call in the aid of the common law as a justification for legislative action.

Among the many to raise a cry of opposition to such dangerous assumptions was John Taylor, soon to leave the political arena to devote an undistracted private life to the cause of localism. Speaking on the point before the Virginia House of Delegates on December 20, 1798, Taylor said, in part: "But the Constitution of the Union did nowhere adopt the common law or refer to it as a rule of construction. . . . it was impossible that the State conventions which assented to the Constitution could ever have supposed that they were establishing a Government which could at pleasure dip their hands into the inexhaustible treasuries of the common law and law of nations and thence extract as much power as they pleased."[76] Shortly afterwards, the committee that drafted and presented to the Virginia Legislature the Report on the Resolutions considered the issue of sufficient importance to fill several pages of their report with historical evidence tending to prove that a federal common law did not exist in the colonial period or in the revolutionary period; nor was it adopted by implication either in the Articles of Confederation or in the Federal Constitution.[77]

[75] A. J. Beveridge, *Life of John Marshall*, III, 23-26.
[76] *Alien and Sedition Laws.* Senate Document 873. 62 Cong., 2 sess., 94. See also,

Thomas Cooper, "On the Sedition Bill" in his *Political Essays*, (1800), 11.
[77] Gaillard Hunt, ed., *Writings of Madison*, VI, 372-382. In *United States v. Hudson*

PRINCIPLE OF LOCAL SELF-GOVERNMENT

In later years, Southern theorists insisted on limiting the jurisdiction of the federal courts to a consideration of "all cases in law and equity" defined to embrace "only such questions as are of a judicial character; — that is, questions in which the parties litigant are amenable to the process of the courts."[78] One of the best statements of this position is found in John Taylor's *New Views of the Constitution:* "Controversies may arise under the constitution between political departments, in relation to their powers; between the legislative and treaty-making departments; between the senate and the house of representatives; between the president and the senate; or between the state and federal departments; but they would not be cases in law and equity, nor is any power to decide them given to the federal judiciary. One species of controversy relates to the form of government; the other flows from its operation. The power by which a government is formed or altered, is not the power by which the law-suits of individuals are tried; and therefore a power to try suits in law and equity, was never supposed to comprise the former power."[79]

(1812) 7 Cranch 32, and *United States* v. *Coolidge*, (1816), 1 Wheaton 415, the United States Supreme Court denied the federal courts jurisdiction over common-law offenses in criminal cases. Felix Frankfurter and J. M. Landis, *The Business of the Supreme Court*, 12. These authors point out other limitations on the national judiciary during the first three decades of Union, particularly those concerning removal of cases from state to federal courts, pp. 10, 11, notes.
[78] John C. Calhoun, *Discourse on the Constitution*, R. K. Crallé, ed., *Works of Calhoun*, I, 259.
[79] *Op. cit.*, p. 134. A somewhat similar statement was once made by John Marshall himself in a speech on the Jonathan Robbins case in the House of Representatives on March 7, 1800. "A case in law or equity," said Marshall, "was a term well understood, and of limited signification. It was a controversy between parties which

had taken a shape for judicial decision. If the Judicial power extended to every question under the Constitution, it would involve almost every subject proper for Legislative discussion and decision; if, to every question under the laws and treaties of the United States, it would involve almost every subject on which the Executive could act." Marshall denied that the judiciary possessed "any political power whatever"; and needless to say his general position in this speech as interpreted by Southern philosophers later became for him a dangerous boomerang, striking, as we shall see, at the very heart of his greatest contribution to national expansion — the doctrine of judicial review. *Annals of Congress*, 6 Cong., 1 sess., 606. There is an account of this incident in A. J. Beveridge, *Life of John Marshall*, II, 462 *et seq.* Marshall was quoted extensively in "The Tribunal of Dernier Resort," *Southern Review*, November, 1830, VI, 493; and in

THE SOUTH AS A CONSCIOUS MINORITY

Meanwhile, the early dilemma between the exclusive use of state courts for the settlement of federal questions, carrying therewith the objectionable right of appeal to the United States Supreme Court, and the use of inferior national courts for the solution of federal issues, prohibiting to that extent the participation of state judges in the interpretation of federal law, brought on the most extreme of all the campaigns waged in defense of local self-government. For the South would grab the two horns of this dilemma, cast aside the undesirable features of each and retain the advantages of both. The demand was for a broad concurrent jurisdiction for state courts over federal questions without the opportunity of appeal to the Supreme Court of the United States!

The case of *Fairfax's Devisee* v. *Hunter's Lessee* [80] was made an issue for the opening of this campaign. The plaintiff claimed title to certain lands in Virginia under treaty rights between the United States and Great Britain; the defendant laid claim to the same lands under a grant from the State of Virginia. In the adjudication of this controversy, which had been before the state courts for more than sixteen years, the Virginia Court of Appeals finally rendered a decision for the defendant in support of the state statute. Under the twenty-fifth section of the Judiciary Act of 1789, the case was brought before the United States Supreme Court on writ of error; and there, in an opinion rendered by Joseph Story on March 15, 1813, the decision of the Virginia Court of Appeals was reversed and a mandate was directed to the judges of the Virginia Court instructing them "to enter judgment for the appellant, Philip Martin [Fairfax's Devisee]."

"The Extent of the Powers of the Federal Judiciary," a chapter in R. J. Turnbull's *Observations on State Sovereignty . . .* (1850), 90. Both these articles deal at length with the meaning of "cases in law and equity." See further on this point, John Taylor, *Tyranny Unmasked*, 264-265; Robert Y. Hayne, Oration at Charleston, South Carolina, 1831. *Hayne's Fourth-of-July Oration*, pamphlet, 27; John C. Calhoun, speech in the Senate, February 15, 1833. *Register of Debates in Congress*, 22 Cong., 2 sess., 519 *et seq.*; and John C. Calhoun, *Discourse on the Constitution*, R K. Crallé, *Works of Calhoun*, I, 338.
[80] United States Supreme Court Reports, 7 Cranch 603 (1813).

The six state judges unanimously refused to obey the mandate, holding, instead, in separate opinions prepared in reply, that so much of Section 25 of the National Judiciary Act as "extends the appellate jurisdiction of the Supreme Court to this court, is not in pursuance of the constitution of the United States." The ablest of these opinions was written by Judge Cabell, who held that since the state and national governments were not dependent upon each other, neither could act compulsively upon the other. Therefore, said he, the state and the national courts, representing coordinate units of government, could not instruct or command each other. From this it followed that the meaning of the National Constitution, laws, and treaties "must, in cases coming before State courts, be decided by the State Judges, *according to their own judgments, and upon their own responsibility.*" If differences in constitutional interpretation developed between the state and national courts, this conflict was to be settled by the sovereign people acting through the constitutional amending process.[81]

President Roane of the Virginia Court of Appeals did not help his own cause when he certified these opinions to the national Supreme Court for review in the case, *Martin v. Hunter's Lessee;* for this gave Story the opportunity to establish more thoroughly, in one of the longest and best opinions that he ever wrote, the principle that the appellate jurisdiction of the Supreme Court embraced every federal case "not exclusively to be decided by way of original jurisdiction." It is the case and not the court that gives jurisdiction, he held; and, furthermore, unless the appellate power of the Supreme Court extended to federal cases arising in the state courts, it could not extend as the Constitution required, "to all cases . . . arising under this Constitution, the Laws of

[81] A. J. Beveridge, *Life of John Marshall*, IV, 152, 157-159.

the United States, and Treaties made, or which shall be made under their Authority." [82]

For a time this issue was overshadowed by other nationalizing decisions of the Supreme Court, but it regained a preeminent place in the controversy over localism five years later when another appeal was taken from the highest court of Virginia to the national Supreme Court. This clash came when Cohens and others were arrested, tried, and convicted by Virginia authorities for selling in the state of Virginia and in violation of state law certain lottery tickets authorized by an ordinance of the City of Washington, D. C. Cohens appealed to the United States Supreme Court; and this time, in the case of *Cohens* v. *Virginia,* it was Marshall who, by entertaining an appeal from the highest state court, asserted a position of supremacy for the national government "in all cases where it is empowered to act" — a supremacy, so he maintained, which from the very nature of government required that the judicial power "must be co-extensive with the legislative, and must be capable of deciding every judicial question which grows out of the constitution and laws." [83]

Against this nationalistic opinion, Spencer Roane reopened the bombardment which he had so furiously conducted two years earlier in the war upon *McCulloch* v. *Maryland.* In a series of five articles published between May 25 and June 18, 1821, in the *Richmond Enquirer,* Roane, now a seasoned veteran from a similar campaign of 1813-1816, employed every artifice to refute Marshall's defense of appellate jurisdiction over state tribunals, even to calling the Constitution a "treaty" between "sovereign governments" under which Virginia was as much a foreign nation as Russia so far as the

---

[82] Constitution, Art. III, Sec. 2. An account of the case together with the quotations herein cited is found in A. J. Beveridge, *Life of John Marshall,* IV. The original is reported in 1 Wheaton 304.

[83] United States Supreme Court Reports, 6 Wheaton 264. An account of the case together with the quotations herein cited may be found in A. J. Beveridge, *Life of John Marshall,* IV, 348, 350.

jurisdiction of the Supreme Court over the judgments of the state courts was concerned.[84]

But if, in the attack upon *McCulloch* v. *Maryland,* Roane lacked the heavy artillery of historical argument which arrived seven years too late under Robert J. Turnbull from South Carolina, he needed even more in this campaign the vital reinforcements of keen constitutional analysis so ably, though so uselessly, contributed by an unknown warrior in the *Southern Review* of 1830. Appellate jurisdiction to the Supreme Court, stated the unknown warrior, can come only from inferior courts; for the word *appellate* necessarily implies the word *inferior.* But the Constitution "recognizes *no tribunal as inferior to that Court,* excepting such as Congress shall *ordain* and *establish.*" Congress cannot "ordain and establish" a state court as an inferior federal tribunal; for to "constitute a tribunal is to define the extent of its jurisdiction, to fix the number of its judges, to prescribe the times and places of its sittings, and to regulate its proceedings, etc." "But," asked the writer, "Can Congress exercise any of these powers in relation to State Courts?" If, then, the whole judicial power of the United States, as the Constitution expressly states, is "vested in one supreme Court, and in such inferior Courts as the Congress may from time to time ordain and establish," and if the whole judicial power of the Supreme Court, as the Constitution likewise designates, is confined to its original jurisdiction and its appellate jurisdiction from *inferior* tribunals, how can appeals lie from the state courts which are in no sense "inferior" federal tribunals and which cannot be made so by an act of Congress?[85]

It is doubtful, however, whether the massed attack of the

[84] A. J. Beveridge, *Life of John Marshall,* IV, 358-359.

[85] "The Tribunal of Dernier Resort," *Southern Review,* November, 1830, VI, no. 12, pp. 442-445. Appleton's *Cyclopedia of American Biography* attributes a treatise by this title to R. J. Turnbull. This principle is discussed, though not so thoroughly, in John Taylor's *Construction Construed and Constitutions Vindicated,* (1820), 130-131.

entire Ante-bellum South could have withstood the wither-
ing fire of centralization directed by a John Marshall through
his biggest guns of judicial expansion of national power:
McCulloch v. *Maryland* (1819), *Dartmouth College* v.
Woodward (1819), *Cohens* v. *Virginia* (1821), and *Gib-
bons* v. *Ogden* (1824).[86] At least Spencer Roane had received all along a substantial backing within his own state.
Jefferson wrote in 1823 that Roane's attack upon the opinion in *Cohens* v. *Virginia* appeared to him "to pulverize every
word which had been delivered by Judge Marshall, of the
extra-judicial part of his opinion"; [87] and the Virginia Assembly supported Roane's position by adopting a resolution
"that the Supreme Court of the United States does not possess appellate jurisdiction in any case decided by a State
court." [88] Other states were soon implicated in troubles of
their own with the Supreme Court: Kentucky opposing the
decision in *Green* v. *Biddle* (1821 and 1823), and Georgia
actually defying the decision in *Worcester* v. *Georgia*
(1832).[89]

Indeed, Spencer Roane, for all he had done, was no more
entitled to be ranked among the leaders in the cause of localism than was his fellow statesman, from whose writings he
quoted — John Taylor of Caroline County, Virginia. Twice
with an opportunity to become a more or less permanent fix-
ture in the United States Senate, Taylor had either resigned
or refused to run for reëlection in order to retire to the quiet
of private life (for his means were adequate) where he might
direct an unharassed but deadly attack upon the enemies of
local self-government. Beginning in 1814 with the publica-

[86] United States Supreme Court Reports:
4 Wheaton 316; 4 Wheaton 518; 6 Wheaton
264; 9 Wheaton 1.
[87] Letter to Johnson, June 12, 1823. P. L.
Ford, ed., *Writings of Jefferson*, X, 229,
note.
[88] Resolutions of February 19, 1821. H. V.

Ames, ed., *State Documents on Federal
Relations*, 104.
[89] United States Supreme Court Reports,
8 Wheaton 1; 6 Peters 515. For the contributions of Georgia to the cause of localism, see U. B. Phillips, *Georgia and State
Rights*, American Historical Association,
Annual Report, 1901, II.

tion of *An Inquiry into the Principles and Policy of the Government of the United States,* a statement of the true principles of the American Government, Taylor produced within the span of a single decade four voluminous works all of which were equally devoted to the cause of localism. His *Construction Construed and Constitutions Vindicated* (1819) followed immediately after Marshall's decision in *McCulloch* v. *Maryland,* and five of its sixteen chapters are devoted to that case. His *Tyranny Unmasked* (1821) is largely directed against centralization embodied in the new tariff bills; and his *A New View of the Constitution* (1823) is primarily a defense of state sovereignty.[90]

In spite of these worthy efforts, Taylor's despair in the cause for which he was fighting is summarily set forth in the closing pages of his *Tyranny Unmasked,* wherein he contrasted the federal system as it had been portrayed in theory with that system as it had come to be in practice:

Theory: "Each State has a right to make its own local laws."
Practice: "Congress and the Court can repeal them, and make local laws for the States."
Theory: "Taxes ought to be imposed for national use."
Practice: "They ought to be imposed to enrich corporations and exclusive privileges."
Theory: "State functionaries cannot discharge their duties, unless they are free."
Practice: "The Federal courts may put them in prison."
Theory: "The Federal department cannot constitutionally invade State rights."
Practice: "It may do so if it pleases."
Theory: "Congress may establish post roads."
Practice: "It may make all roads."
Theory: "It may make war;"
Practice: "that is, it may make canals."
Theory: "It may dispose of public lands;"

[90] Jefferson once stated that each state should place a copy of Taylor's *Construction Construed* in the hands of its members of Congress as a standing instruction. W. F. Dodd, "Taylor, Prophet of Secession," *John P. Branch Historical Papers,* June, 1908, II, nos. 3 and 4, p. 243. Extracts from Taylor's writings may be conveniently found in B. F. Wright, Jr., ed., *A Source Book of American Political Theory,* 343-365.

Practice: "that is, it may give them away."
Theory: "It was instituted for common defence, general welfare, and to preserve the blessings of liberty."
Practice: "It was also instituted to establish monopolies, exclusive privileges, bounties, sinecures, pensions, lotteries, and to give away the public money."

"Such is the chaos," concludes Taylor, "which is obscuring the original effulgence of our system of government, and gradually intercepting the genial warmth it imparted, whilst inspired by home-bred principles." [91]

Taylor's charge, largely directed against Congress, was no more severe than Jefferson on a dozen different occasions had hurled at the judiciary. "The judiciary of the United States is the subtle corps of sappers and miners constantly working under ground to undermine the foundations of our confederated fabric," so he wrote Thomas Ritchie, editor of the *Richmond Enquirer*. Four weeks later, after reading Roane's essays and Taylor's *Tyranny Unmasked*, Jefferson wrote in approval: "The judiciary branch is the instrument which, working like gravity, without intermission, is to press us at last into one consolidated mass." [92]

By this time the executive department with its expanding patronage had also been added to the mill of national consolidation. A select committee reporting to the Senate on May 4, 1826, found as a result of its investigations that "in no part of the practical operation of the Federal Government, has the predictions of its ablest advocates been more completely falsified, than in this subject of patronage." The committee then quoted extensively from Madison's words in

[91] John Taylor, *Tyrany Unmasked*, 343-344, 345.
[92] Letter to Thomas Ritchie, December 25, 1820, and to Archibald Thweat, January 19, 1821. P. L. Ford, ed., *Writings of Jefferson*, X, 170, 184. Jefferson's numerous attacks upon the judiciary are brought together in Charles S. Thomas, "Jefferson and the Judiciary," H. C. Black, ed., *Constitutional Review*, April, 1926, X, 67-76. See also John Rowan of Kentucky, Speech in the Senate, April 10, 1826: "The evil apprehended is the absorption of the powers of the States by the General Government, through the instrumentality of its Judges. . . ." *Register of Debates in Congress*, 19 Cong., 1 sess., 428. Also, 436.

PRINCIPLE OF LOCAL SELF-GOVERNMENT

The Federalist, no. 45, in order to "exhibit the difference which a few short years have developed, between the theoretical and the practical Government of this Union." After submitting a Blue Book showing "the whole number of persons employed, and the whole amount of money paid out" under the direction of each department, the committee added .that the Senate should discover from this compilation sufficient evidence "to show that the predictions of those who were not blind to the defects of the Constitution, are ready to be realized; that the power and influence of *Federal* patronage, contrary to the argument in the '*Federalist*,' is an overmatch for the power and influence of *State* patronage; that its workings will contaminate the purity of all elections, and enable the Federal Government, eventually, to govern throughout the States, as effectually as if they were so many provinces of one vast empire." [93]

Thomas Jefferson, now with over fifty years in the public service, but with far less enthusiasm for the Constitution than characterized his letters from Paris in 1787, brought together on December 26, 1825, six months before his death, the work of the three departments of the national government in misapplying his original conception of a distribution of powers in the federal system. To his friend William Giles he wrote: "I see, as you do, and with the deepest affliction, the rapid strides with which the federal branch of our government is advancing towards the usurpation of all the rights reserved to the States, and the consolidation in itself of all powers, foreign and domestic; and that, too, by constructions

[93] *Register of Debates in Congress,* 19 Cong., 1 sess., Appendix, 136. A more elaborate treatment concerning the expansion of national patronage was presented to the House on March 23, 1830, by P. P. Barbour of Virginia, who set out to prove "that there is not a county, city, town, village, or even hamlet, in the United States, which the federal arm does not reach; . . . that, in point of official patronage, that of this Government is immeasurably beyond that of the States." *Register of Debates in Congress,* 21 Cong., 1 sess., 654. For later attacks, see John C. Calhoun, speech in the Senate, February 9, 1835. *Register of Debates in Congress,* 23 Cong., 2 sess., Appendix, 222; and Jefferson Davis, speech in the Senate, May 17, 1860. *Congressional Globe,* 36 Cong., 1 sess., 2156.

which, if legitimate, leave no limits to their power. Take together the decisions of the federal court, the doctrines of the President, and the misconstructions of the constitutional compact acted on by the legislature of the federal branch, and it is but too evident, that the three ruling branches of that department are in combination to strip their colleagues, the State authorities, of the powers reserved by them, and to exercise themselves all functions foreign and domestic." [94]

The constitutional provisions for local self-government upon which the South as a sectional minority had relied for protection since the formation of the Union were now largely abandoned. Bitter attacks more pointed than those of Jefferson or Roane or Taylor were launched against "paper guarantees." During the tariff controversy of 1824, John Randolph exclaimed in the House: "I have no faith in parchment sir; I have no faith in the abracadabra of the Constitution; I have no faith in it." [95] Four years later in the Senate, Nathaniel Macon of North Carolina, after hearing Robert Y. Hayne's *constitutional* objections to a federal grant for education, remarked: "I don't like to hear members talk about the Constitution. . . . It is useless. I have taken my leave of it some years ago." [96] And nine years later a new leader in a new campaign, John C. Calhoun, justified his departure upon a new highway of protection by declaring "that the constitution has gradually become a dead letter, and that all restrictions upon the power of Government have been virtually removed, so as practically to convert the General Government into a Government of an absolute majority, without check or limitation." [97]

[94] P. L. Ford, ed., *Writings of Jefferson,* X, 354-355.

[95] *Annals of Congress,* 18 Cong., 1 sess., 2361.

[96] Remarks on March 28, 1828. *Register of Debates in Congress,* 20 Cong., 1 sess., 549.

[97] Speech in the Senate, February 15, 1833. *Register of Debates in Congress,* 22 Cong., 2 sess., 548. See Thomas Cooper, *Consolidation An Account of Parties in the United States,* preface to the second edition, (1830).

CHAPTER IV

THE PRINCIPLE OF THE CONCURRENT VOICE

"THE adoption of some restriction or limitation, which shall so effectually prevent any one interest, or combination of interests, from obtaining the exclusive control of the government, . . . can be accomplished only in one way, — and that is, by such an organism of the government . . . as will, by dividing and distributing the powers of government, give to each division or interest, through its appropriate organ, either a concurrent voice in making and executing the laws, or a veto on their execution. . . . it is only by the one or the other that the different interests, orders, classes, or portions, into which the community may be divided, can be protected, and all conflict and struggle between them prevented. . . ." These are the words of John C. Calhoun taken from his *Disquisition on Government,* written in 1848.[1] They contain two additional possibilities for Southern minority protection within the Union; and the first of these — "a concurrent voice in making and executing the laws" — becomes the subject of our attention in the present chapter.

THE PRINCIPLE EXPLAINED AND DEFENDED

The idea of the concurrent voice was not new with Calhoun in 1848, for he had often discussed the theory in the early thirties. In his important letter to Governor Hamilton on August 28, 1832, he had written that the "principle of the concurring majority has sometimes been incorporated in the regular and ordinary operation of the Government — each

---

[1] R. K. Crallé, ed., *Works of Calhoun,* I, 24-25. See also, Calhoun's *Discourse on* the Constitution, *Ibid.,* 266-267.

interest having a distinct organization — and a combination of the whole forming the Government; but still requiring the consent of each, within its proper sphere, to give validity to the measures of Government." [2]

Just what Calhoun had in mind, he perhaps explained best in a number of simple hypothetical situations which he presented to the Senate on February 15, 1833: Calhoun supposed "a small community of five persons, separated from the rest of the world; and . . . that they determine to govern the community by the will of a majority; and . . . that a majority, in order to meet the expenses of the Government, lay an equal tax, say of one hundred dollars, on each individual of this little community." From this premise, Calhoun proceeded to explain why a concurrent voice was necessary to protect the interests of the minority in his presumed community: "Their treasury would contain five hundred dollars. Three are a majority; and they, by supposition, have contributed three hundred as their portion, and the other two, (the minority,) two hundred. The three have the right to make the appropriations as they may think proper. The question is, how would the principle of the absolute and unchecked majority operate, under these circumstances, in this little community? . . . should they [the majority] appropriate the money in a manner to benefit their own particular interest, without regard to the interest of the two; (and that they will so act, unless there be some efficient check, he who best knows human nature will least doubt,) who does not see that the three and the two would have directly opposite interests, in reference to the action of the Government?" Calhoun then enlarged his presumed community to one of twenty-four members and restated the process whereby the majority (thirteen in this case) would encroach upon the minority unless some means were devised to prevent it.

Having diagnosed the evil, Calhoun proceeded to the

[2] The Fort Hill Letter. R. K. Crallé, ed., *Works of Calhoun*, VI, 183.

remedy: "There is a remedy, and but one, the effect of which, whatever may be the form, is to organize society in reference to this conflict of interests, which springs out of the action of Government; and . . . upon all questions tending to bring the parts into conflict, the thirteen against the eleven, take the will, not of the twenty-four as a unit, but that of the thirteen and that of the eleven separately, the majority of each governing the parts; and, where they concur, governing the whole; and where they disagree, arresting the action of the Government." [3]

This principle was not entirely new to the Senate in 1833, for it had been thoroughly thrashed out in the Virginia Constitutional Convention of 1829-1830, wherein a minority East fought for protection within the state government against a majority West, just as a minority South was fighting for protection in the national government against a majority North. Some of the leaders in this Convention were also leaders in the movement for Southern protection within the Union; so that the ideas applicable to the state must have been considered equally applicable to the nation. There James Madison, for example, explained the principle of the concurrent voice in these terms: "In republics, the great danger is, that the majority may not sufficiently respect the rights of the minority . . . We all know that conscience is not a sufficient safe-guard; . . . These favourable attributes of the human character . . . can never be relied on as a guarantee of the rights of the minority against a majority disposed to take unjust advantage of its power. The only effectual safeguard to the rights of the minority, must be laid in such a basis and structure of the Government itself, as may afford, in a certain degree, directly or indirectly, a defensive authority in behalf of a minority having right on its side." [4]

[3] *Register of Debates in Congress*, 22 Cong., 2 sess., 545-547.
[4] *Debates of the Virginia Constitutional Convention 1829-1830*, 537, 538. Also pp. 63-79. Madison suggested this principle with direct reference to the national gov-

Other Southern political thinkers of the middle decades expressed their approval of the principle. In 1824, John Randolph, after taking leave of the Constitution as an adequate protection to local self-government, turned to the concurrent voice by asserting that "those governments only are tolerable where, by the necessary construction of the political machine, the interest of all the parts are obliged to be protected by it."[5] In 1837, A. B. Longstreet wrote from Augusta, Georgia, to his friend Mirabeau B. Lamar a letter so rich in the theory of government and so vital to the interests of the South that it should have become the common Southern property of that day, instead of being relegated to Lamar's files until recently brought to light. Though the immediate subject of the letter was the question of the admission of Texas into the Union, the writer wandered away into fundamental concepts of political power when he maintained: "the great security for all interests in a government, is in having all interests *represented,* and so represented, that every interest may act as a check upon others — Thus if you put farmers and manufacturers together, and say that they shall be governed by the vote of the majority, why then, whichever class has the majority, will favor itself, and oppress the other. But if you say that they should form two distinct bodies and that nothing shall become a law, that has not the sanction of both, it is impossible that either can favor

ernment in the Federal Convention of 1787: Max Farrand, ed., *Records,* I, 486-487; and again in his letter to Jefferson, October 17, 1788: Gaillard Hunt, ed., *Writings of Madison,* V, 272. See also IX, 359, note. On June 25, 1798, John Taylor had written to Vice-President Thomas Jefferson these lines: "Constitutional paper vetos, are nothing, compared with a solid check, so woven into the form of government, as to be incapable of a separation from it." "Letters of John Taylor of Caroline County, Virginia," *John P. Branch Historical Papers,* June, 1908. II, nos.

3 and 4, p. 274. Compare this early statement with the following one made in a letter of L. Q. C. Lamar to P. F. Liddell on December 10, 1860: "Liberty does not exist where rights are on one side and power on the other. To be liberty, rights must be armed with vital powers. A people cannot be free who do not participate in the control of the government which operates upon them." Edward Mayes, *L. Q. C. Lamar: His Life, Times, and Speeches,* 635.
[5] Speech in the House, April 15, 1824. *Annals of Congress,* 18 Cong., 1 sess., 2360.

itself or oppress the other." [6] Again in 1842, R. B. Rhett, aggressive advocate of Southern co-operation and later chairman of the committee that reported the Confederate Constitution, expressed his conviction based upon the similar experiences of the American Colonies in their conflict with Great Britain, that representation of a Southern minority in Congress without some effective check within the machinery of the national government, "would be rather worse than no representation at all; for, from being a party to the legislation, it will afford the semblance of self-taxation, without the least reality." [7]

The justification for the principle of the concurrent voice was based upon a philosophical opposition to numerical majority rule. Rhett, continuing his discussion in 1842, finds this opposition embodied in the Instrument of the "fathers": "The Constitution of the United States was not framed to enforce the will of a majority merely. It aims far higher in its pretensions. Its object is, to enable the *whole* of the people of the United States — not a *part* only — to rule themselves." [8] John C. Calhoun, whose passion for thoroughness was always leading him back to fundamental principles, declared in 1833: "The first mistake was, in supposing that the Government of the absolute majority is the Government of this people; . . . There could be no greater error; the Government of the people is the Government of the whole community. . . . The Government of the absolute majority, instead of the Government of the people, is but the Government of the strongest interests; and when not efficiently checked, is the most tyrannical and oppressive that can be devised." [9]

A third active participant in the struggles of the middle

[6] C. A. Gulick, Jr., ed., *Papers of Mirabeau Buonaparte Lamar*, II, 3.
[7] Speech in the House, July 1, 1842. *Appendix to the Congressional Globe*, 27 Cong., 2 sess., 607.
[8] *Ibid.*
[9] Speech in the Senate, February 15, 1833. *Register of Debates in Congress*, 22 Cong., 2 sess., 547.

decades, though one whose greatest contributions were reserved for the fifties, best explained his opinions on this issue
years later in a letter quite characteristic of his unconquer-
able convictions, even during the War between the States.
In 1864, Alexander H. Stephens wrote: "No doctrine or
principle is more unjust or pernicious than that 'of the greatest good to the greatest number.' The true rule is the greatest good to all, to each and every one, without injury to any.
No one hundred men on earth have the moral right to govern any other ninety-nine men or, less number, and to make
the interests of the ninety-nine, or less number, subservient
to the interests of the hundred, because thereby the greatest
good to the greatest number will be promoted." [10]

THE PRINCIPLE OF CHECKS AND BALANCES: THE BASIS OF ITS APPLICATION

The application of the principle of the concurrent voice
depended upon the maintenance of the constitutional system
of checks and balances. Whatever the purpose for which
this system was originally devised — and there is strong
evidence that protection to minorities was an important factor [11] — the South by the decade of the thirties had come
to look upon the system as essential to its security against
the inroads of a Northern majority. In the course of a
Fourth-of-July Oration (1831), Robert Y. Hayne thus addressed an audience in Charleston, South Carolina: "But
though the minority may not govern, the Constitution expressly provides for numerous cases in which they may arrest
the progress of the majority. The President (who is but an

---

[10] Letter to A. J. Marshall, November 4, 1864. Henry Cleveland, ed., *Stephens in Public and Private with Letters and Speeches,* 802. See further, G. J. McRee, *Life and Correspondence of Iredell,* II, 356; Thomas Cooper, *Foundations of Civil Government,* 16-18; Robert Toombs, Address at Emory College, Georgia, U. B. Phillips, *Life of Toombs,* 157; Jefferson Davis, speech in the Senate, December 10, 1860. *Congressional Globe,* 36 Cong., 2 sess., 29.

[11] See Max Farrand, ed., *Records,* II, 451-452; Jonathan Elliot, ed., *Debates,* (2 ed.), IV, 257.

individual, and may as in the case of Mr. Adams be the representative of a minority,) may by his simple *veto,* arrest the progress of a majority of both houses of Congress and of the whole nation; a majority of the Senate, representing a small minority of the people, may arrest the progress of any other department, and half a dozen Judges are in the constant habit of nullifying the acts of Congress at their pleasure." [12]

So obviously a useful tool in the hands of a minority, it is not surprising that the South vigorously supported the system of checks and balances in the national government. In order to maintain the system, it was necessary to support the principle of a separation of powers. "The constitution," as Felix Grundy of Tennessee explained to the Senate on February 18, 1835, "provides three separate, distinct, and independent departments of Government — legislative, executive, and judicial; and, by this division of power, the wisest lawgivers and statesmen have supposed the best security for liberty was secured. . . ." [13] Therefore — to quote the words of Thomas H. Hall of North Carolina, spoken ten months earlier in the House —"Does not every one see that if the Executive, the Judicial, and the Legislative departments are fused or intermingled, the genius of the Government is changed; that instead of a Government of three centers, acting as mutual and salutary checks on each other, you unite the Executive, the Legislative, and Judicial into one, which is the very definition of despotism." [14]

[12] *Hayne's Fourth of July Oration at Charleston, South Carolina, 1831,* pamphlet, 29-30. "The Checks and balances of our noble Constitution, it is true, were designed to keep down and to control all those sectional elements that have arisen in the States of the Union." William L. Yancey, speech at Columbus, Georgia, 1855. J. W. DuBose, *Life and Times of Yancey,* 300.
[13] *Register of Debates in Congress,* 23 Cong., 2 sess., 528-529.

[14] Speech in the House, April 28, 1834. *Register of Debates in Congress,* 23 Cong., 1 sess., 3824-3825. For earlier statements, see Thomas Jefferson, Letter to John Adams, September 28, 1787. P. L. Ford, ed., *Writings of Jefferson,* IV, 454; James Madison, *The Federalist,* no. 47, H. C. Lodge, ed., *The Federalist,* 300; Charles Pinckney, speeches in the Senate, March 5 and 28, 1800. *Annals of Congress,* 6 Cong., 1 sess., 97, 98, 130.

THE SOUTH AS A CONSCIOUS MINORITY

Upon this separation of powers as a means to an end, R. B. Rhett was able to explain how the Constitution was formed to benefit the whole people of the United States "by the checks and vetoes it has provided." In his speech before the House on July 1, 1842, Rhett carefully emphasized these features of the instrument: "The whole Constitution, indeed, is but a bundle of the most cautiously-bestowed grants of power, on the one hand, and accumulated vetoes to prevent its abuse, on the other . . . it says to this House, 'You may veto the acts of the Senate'; and to the Senate, 'You may veto the acts of the House'; whilst, to the President, it gives the power of a qualified veto on the acts of both. . . . To all its functionaries, legislative, judicial, and executive, in prescribing the powers of each towards the other, and the people, it says, 'I forbid'; . . . At the worst, a veto by any department, is only a negative evil — a suspension of good, if properly exercised — for a limited time only." [15]

In the maintenance of the check-and-balance principle, the South possessed three possibilities of establishing a concurrent voice in the machinery of the national government; for with each department possessing checks upon the other two, any effective Southern control in any of the three departments would subject the entire work of the central government to the concurring voice of a Southern minority. For this reason, the South of the twenties, thirties, and forties was striving to prevent usurpations of power by any of the departments with respect to the other two, just as the South of the first three decades was fighting to stave off the assumption of power by the central government at the expense of the state governments.

Along with the earlier fear of judicial encroachments upon

[15] *Appendix to the Congressional Globe*, 27 Cong., 2 sess., 607, 606. "The *balances* and *checks* which exist in the federal constitution, have no other effect than to offer salutary impediments to the different departments of the same government, when disposed to trespass upon the prerogatives of each other." R. J. Turnbull, *Observations on State Sovereignty* (1850), 104. See also pp. 85-86.

local autonomy, for example, there had arisen the danger of judicial domination of the other two departments. During the transition period from local self-government to the concurrent voice, Jefferson had rendered service in the new cause by raising a cry against judicial control of the executive and legislative departments under the false presumption that the "judiciary is the last resort in relation *to the other departments* of the government." To Spencer Roane he wrote in 1819: "If this opinion be sound, then indeed is our constitution a complete *felo de se*. For intending to establish three departments, co-ordinate and independent, that they might check and balance one another, it has given, according to this opinion, to one of them alone, the right to prescribe rules for the government of the others." [16]

The danger of judicial supremacy did not exceed that of congressional domination. Especially to be feared was the tendency towards congressional control of the executive through an undue influence in the selection of presidential nominees. Both Tennessee and North Carolina attacked the congressional caucus because it interfered with a proper separation of powers. After the former state had adopted resolutions holding this caucus unconstitutional, one Fisher presented similar resolutions to the North Carolina House of Commons and therewith defended his proposals by showing that the Constitution expressly forbids members of Congress to act as electors for President; and yet, so he explained, "by the practice of Caucusing, these Members of Congress indirectly do, what by the Constitution they are prohibited from doing directly." This practice, he further contended, was also out of harmony with the general purpose and spirit of the Constitution: "The Constitution of the Nation is one of checks and of balances; its framers knew the frailties of mankind, and to preserve pure the integrity of its agents, it contemplates keeping separate and

[16] P. L. Ford, ed., *Writings of Jefferson*, X, 140, 141.

distinct from each other, the Legislative and Executive branches of the Government. Members of Congress are chosen by the people for certain specific and defined purposes — to exercise the functions of legislation, and not to elect or to nominate Presidents, except in the event as provided by the Constitution." [17]

Though after a heated debate Fisher's resolutions were tabled at that time, the congressional caucus there under attack was ultimately succeeded in the thirties by the national nominating convention as an institution for selecting presidential candidates. It is furthermore interesting to note that a number of constitutional amendments were advanced in the middle decades to obviate congressional influence in the selection of the President even in the event that no candidate received a majority of the electoral vote. [18] "The Executive," later wrote E. W. Hubard to R. M. T. Hunter, "must in inception, election, and action be distinct from Congress. Let the Congress indicate Candidates, which is tantamount to an election, the next step will be for the President to humble himself to his *real* master. Thus the judiciary will also fall under the influence of Congress. Then a congressional majority will decide and continue the fate of the country." [19]

In the middle period the danger of congressional tyranny was overshadowed by the extensions of the executive power. President Jackson, whose dictatorial methods won for him the title of "King Andrew," gave the whole country reason to fear the unbalancing of the nice adjustments of the Constitution. Over Congress he wielded an extensive veto power,

[17] *Debate on Mr. Fisher's Resolutions against Caucuses in the House of Commons of North Carolina in December, 1823*, pamphlet, 3.
[18] H. V. Ames, *Proposed Amendments to the Constitution*, American Historical Association, *Annual Report*, 1896, II, 90, 108. The Constitution requires that in event no candidate gets a majority of the electoral vote, election from the three highest candidates shall be completed by the House of Representatives voting by states. Amendment XII.
[19] Letter dated May 8, 1852. C. H. Ambler, ed., *Correspondence of Hunter*, American Historical Association, *Annual Report*, 1916, II, 141.

effective, because until then never overridden. To the Supreme Court Jackson is said to have exclaimed, "Well, John Marshall has made his decision, now let him enforce it!" [20] And to insure the co-operation of his own department, Jackson exercised over his entire staff an unlimited power of removal through which he dictated orders to his men as the occasion required. Twice he removed the Secretary of the Treasury for refusing to transfer the government funds from the national bank; and for so doing, he not only received the official censure of the Senate, but, what is more important, he also opened anew the whole question of the nature and function of the check-and-balance principle as applied to the machinery of the national government.

Many times during the spring of 1834, the implications of this check-and-balance principle were debated upon the floors of Congress under the cloak of the removal-of-deposits issue. And if, as was said at the time, "one universal cry of indignation has been raised, from the Potomac to the Gulf of Mexico, against the usurpations of the Executive in this matter," [21] it was raised without "a thought of the question of whether the deposites ought to be removed," [22] but as "a question involving the separation of the powers of a free constitution." [23] In presenting to the House of Representatives certain resolutions of the Virginia Assembly attacking the removal of deposits as "an unauthorized assumption, and a dangerous exercise of executive power," William F. Gordon, on March 3, 1834, spoke as follows: "There is already a fearful proclivity of power towards the Executive Magistrate; and if a construction be given to the constitution

---

[20] A statement attributed to Jackson by a Massachusetts Congressman and uttered in reply to Marshall's decision in the Cherokee Indian Cases. Charles Warren, *The Supreme Court in United States History*, (rev. ed.) I, 759, note.

[21] A statement which J. M. Patton, representative from Virginia, declared during debates in the House on March 3, 1834,

to have been previously made. *Register of Debates in Congress*, 23 Cong., 1 sess., 2850.

[22] J. M. Patton, speech in the House, March 3, 1834. *Register of Debates in Congress*, 23 Cong., 1 sess., 2862.

[23] W. F. Gordon, speech in the House, March 3, 1834. *Register of Debates in Congress*, 23 Cong., 1 sess., 2843.

by which the President would have the power to appoint and displace, at his mere will, or under the pretext of seeing that the laws are faithfully executed, I should feel that the power given to the Legislative Department of the Government was absorbed in the pretended execution of the laws, and the representatives of the people had as well depart to their idle homes." [24]

With an equal desire to preserve the proper balance between the departments, John M. Patton, also of Virginia, immediately moved to lay the resolutions upon the table; and in so doing he introduced numerous quotations from James Madison, among which were these: "The Legislative Department is every where extending the sphere of its activity, and drawing all power into its impetuous vortex"; and if, by senatorial confirmation of removals, "it should happen that the officers connect themselves with the Senate, they may naturally support each other, and, for want of efficacy, reduce the power of the President to a mere vapor; in which case, his responsibility would be annihilated." [25]

In the following year, the attack swung to the veto power of "King Andrew." In the Senate, Joseph Kent of Maryland pointed out that bills of great importance had always passed in Congress by bare majorities, and that experience had shown the veto power as provided in the Constitution to be absolute. "Let this veto power be exerted in all its extent," he said, "and the legislative power vested in Congress by the constitution is no more. Restrict the President in whatever other way you please, still from that moment

[24] *Register of Debates in Congress*, 23 Cong., 1 sess., 2842.
[25] *Register of Debates in Congress*, 23 Cong., 1 sess., 2851, 2856. The first quotation he takes from *The Federalist*, no. 48; the second from *Lloyd's Debates* of the Senate in 1789 on the executive power of removal. During these spring debates, another example of discrepancies in Southern political thought concerning the appropriate means to a common end developed between Richard H. Wilde of Georgia, who held that the Secretary of the Treasury was subject to the control of Congress since "the power over the place of deposite for the public money is a legislative power," and William C. Rives of Virginia, who was inclined to ridicule the "extraordinary novelty . . . that the Secretary of the Treasury is not an executive officer." *Register of Debates in Congress*, 23 Cong., 1 sess., 3038, 286.

he becomes absolute in his actions, a monarch, a dictator, a despot." [26] As a solution to this threat, Kent proposed a constitutional amendment permitting the presidential veto to be overridden by a bare majority vote in Congress. Between the years 1833 and 1842, there were nine other such proposals introduced in Congress.[27]

By 1840 Abel P. Upshur, soon to be appointed Secretary of the Navy under President Tyler, lamented the encroachments of the Executive Department upon Congress and the Courts. "One by one," he wrote, "the powers of the other departments are swept away, or are wielded only at the will of the executive, . . . That officer is not, by the Constitution, and never was designed to be, any thing more than a simple executive of the laws; . . . The boasted *balance,* which is supposed to be found in the separation and independence of the departments, is proved, even by our own experience, apart from all reasoning, to afford no sufficient security against this accumulation of powers." [28]

APPLICATIONS IN THE EXECUTIVE DEPARTMENT

In the executive department lay at once the greatest hope and the greatest fear of the South, for this department alone was ultimately in the hands of one man — the President. If the South, therefore, were to be represented at all in the highest office, it might control the department entirely — and herein lay the hope. Short of control of the presidency, however, the South would be left without any decisive

---

[26] Speech in the Senate, February 20, 1835. *Register of Debates in Congress,* 23 Cong., 2 sess., 549. For another strong attack upon the presidential veto because of its tendency to destroy the check-and-balance principle, see Henry Clay, speech in the Senate, January 24, 1842. *Congressional Globe,* 27 Cong., 2 sess., 164-167. A general treatment is found in E. C. Mason, *The Veto Power.*

[27] H. V. Ames, *Proposed Amendments to the Constitution,* American Historical Asso-

ciation, *Annual Report,* 1896, II, 130.

[28] A. P. Upshur, *Inquiry into the Character of the Federal Government,* 126, 127. Further material on this section may be found in *Register of Debates in Congress,* 23 Cong., 2 sess., Appendix, 219 *et seq.,* especially 222. *Congressional Globe,* 30 Cong., 1 sess., 962; *Appendix to the Congressional Globe,* 30 Cong., 1 sess., 939; C. H. Ambler, *Correspondence of Hunter,* American Historical Association, *Annual Report,* 1916, II, 141.

power — and herein lay the fear. The history of the Ante-bellum Period reveals that in all but twenty of the seventy years of Union under the Federal Constitution, a Southern president occupied the White House. And for a good percentage of those remaining twenty years, the Northern president was a man with Southern sympathies.[29]

This continued Southern control of the presidency created certain sentiment for reliance upon the executive department, as constituted, for the protection of the South. In the early forties, Henry A. Wise of Virginia is said to have worked in Congress for the preservation of the presidential veto "in all its force and power, that it may hereafter be wielded in defence of the South, when fanaticism shall have secured a majority here, [in Congress] and shall attempt to deprive us of our rights."[30] In 1848, Jefferson Davis thus commended the presidential veto as a source of Southern protection: "its great object and use is to restrain irresponsible majorities from unconstitutional aggression on minorities, . . . The veto of the president gives to a considerable minority a power which may be relied on to shield it from legislative invasion of a vital right." Davis then discusses the possibility of protecting negro slavery in the South by electing a President "pledged, by his constitutional veto, to prevent [t]he passage of a law which would violate a right, paramount with us to all other considerations."[31]

Aptly enough, that is just what happened five months later, or, to be exact, on the night of March 3, 1849, during the closing hours of the last session of the Thirtieth Congress. The President, James K. Polk, very effectively tells in his diary the story of what occurred on that night: "At a late hour of the night I learned that the Ho[use of] Repts.

[29] Only the two Adamses, Van Buren, Harrison, Fillmore, Pierce, and Buchanan were Northern; and the last three were eminently satisfactory to the South.
[30] Statement of Kenneth Rayner of North Carolina in the House, August 18, 1842.

Appendix to the Congressional Globe, 27 Cong., 2 sess., 936.
[31] Letter to H. R. Davis, October 6, 1848. Dunbar Rowland, ed., *Davis, Constitutionalist,* I, 215.

had by a vote adopted an amendment to Walker's provision for the Government of California and New Mexico, the substance of which was to declare all the laws of Mexico in force in these territories before their acquisition by the U. S. to continue in force until altered or changed by Congress. . . . Many of the Southern members of Congress of both Houses came into my room in great excitement about it. The effect of the amendment was to sanction the law of Mexico abolishing slavery in that Republic and to sanction other very obnoxious laws. . . . Among others Gen'l Bayley of Va. & Gen'l George S. Houston of Alabama, Lynn Boyd of Ky., [and] Cobb of Georgia came in & earnestly urged me to veto the Bill. . . . Some minutes after they retired Mr. Houston returned and informed me that the excitement among the Southern men of the Ho[use of] Repts. was intense, and that they were signing a paper addressed to me requesting me to veto the Bill. I at once told him to return to the House and stop the signatures to the paper, for the President could not perform a high Constitutional duty of this kind upon a petition. I then told him he might rest easy, that I was prepared with a veto message in my pocket and that I should veto the Bill if it came to me. He was greatly rejoiced, immediately left my room, & I heard nothing more of the petition." [32]

All arguments involving Southern reliance for protection upon the executive department were ably refuted, however, by those who appreciated the true status of the Southern control of the presidency. In opposing the presidential veto

[32] M. M. Quaife, ed., *The Diary of James K. Polk,* IV, 365, 366. An earlier example is found in a letter dated February 16, 1820, from Spencer Roane to President James Monroe concerning the dispute over slavery restriction in Missouri: "I have seen Mr. Ritchie & Many other respectable citizens. . . . They are averse to be dammed up in a land of Slaves, by the Eastern people. . . . They confide in you to resist the menaced restriction in whatever form it may approach you;—whether in relation to States or to territories which are shortly to become States. We are in quest of real safety, and are not to be quibbled out of our rights. . . . You are counted upon I assure you, with unabated Confidence." "Letters of Spencer Roane," *Bulletin of the New York Public Library,* March, 1906, X, no. 3, p. 175.

as an effective weapon of Southern defense, Kenneth Rayner of North Carolina spoke in the House on August 18, 1842, to this effect: "Will not the same overwhelming anti-slavery interest that is to send a majority here to break down the barriers of the Constitution, also elect a President who will co-operate with them in this work of ruin? Is it not as reasonable to suppose that we shall have a Congress with us, and a President against us, as that we shall have a President for us, and Congress against us? . . . This argument cuts both ways — what might be for our temporary benefit today, might be used for our utter destruction tomorrow." [33] Jefferson Davis also lost faith in the executive department as an agency for Southern protection, for in 1860 he questions the value of James S. Green's proposal for establishing an armed force under the control of the executive on the boundary-line between the two sections: "But how long might it be," he asked, "before that same military force would be turned against the minority section which had sought its protection; and that minority thus become mere subjugated provinces under the great military government that it had thus contributed to establish?" [34]

Still others felt that the executive department, though dominated by Southern men, could never be relied upon for effective protection because the North always "has a 'sly and dishonest way' of making Southern men presidents" so that "by means of this delicate flattery" the Southern people might not, for a long time, at least, become aware "that they were little else than the 'milch-cow' of the Union" in supporting the programme of paternalistic legislation for the benefit of the Northern states.[35] In no uncertain tones E. W. Hubard expressed himself upon this issue when he wrote in

[33] *Appendix to the Congressional Globe*, 27 Cong., 2 sess., 936.

[34] Speech in the Senate, December 10, 1860. *Congressional Globe*, 36 Cong., 2 sess., 30.

[35] These quotations are from L. G. Tyler, *Letters and Times of the Tylers*, I, 381. The work was published after the Civil War. See the letter of William Grayson to Patrick Henry, June 12, 1789, I, 165-169.

1852 that the North has "fattened and grown strong upon the substantials, while we are starving and growing weak upon honors." Continuing, Hubard further stated his views: "Now I am for a change. Give me sound and reliable Northern or free State men, and so far as I am concerned they may enjoy *all* the honors. We want the real solid benefits of government and if they have the honors, it will be the most powerful motive with their aspirants on both sides to keep down the slavery agitation and also to so make the machinery of government as to rebuild the south. . . . When the south held the Posts of honor, she had to throw all the crumbs of government to conciliate distant support. Now give the free States the honors and then they will do justice to gain our confidence and support. . . ." [36] With more vehemence did William L. Yancey decry: "What a sad comment upon the condition of the South! Manacled and robbed, she is exhorted to be quiet, for lost rights are but as spilt milk! Debauched and humbled, she is persuaded that her best course is to go to work and sustain a party, which will, perhaps, choose one of her sons to be President or vice-President, and others to be Cabinet officers and foreign ministers!" [37]

[36] C. H. Ambler, ed., *Correspondence of Hunter*, American Historical Association, *Annual Report*, 1916, II, 141.

[37] Letter to J. D. Meadows, June 16, 1859. J. W. DuBose, *Life and Times of Yancey*, 388.

As early as 1823, John Stanly, observing in the North Carolina House of Commons that "the Southern States have given four out of five of the Presidents we have had," favored the selection of John Quincy Adams, since the election of the president "from the Northern section may serve to remove discontent, cultivate harmony and strengthen the Union." *Debate on Mr. Fisher's Resolutions against Caucuses in the House of Commons of North Carolina in December, 1823*, pamphlet, 67.

On September 11, 1844, Langdon Cheves thus wrote to the Charleston *Mercury* concerning the proper attitude of the South towards the forthcoming general election of that year: "Renounce absolutely and unreservedly, during this contest, all pretensions to the high honors of the Union. Fill no office under the General Government, except in the Legislative Halls." *Letter of the Hon. Langdon Cheves, . . .* pamphlet, 3.

On December 11, 1850, Benj. F. Perry addressing the South Carolina House of Representatives observed "that whilst the high offices have been filled by Southern men, . . . the expenditures of money have been mostly in the Northern States. This is owing to a variety of causes, and no doubt a most powerful one is, the eagerness of the Northern people to get money, whilst the Southern people are thinking of office and distinction." *Speech of Hon. B. F. Perry . . . ,* pamphlet, 13.

Enough has been disclosed to indicate the Southern despair of the executive department as originally constituted. Meanwhile the more farsighted were engaged in devising some interesting plans for the reorganization of the structure of the department along lines more favorable to the protection of the South. Even in the Federal Convention of 1787, objection had been raised to the single executive upon sectional grounds; for James Madison in his Notes thus records the position taken by Hugh Williamson of North Carolina on July 24: "He did not like the Unity in the Executive. He had wished the Executive power to be lodged in three men taken from three districts into which the States should be divided. As the Executive is to have a kind of veto on the laws, and there is an essential difference of interests between the N. & S. States, particularly in the carrying trade, the power will be dangerous, if the Executive is to be taken from part of the Union, to the part from which he is not taken. The case is different here from what it is in England; where there is a sameness of interests throughout the Kingdom." There also George Mason suggested a council of State "to consist of 6 members — two from the Eastern, two from the middle and two from the Southern States — who should in conjunction with the President make all appointments and be an advisory body." [38]

Whether Calhoun had these early proposals before him when he prepared his *Discourse on the Constitution of the United States* is not known; at all events, he included in this work a plan for a dual executive as an essential part of his scheme for applying the principle of the concurrent voice in the national government. "The nature of the disease is such," so he wrote, "that nothing can reach it, short of some organic change, — a change which shall so modify the constitution, as to give to the weaker section, in some one form

[38] *Documents Illustrative of the Formation of the Union,* House Document, no. 398,   69 Cong., 1 sess., 443, 949.

or another, a negative on the action of the government. . . . it might be effected through a reorganization of the executive department; so that its powers, instead of being vested, as they now are, in a single officer, should be vested in two; — to be so elected, as that the two should be constituted the special organs and representatives of the respective sections, in the executive department of the government; and requiring each to approve all the acts of Congress before they shall become laws."

Calhoun then proceeded to defend this proposal: "The effect . . . would be . . . to insure harmony and concord between the two sections, and through them, in the government. For as no act of Congress could become a law without the assent of the chief magistrates representing both sections, each, in the elections, would choose the candidate, who, in addition to being faithful to its interests, would best command the esteem and confidence of the other section. And thus, the presidential election, instead of dividing the Union into hostile geographical parties, the stronger struggling to enlarge its powers, and the weaker to defend its rights, — as is now the case, — would become the means of restoring harmony and concord to the country and the government." [39]

At first thought, it appears strange that other proposals were not advanced in the thirties and forties for applying the concurrent voice to a reorganized executive department; but Calhoun himself explained the secret when he wrote that the South "cannot be responsible for an act which requires the concurrence of two thirds of both houses of Congress, or two thirds of the States to originate, and three fourths of the latter to consummate. With such difficulties in their way, the States of the weaker section can do nothing, however disposed, to save the Union and the government, without the

[39] R. K. Crallé, ed., *Works of Calhoun*, I, 391, 392, 395.

aid and co-operation of the States composing the stronger section: but with their aid and co-operation both may be saved. On the latter, therefore, rests the responsibility of invoking the high power, which alone can apply the remedy." [40]

That the possibilities of application were widely known, however, becomes apparent from the large number of proposals similar to Calhoun's scheme, which flooded the country in the crisis of 1860-1861, when the South, clutching at straws to save itself by any means whatsoever, forced into possible use all sources of protection upon which it, as a minority, had relied throughout the entire Ante-bellum Period. On December 12, 1860, Albert G. Jenkins from Virginia and John W. Noell from Missouri introduced into Congress two proposals for such a radical alteration of the executive department as would insure a concurrent voice to a Southern minority: the former would have used the dual executive principle; the latter would have abolished the presidency and replaced it by an executive council of three elected from contiguous districts with each holding a veto power over the acts of the others. [41] On the following day, Andrew Johnson of Tennessee proposed to the Senate a resolution to provide for "alternating the President and Vice-President every four years between the slaveholding and the non-slaveholding States during the continuance of the Government"; [42] and on January 11, 1861, by far the most elaborately analyzed plan for a dual executive was presented to Congress by R. M. T. Hunter of Virginia. [43] As late as March 20, 1861, the Convention of the People of Arkansas resolved that "the President and Vice President of the United States shall each be chosen alternately from a slave-

---

[40] R. K. Crallé, ed., *Works of Calhoun*, I, 396.

[41] *Congressional Globe*, 36 Cong., 2 sess.,

77, 78.

[42] *Ibid.*, 82-83.

[43] *Ibid.*, 329.

holding and non-slaveholding State: but in no case shall both be chosen from slaveholding or non-slaveholding States." [44]

APPLICATIONS IN THE JUDICIAL DEPARTMENT

The possibilities of the judicial department were quite similar to those of the executive. To establish a check within the machinery of the judiciary was to control in no small degree the nature and scope of national activities. And as was true of the presidency, so here the South did maintain representation out of all proportion to its strength, for until 1860 "the major part of the Justices of the Supreme Court of the United States had been Southern in every year of its existence." [45] Although it is true that sectionalism played a negligible rôle on the Supreme Court Bench, and although it is furthermore true that John Marshall of Virginia probably did more than any other one man to destroy Southern reliance upon the principle of local self-government, it cannot be denied that Southern political thought more than once received recognition in the opinions and decisions of this Court.[46]

Yet the South could no more rely upon continued control over the judiciary as originally constituted than it could upon continued control of the presidency; for, as was often pointed out, the judiciary, like the other two departments, was susceptible to Northern domination whenever the will existed in the North to exercise this control. Never was this possibility more plainly presented than in the *Southern Review* of 1830: "Without, however, supposing any liability to change, or even to modify an opinion from the mere influence of office, it must be obvious to all who study the operation of our government, that it is in the power of its authorities, by appointment, to shape the opinion of the Supreme Court in such a manner, that, after a given time,

[44] From p. 10 of the resolutions which compose Document 16 of the Virginia Constitutional Convention of 1861.

[45] Edward Channing, *History of the United States*, VI, 2.
[46] *Cf., infra.*, p. 145.

it shall respond to any decision of a permanent majority, and uphold their doctrines. Independently of the variations which office may be suspected to produce, who can doubt, that as vacancies occur, men will be selected to fill this high station, for *opinion's* sake, as well as for their talents; and that none will be called to construe the Constitution, whose doctrinal views shall not have been previously known and considered. . . . Such as are disposed to resist the assumption of power, or, in a word, the minority, must not, for a moment, think of confiding their rights to the decision of such a tribunal. They must, at once, plead to the jurisdiction." [47]

As in the executive, so here adequate protection for the South from the judiciary demanded a reorganization of the structure of that department. Proposals to that end, though more numerous during the middle period than those for executive reorganization, were of less consequence. In 1822, Thomas Ritchie came out in the *Richmond Enquirer* with a proposal to abolish the Supreme Court entirely, and to substitute in its place an elective council or tribunal selected by the state legislatures. Such a tribunal, he thought, would guard the rights of the states as well as those of the central government.[48] A number of other proposals were advocated for establishing some tribunal above the Supreme Court to settle disputes between the central and local units of government, but these ideas were seldom developed sufficiently to show their utility in the application of the principle of the concurrent voice.[49]

But when a drowning South of 1860 was clutching desperately at every hope of safety, however futile, several concrete propositions were advanced for a reorganization of the judiciary along sectional lines. R. M. T. Hunter presented

[47] "The Tribunal of Dernier Resort," *Southern Review*, November, 1830. VI, 430, 431.
[48] C. H. Ambler, *Thomas Ritchie*, 81.

[49] H. V. Ames, *Proposed Amendments to the Constitution*, American Historical Association, *Annual Report*, 1896, II, 160-161.

such a proposal along with his scheme for changes in the executive department. The Supreme Court, he thought, "should consist of ten judges — five from each section — the Chief Justice to be one of the five." And furthermore, in order "to make this check efficient, it should be provided that the judges of the Supreme Court in each section should be appointed by the President from that section." [50] Likewise, Andrew Johnson, as a part of his joint resolution for changes in the structure of the national government, proposed to divide the Supreme Court into three classes, with the judges of each class to be appointed for a twelve-year term, *"Provided, however,* That all vacancies occurring under the provisions of this section shall be filled by persons, one half of whom shall be chosen from the slaveholding States, and the other half with persons chosen from the non-slaveholding States, so that the Supreme Court will be equally divided between the slaveholding and the non-slaveholding States." [51]

Inasmuch as the application of any of the executive or judicial plans for reorganizing the structure of the law-enforcing and law-interpreting branches of the national government depended in the first instance upon the adoption of these plans by Congress, the South turned to the legislature as the only department possessing possibilities of putting into operation effectively the principle of the concurrent voice in the structure or proceedings of the national government.

APPLICATIONS IN THE LEGISLATIVE DEPARTMENT

In the provisions of the Constitution requiring more than a numerical majority vote for congressional action is found one source of protection for a Southern minority — a source that was recognized as such even at the time the Constitution was framed and adopted. For, in the Constitutional

---

[50] Speech in the Senate, January 11, 1861. *Congressional Globe,* 36 Cong., 2 sess., pp. 329, 330.   [51] *Ibid.,* 83. Remarks in the Senate, December 13, 1860.

Convention of 1787, a heated sectional debate developed between an agricultural South and a commercial North over, the regulation of commerce by an extra-majority vote, wherein the Southern members finally yielded to the bare-majority principle only in return for guarantees against legislative interference with the slave-trade before 1808.[52] George Mason, however, was not satisfied with this compromise; so, in his *Objections to the Federal Constitution,* he maintained that by "requiring only a majority to make all commercial and navigation laws, the five Southern States, whose produce and circumstances are wholly different from that of the eight Northern and Eastern States, may be ruined. . . . Whereas requiring two-thirds of the members present in both Houses would have produced mutual moderation, promoted the general interest, and removed an insuperable objection to the adoption of this government." [53]

Though the Southern members of the Convention were defeated in their attempts to apply the extra-majority principle to the regulation of commerce, they were influential in successfully introducing the idea into other provisions of the Constitution. In seeking to justify a similar application of the concurrent voice to his own state, Abel P. Upshur explained to the Virginia Constitutional Convention on October 29, 1829, how the extra-majority principle had been effectively utilized in the Federal Constitution as an instrument for minority protection: "Look first at the Federal Government, whether in its Executive, its Legislative, or its Judicial Department; and we shall find, that a majority is, in many instances, subject to the control of a minority, greater, but by a single unit, than *one-third* of the whole.

[52] Max Farrand, ed., *Records,* II, 449-453. The fear of numerical majority control of navigation of the Mississippi led the Virginia Ratifying Convention to propose as a constitutional amendment that no treaty regulating the right of navigation on American rivers should be ratified "without the concurrence of three fourths of the whole number of the members of both houses respectively." Jonathan Elliot, ed., *Debates,* (2 ed.) III, 660, 499-516.
[53] K. M. Rowland, *Life of George Mason,* II, Appendix, 389.

If the President of the United States, shall refuse to sign a bill, passed by both Houses of Congress, and shall return that bill to them with his reasons for such refusal, the consent of two-thirds of the members of both houses is requisite before such bill can become a law. The Senate of the United States hold a double capacity, being a branch, as well of the Executive, as of the Legislative Department of Government, and when it acts in its Executive capacity, two-thirds of the members present must concur, before any treaty formed by the President, can receive its due ratification. Here, again, and in concerns too, of the utmost importance, a majority is subject to the will of the minority. So, in the Judicial Department, (the quasi Judicial, at any rate, for the Senate when it sits to try impeachments, is, in fact, a Judicative power, and acts entirely in a Judicial character;) when the Senate thus sits, two-thirds of the members present are necessary to convict the party impeached. Here, again, is found a minority, controlling the will of the majority." [54]

A second proposal for establishing a concurrent voice in Congress was based upon the bicameral principle of legislative structure. With Congress divided into the two branches, a House and a Senate, this plan provided that the North should control one branch; the South, the other. Then, since the concurrence of both houses was necessary for the enactment of national legislation, no measure would become law without the consent of both sections of the Union. This suggestion also had its origin in the Federal Convention, for on June 30, 1787, after discussing the division of interest between the Northern and Southern states, and after further declaring that "if any defensive power were necessary, it ought to be mutually given to these two interests," James Madison proposed that the people "should be represented in one branch according to the number of free inhabitants only; and in the other according to the

[54] *Proceedings and Debates of the Virginia Convention of 1829-1830*, 93.

whole no. counting the slaves as if free." By such an arrangement, so he explained, "the Southern Scale would have the advantage in one House, and the Northern in the other." [55]

Madison's proposal received little consideration in 1787, but in the middle decades of the Ante-bellum Period, the South revived the principle with added interest. Thus, in 1848, John C. Calhoun pointed out how the controversy between the upland and lowland sections of his own State of South Carolina had been settled by giving the lower section a decided preponderance in the Senate and the upper section "a preponderance, equally decisive, in the House of Representatives." And by so doing, "an equilibrium was established between the two sections in the legislative department of the government; and, . . . the government . . . was converted into that of the concurrent majority, and made, emphatically, the government of the entire population, — of the whole people of South Carolina; — and not of one portion of its people over another portion. The consequence was, the almost instantaneous restoration of harmony and concord between the two sections." [56]

In 1850, the concurrent majority principle applied to the bicameral feature in the structure of Congress was twice ably defended as an effective protection to the South. In that year, both Jefferson Davis and David L. Yulee argued for the adoption of this phase of the theory in their speeches before the United States Senate. From early experiences that transcended state boundaries, both these men were peculiarly devoted to the South as a section. David L. Yulee, two years the younger, was born on June 10, 1810, in St. Thomas, West Indies, brought up in Norfolk, Virginia, and studied law in St. Augustine, Florida; whereas, Jefferson Davis, though born and educated in Kentucky, lived for

[55] Max Farrand, ed., *Records,* I, 486-487.   Crallé, ed., *Works of Calhoun,* I, 404, 405.
[56] *Discourse on the Constitution,* R. K.

the greater part of his life upon a large plantation in Mississippi. Both men entered public life in the forties, and both preceded their election to the Senate by an apprenticeship in the House of Representatives, though Davis interpolated his rise from the House to the Senate with gallant service in the Mexican War. Now, in 1850, they were fighting on the floor of the Senate shoulder to shoulder in defense of the South. Incidentally, both were to leave the Senate in 1851, until re-elected for further service in the later years of the decade; and, oddly enough, both were to bid farewell to the Senate together on January 21, 1861, to take up important positions in the new government of the Southern Confederacy.

On February 13, 1850, Davis spoke as follows: "I believe, Mr. President, it is essential that neither section have such power in Congress as would render them able to trample upon the rights of the other section of this Union. It would be a blessing, an essential means to preserve the Confederacy, that in one branch of Congress the North and in the other the South should have a majority of representation. . . . if legislation was restricted and balanced in the mode I have suggested, Congress would never be able to encroach upon the rights and institutions of any portion of the Union, nor could its acts ever meet with resistance from any part of it. . . . Whenever you take from the people of this country the confidence that this is their Government, that it reflects their will, that it looks to their interests, the foundation upon which it was laid is destroyed and the fabric falls to the ground." [57] Six months later, Yulee maintained that to "produce a perfect check or counterpoise — an effective balance — by a means to which a legislative policy is competent, each section should have control of one of the legislative branches; and as the North is in admitted ascen-

[57] *Appendix to the Congressional Globe,* 31 Cong., 1 sess., 150.

dency in the popular branch, the South should be allowed a preponderance in this body." [58]

Failing in all attempts to apply these principles, the South of the middle decades was forced to concentrate its attention on that single aspect of the concurrent voice actually in operation in the legislative department; namely, the principle of the sectional equilibrium in the Senate. In the speech from which excerpts have been quoted above, Yulee doubted whether "in the progressive fierceness which seems to mark the antagonism of the sections, anything that is competent to legislative power, short of the surrender of one branch to each section" would suffice to maintain peace and harmony; but he admitted that "thus far an equality of representation in this body has been deemed sufficient, and has answered to a certain extent, though not in a perfect degree, the purpose of a practical check in the power of the two sections." [59]

The sectional equilibrium in the Senate is a product of the Missouri Compromise of 1820, and as such, it marks the point of transition from dependence upon local self-government to dependence upon the concurrent voice as the chief source of protection to Southern minority interests within the Union. From the protracted congressional debates of 1819-1820 that revolved around the topics of Missouri, slavery, and the territories, David L. Yulee in 1850 extracted sufficient evidence for a convincing argument to prove that the South, in renouncing its constitutional claim to the protection of slavery in all the territories, received in return a guarantee of a sectional equilibrium in the Senate to be secured by carving only slave states from the territory to the south of the north latitude line 36° 30′ and only free states from the territory to the north of that line. As was true with the plans for the admission of Maine and Missouri

[58] *Ibid.*, 1162.   [59] *Ibid.*, 1162.

at that time, the sectional equilibrium was to be maintained by admitting slave and free states in pairs.[60]

To what degree this principle established in 1820 was applied thereafter, James F. Dowdell, a representative from Alabama who was born in Georgia and educated in Virginia, related in an historical review presented to the House on July 28, 1856: "Missouri . . . adjusted the scales, and each section had twelve States. Michigan came in in 1837, and Arkansas in 1836. Iowa and Florida were embraced in the same bill, but owing to a disputed boundary between Iowa and Missouri, Iowa was not admitted until 1846. Florida came in the year previous, 1845. Texas was admitted in 1845, and Wisconsin in 1848. . . . By its [i. e., Texas's] acquisition the South was enabled to maintain her relative strength — a matter of vital import to the safety of her rights under the circumstances, when a large party was struggling for supremacy in the northern States, for the purpose of controlling the Federal Government, to circumscribe and destroy southern institutions. The addition of the six States last mentioned left the two sections in 1848 with fifteen States each. . . . The two sections were equal in the number of States, and therefore possessed equal political power in the Senate." [61]

David L. Yulee, in the course of a similar review on August 6, 1850, declared that temporary irregularities in the application of the principle were "rendered immaterial, because, whenever that was the case, it was well understood that a balancing State was in progress of formation, soon to restore the equality." [62] That the operation of the prin-

[60] *Ibid.*, 1162-1163. On February 20, 1820, William Plumer, Jr., representative from New Hampshire, thus wrote to his father concerning proceedings in the House: "Many of the Southern members openly avow their intention — They say they have now an equality in the Senate, eleven slave holding, & eleven free state, & they are determined not to admit a free state without bringing in at the same time a slave state to preserve the balance." E. S. Brown, ed., *The Missouri Compromises and Presidential Politics, 1820-1825. From the Letters of William Plumer, Jr.,* 11.

[61] *Appendix to the Congressional Globe,* 34 Cong., 1 sess., 1059.

[62] *Appendix to the Congressional Globe,* 31 Cong., 1 sess., 1162.

ciple was well known and generally conceded appears from a report of a committee on territories concerning the admission of Florida into the Union made to the House on June 17, 1844: "The practice has now, since the date of the Missouri Compromise, very properly become one of settled policy to preserve, as nearly as possible, in one of the branches of the Legislature of the Union, that balance of power between two of the great divisions of the republic, which is so important to the harmony and security of the whole, and to the permanency of the Union. It is right that every section of this happy and prosperous confederacy should not only be, but feel itself to be, secure against any unjust or unequal action of the Federal Legislature upon those of their interests which may in somewise conflict with the interests, policy, or prejudices of other portions. It is only thus that there can be preserved that entire confidence and happy harmony which is so desirable to be maintained by all just and conciliatory means." [63]

How intensively did the South rely upon the sectional equilibrium in the Senate as a source of protection after 1820? This question may be answered first, by the Southern support accorded the Missouri Compromise line separating the new Northern free states from the new Southern slave states by the north latitude of 36° 30'; and, secondly, by the vigorous Southern defense of this principle when it was threatened with destruction by the admission of California in 1850.

As a basis for the maintenance of sectional equality in the Senate, the South defended the Missouri Compromise line almost with unanimity. At least, such was the conclusion of Alexander H. Stephens, who made a study of the subject the results of which he laid before the House on February 17, 1854. At that time, Stephens provided an adequate answer to our first inquiry when he spoke in part as follows: "The

[63] House Report, III, no. 577. 28 Cong., 1 sess., 3.

first time that this question came up afterwards, was within twelve months from the date of the act itself, and before the same Congress. It came up on the application of Missouri for admission. . . . The whole South were for letting her be admitted, and the entire North, nearly, were against it. . . . on the direct vote for the admission of Arkansas with a constitution tolerating slavery, though she was south of 36° 30', there are fifty-two names, under the lead of Mr. Adams, in the negative — every one of them, I believe, from the North. . . . When, therefore, the bill to organize a territorial government for Oregon came up in this House on the 15th of January, 1847, Mr. Burt, of South Carolina, to take the sense of the North directly upon the question of *abiding* by this line of 36° 30', moved, as an amendment to that clause in the bill which excluded slavery forever from the Territories, these words: — 'inasmuch as the whole of said Territory lies north of 36° 30' north latitude, known as the line of the Missouri compromise.' . . . Here is the vote upon this question: there were in this House then 82 votes for Mr. Burt's amendment, and 113 against it! Of these noes, every man was from the North. Every southern man in the House voted for it. . . . This proposition in the Senate was moved by Mr. Douglas. It received every southern vote in that body, . . . The proposition was made in this House, on the part of the South, for the last time, on the 13th day of June, 1850. . . . This proposition was rejected in Committee of the Whole upon a count by tellers — ayes 78, noes 89. It was the last time, sir, it was ever offered." [64]

The Southern stand for the sectional equilibrium was even more impressively revealed in the defense of that principle during the congressional debates of 1850 over the admission of California into the Union as a free state. Never did a Congress so exhaust its intellectual resources upon the science of effective minority control in government as dur-

[64] *Appendix to the Congressional Globe,* 33 Cong., 1 sess., 193, 194, 195.

ing those first eight months of 1850. Among the outstanding
leaders in the Southern cause at this time was Henry Washington Hilliard, representative from Alabama. Born in
Cumberland County, North Carolina, in 1808 — the year
that gave birth to Jefferson Davis across the mountains in
Kentucky — Hilliard, like so many other leaders in Southern thought, soon joined the caravan of prosperity seekers
that moved into the new Southwest. He stopped over at
Columbia, South Carolina, long enough to be graduated
from what is now the State University, and again at Athens,
Georgia, for a brief practice of law before he proceeded to
Tuscaloosa to become a professor at the University of Alabama. In 1836, he entered upon a colorful political career
that was to be brought to a close forty-five years later with
the termination of his ministry to Brazil.

On February 14, 1850, with the conflict over California
already at white heat, Hilliard addressed the House of Representatives: "If we should admit California into the Union
as a State, with the boundaries now claimed by its inhabitants, without receiving guarantees for the protection of our
rights in other portions of the territories belonging to us,
we should transfer the scepter of political power at once and
forever into the hands of the enemies of our institutions,
and the slaveholding States would enter upon a fixed, dreary,
hopeless minority in the face of a growing aggression which
threatens our very existence. To-day we hold a balance in
the Senate of the United States, but the entrance of another
non-slaveholding State into the Union would turn that balance against us. We shall never be stronger than we are
to-day." [65]

Six months later, Florida's greatest exponent of the South-

---

[65] *Congressional Globe,* 31 Cong., 1 sess.,
358–359. "Sir, the day that the balance
between the two sections of the country —
the slaveholding States and the non-
slaveholding States — is destroyed, is a
day that will not be far removed from political revolution, anarchy, civil war, and
widespread disaster." John C. Calhoun,
speech in the Senate, February 19, 1847.
Ibid., 29 Cong., 2 sess., 454.

ern cause, David L. Yulee, undaunted by the prolonged struggle that was growing more hopeless every day, again struck for the South upon the floor of the Senate: "While the increase of power in the Senate is not necessary to the North, it is vital to the South. In the first place the North is in undisputed and unchangeable possession of the House of Representatives. Her power of defence is therefore perfect. The South has no such element of power in the Government. In the next place, the South has an interest [slavery] much more sensitive than that which distinguishes the Northern section. . . . A defensive power, therefore, is more essential to us than to them." [66]

Another week of excitement passed in the Senate, and on August 13, the very day that the Senate voted to admit California as a free state, Jefferson Davis again spoke out strongly in defense of the South: "We stand on the verge of an act which is to form an era in the history of our country. Now, for the first time, we are about permanently to destroy the balance of power between the sections of the Union, by securing a majority to one, in both Houses of Congress; this, too, when sectional spirit is rife over the land, and when those who are to have the control in both Houses of Congress will also have the Executive power in their hands. . . . When that barrier for the protection of the minority is about to be obliterated, I feel we have reached

[66] Speech on August 6. *Appendix to the Congressional Globe,* 31 Cong., 1 sess., 1162. For a typical attack upon the maintenance of the sectional equilibrium in the Senate, note the following lines from William H. Seward's speech in the Senate on March 11, 1850. "What is proposed, is a *political* equilibrium. Every political equilibrium requires a physical equilibrium to rest upon, and is valueless without it. To constitute a physical equilibrium between the slave States, and the free States, requires first an equality of territory, or some near approximation; and this is already lost. But it requires much more than this; it requires an equality or a proximate equality, in the number of slaves and freemen. And this must be perpetual! . . . The theory of a new political equilibrium claims that it once existed, and has been lost. When lost, and how? It began to be lost in 1787, when preliminary arrangements were made to admit five new free States in the Northwest territory, two years before the Constitution was finally adopted — that is it began to be lost two years before it began to exist!" *Appendix to the Congressional Globe,* 31 Cong., 1 sess., 263.

the point at which the decline of our Government has commenced." [67]

That the sectional equilibrium in the Senate was the last hope of the South in maintaining a concurrent voice in any of the three departments of the national government appeared beyond question to David L. Yulee who spoke to this effect in the Senate on August 6: "But it may be said that because the political balance in the Senate is lost, all is not lost — that the Executive and Judicial departments are competent, by the veto of the one and the judicial intervention of the other, to prevent unconstitutional legislation to our prejudice. . . . To the same extent to which the North is in the ascendant in the two branches of Congress will it be in the ascendant in the Electoral Colleges. With the power to make a President in defiance of Southern opposition, the North may effectually reduce to her control the Executive department. With a Northern Executive to nominate Judges, and a Northern Senate to confirm, how long would it be before the Supreme Bench might be filled with judges imbued with Northern sentiments and bias, and instrumental to Northern purposes of aggression? . . . There is no shield, then, for our rights in the Executive or Judicial departments, when the full control of the Legislative depa[r]tment shall have settled down in the North. When that time comes, the whole unchecked power of the Government will be consolidated in the North, and the South will hold her existence at the mercy of that dominant power." [68]

On September 9, 1850, California was admitted into the Union. Two months later, Langdon Cheves, active at the age of seventy-four, remarked in the Nashville Convention, which had been called to consider the sources of Southern protection within the Union: "the balance of the Govern-

[67] *Appendix to the Congressional Globe,* 31 Cong., 1 sess., 1533.
[68] *Appendix to the Congressional Globe,* 31 Cong., 1 sess., 1162. Calhoun had earlier presented a similar argument in his farewell address to the Senate, March 4, 1850. *Congressional Globe,* 31 Cong., 1 sess., 452.

ment is destroyed forever; and it is beyond the power of our opponents to restore it, even if they had the wish to do so." [69] Another two months passed, and the *Southern Quarterly Review* came out with an article entitled "Is Southern Civilization Worth Preserving?" wherein it was recognized that the death-knell of the concurrent voice in the three departments of the national government had been sounded. "Between slavery and non-slavery the balance of power was nicely poised, and its equilibrium adjusted. . . . Is it so now? . . . The North is the government; the South holds nothing under the constitution — bare sufferance is her only tenure." After showing the futility of reliance upon the executive or the courts, the article reverted to the Senate as the last stronghold of the South: "The last, the best, the strongest guarantee, senatorial equality, has gone. The admission of California has at once, and forever, destroyed the equality between the sections, which had existed from the adoption of the constitution." [70]

For a decade yet, seeds of a restoration of the sectional

[69] *Speech of the Hon. Langdon Cheves in the Nashville Convention,* November 15, 1850, pamphlet, 16.

[70] A reprint from the *Southern Quarterly Review,* January, 1851, published as a pamphlet by the Southern Rights Association at Charleston, South Carolina, 1851, pp. 6, 27. It is most surprising that throughout the entire struggle for the maintenance of the sectional equilibrium in the Senate, no attention was given to the dominating position of the Vice-President, who possessed the constitutional power to cast the deciding vote in case of a tie. Twice this decisive power was exercised in settling issues that had a direct bearing upon the sectional controversy. On February 20, 1811, Vice-President Clinton, a state-rights Democrat of New York, cast the deciding vote that defeated the measure designed to renew the charter of the first United States Bank; and on July 28, 1846, Vice-President G. M. Dallas, a Democrat of Pennsylvania, cast two deciding votes that were responsible for the success of the Walker Tariff Bill. H. B. Learned, "Casting Votes of the Vice Presidents 1789-1915," *American Historical Review,* April 15, 1915. Vol. XX, 574. Otherwise the casting votes of the Vice-Presidents were not significant in the sectional controversy. It would seem that if the doctrine of the sectional equilibrium were carried to its logical conclusion, every issue of sectional importance would be finally decided by the casting vote of the Vice-President. In this connection, it is interesting to note that the office of Vice-President was created in order not to disturb the equality of state representation in the Senate by having to choose a presiding officer from among the regular members. In any event the Vice-President must come from one of the states, but under the plan adopted he would be elected by all the people and represent all the people. A. J. Beveridge, "The Fifth Wheel in Our Government," *The Century Magazine,* December, 1909, Vol. 79, p. 209.

equilibrium were strewed broadcast over the land; but, without the Northern desire to restore this equilibrium, they were as seed sown upon barren ground. And the South as a whole now cared little for the sowing.[71]

APPLICATIONS IN POLITICAL PARTIES

Aside from the three great departments of the national government, there existed one other institution through which the South might establish its concurrent voice in the realm of national governmental activities. That institution had developed entirely through custom and beyond the pale of the law; yet it had wielded an ever increasing influence in the central government — an influence so great that to control this institution was ultimately to dominate all the machinery of the national government; for that extra-legal governmental agency was the institution of political parties. "If the dominant party finds the senate in their way," wrote A. B. Longstreet in 1837, "the senate will be *instructed* out of the way — If the Supreme Court stand in their way; the party makes the President and the President makes the Judges, and he will soon mold them at his will — or they will lay off new circuits enough, to put a majority of new judges on the bench. It it certainly true that [there] is not a more irrespo[n]sible unapproachable despotism under heaven, than a dominant party united by local interests and acting under a constitutional form of Government." [72] Of like mind was John C. Calhoun, for in his *Discourse on the Constitution* he wrote: "Nor can the veto power of the

[71] For attempts at restoration, see C. H. Ambler, ed., *Correspondence of Hunter*, American Historical Association, *Annual Report*, 1916, II, 265; Henry Cleveland, ed., *Stephens in Public and Private with Letters and Speeches*, 646; H. D. Capers, *Life and Times of Memminger*, 276; L. E. Chittenden, *Proceedings of the [Peace] Convention*, 447; E. A. Pollard, *Lost Cause*, 94; U. B. Phillips, *Life of Toombs*, 210; "Barbarossa" [John Scott], *The Lost Prin-*ciple or the Sectional Equilibrium: How It Was Created — How Destroyed — How It May Be Restored; and the *Journal of the Virginia Convention of 1861*, Appendix, Journal of the Committee of the Whole, 127-132. Further material may be found in R. R. Russel, "Economic Aspects of Southern Sectionalism," *Illinois University Studies*, XI, 58, 217.
[72] Letter to M. B. Lamar. C. A. Gulick, Jr., ed., *Papers of Lamar*, II, 2.

President, or the power of the Judges to decide on the constitutionality of the acts of the other departments, furnish adequate means [of protection] . . . for the plain reason, that the party combinations which are sufficient to control the two majorities constituting the elements of the government of the United States, must, habitually, control all the departments." [73]

With the political party, therefore, the South, seeking protection for its minority interests, was forced to contend, hoping by some process to convert it from a threatening instrument of encroachment to a possible vehicle of protection. This conversion was everywhere deemed essential, since the South entertained no hope of abolishing parties entirely. "It is in vain to say the monster party may be destroyed," wrote Thomas Cooper, the versatile South Carolinian, in 1830, "people who honestly, and with views and intentions equally honest, *differ on principle,* must ever remain two parties." [74] In 1847, Thomas L. Clingman maintained that in "a country like this, political parties will always exist"; [75] and in 1852, Alexander H. Stephens insisted that "in all free countries where the principle of representation is recognized and acted upon, there will necessarily be parties. Because perfect agreement upon public questions and measures can hardly be expected. And the friends and opponents of measures will act in opposition to each other." [76]

The peculiarly *Southern* problem of the political party was that of preventing organization along sectional lines. Perhaps no problem in Southern political thought was more widely appreciated or more often discussed. At the begin-

[73] R. K. Crallé, ed., *Works of Calhoun,* I, 235.
[74] Thomas Cooper, *Consolidation. An Account of Parties in the United States* (2 ed.), 26.
[75] Speech in the House, December 22, 1847. *Appendix to the Congressional Globe,* 30 Cong., 1 sess., 45.
[76] Speech in the House, April 27, 1852.

Appendix to the Congressional Globe, 32 Cong., 1 sess., 460. Like sentiments were expressed by Thomas Jefferson, Notes for an Inaugural Address, P. L. Ford, ed., *Writings of Jefferson,* VIII, 1, note; and by James Madison, Letter to Robert Walsh, November 17, 1819. Gaillard Hunt, ed., *Writings of Madison,* IX, 12.

ning of the middle decades two old leaders in the school of state rights offered their warnings. In 1819 James Madison queried: "Should a State of parties arise, founded on geographical boundaries and other Physical & permanent distinctions which happen to coincide with them, what is to controul those great repulsive Masses from awful shocks ag^st each other?" [77] During the following year, Thomas Jefferson, after paying due respect to the uniting effect of parties in the past, expressed the fear of a reorganization over the slavery issue and along sectional lines, until strife between these parties "would kindle such mutual and mortal hatred, as to render separation preferable to eternal discord." [78]

Other leaders in the South were willing to carry on this note of warning. In 1847, Jefferson Davis hoped that the Southern Democrats "will happily avoid the worst of all political divisions — one made by geographical lines merely"; [79] two months later Thomas L. Clingman contended that whenever "you see political parties divided by strict geographical lines, the Union is virtually at an end"; [80] and in 1849, Howell Cobb and others in a general letter to their constituents in Georgia, opposed the Southern Address of that year because it "seemed to us to foreshadow a result in the organization of a sectional party, which would neither promote the interests nor strengthen the securities of the South." [81]

---

[77] Gaillard Hunt, ed., *Writings of Madison*, IX, 12.

[78] Letter dated April 13, 1820. Virginia Mason, *Life and Correspondence of James M. Mason*, 61. See also, Nathaniel Macon of North Carolina, speech in the Senate, January 20, 1820. *Annals of Congress*, 16 Cong., 1 sess., 220. Macon, as did others, referred to Washington's admonition to avoid geographical parties. Washington's Farewell Address, September 17, 1796. J. D. Richardson, ed., *Messages and Papers*, I, 216.

[79] Letter to C. J. Searles, September 19, 1857. Dunbar Rowland, ed., *Davis, Constitutionalist*, I, 95.

[80] Speech in the House, December 22, 1847. *Appendix to the Congressional Globe*, 30 Cong., 1 sess., 47.

[81] R. C. Brooks, ed., "Howell Cobb Papers," *Georgia Historical Quarterly*, June, 1921. V, no. 2, p. 40.
In the early fifties, James A. Seddon wrote R. M. T. Hunter that Southern protection cannot lie in a separate political organization, for "it is apparent, their

PRINCIPLE OF THE CONCURRENT VOICE

Having set out to prevent the organization of sectional parties, the Southern political philosopher developed a theory of ideal party combinations directed to that end. Thomas L. Clingman, who was elected as a Whig from North Carolina to the Twenty-eighth Congress (1843-1845) and as a Democrat from the same State to the Thirtieth Congress (1847-1849) was well qualified both from experience and by training — for he was graduated from the University of North Carolina — to present an acceptable philosophy of party combinations. This he did in a speech before the House of Representatives on December 22, 1847: "Unquestionably, the safest and best parties are those based upon differences of opinion as to the mode of administering the Government, and as to the measures it should carry out; . . . because such is the nature of the human mind that such parties will have members in every class of society and every section of the country. States, counties, neighborhoods, and even families, are divided, and the minorities, as well as the majorities, in their zeal to defend their views and make converts out of opponents, diffuse in every section correct notions as to their respective opinions; so that, by this interchange of sentiment, produced by a collision ramifying itself into every portion of the community, the excitement is kept within due bounds, and both parties are satisfied as to the honesty and patriotism of their opponents, as classes, and are rendered tolerant and liberal in their intercourse with each other. . . . every great party has numbered among its members men of all classes and pursuits, as well as of all sections of [the] country." [82]

In this position Clingman was ably supported by Samuel J. Tilden, even though the latter did not express his opin-

---

cause as a political one is lost and thus separate action would be more than preposterous — would be suicidal." C. H. Ambler, ed., Correspondence of Hunter, American Historical Association, Annual Report, 1916, II, 137. See also the Whig platform of 1856. K. H. Porter, ed., National Party Platforms, 50.

[82] Appendix to the Congressional Globe, 30 Cong., 1 sess., 45, 46.

ions upon the subject in a comprehensive way until 1860. In a letter to William Kent, dated October 26, of that year, Tilden, whose place in history belongs more properly to the post-war period, thus expressed himself: "The tendency of parties is to draw the various political elements into two divisions and to equalize those divisions. The minority adopts enough of the ideas of the majority to attract those who are nearest to the line of division; and the majority, struggling to retain them, makes concessions. The issue is thus constantly shifting 'with the wavering tide of battle,' until the policy which at last prevails has become adjusted so as nearly to represent the average sense of the whole people. . . . In shaping the policy which emerges from the conflict, the minority acts a part scarcely less important than the majority; and the dissentients are thus prepared to accept the result. Such is the process by which the will of all the parts of the community is collected, averaged, and represented in the policy finally agreed upon." [83]

How to apply this theory was the real problem facing the Southern politician — a problem that was all the more difficult because of the growing intensity of sectional peculiarities separating the North from the South. It was not an easy matter to obliterate the identity of the two sections in order to maintain political parties on broad national lines; but it was in this endeavor that John C. Calhoun justified his nationalism in 1817; for in defense of his position at that time he declared that whatever "impedes the intercourse of the extremes with this, the center of the Republic, weakens the Union. The more enlarged the sphere of commercial circulation, the more extended that of social intercourse; the more strongly are we bound together; the more inseparable are our destinies." [84] Alexander H. Stephens took a similar position in 1848 when he advocated national ap-

[83] John Bigelow, *Writings and Speeches of Samuel J. Tilden,* I, 290.

[84] Speech in the Senate, February 4, 1817. *Annals of Congress,* 14 Cong., 2 sess., 854.

propriations for a telegraph. He hoped to see the day "when our whole body politic would be knit together, and the wires communicating intelligence from one extremity to the other, would make us more and more one people." [85]

But whatever was lacking in the fundamental bases for genuine national political parties cutting athwart sectional lines was more than offset by the skill of Southern politicians. "It is true," wrote Edward A. Pollard of Virginia, just after the Civil War, "that the numerical majority of the North the South held long in check by superior and consummate political skill. Party complications were thrown around the Sectional Animosity." [86] These complications were found in the two major political parties of the middle period, the Whigs and the Democrats, both organized on national principles and receiving support from all sections of the Union. Leaders in the defense of the South were found in opposite political camps, often voting against each other on important political issues. "You see Southern Senators voting for a tariff which they themselves repeatedly condemned and reprobated," wrote Langdon Cheves in disgust at party influences in 1844; [87] but what did these shifting divisions among Southern leaders matter if more was to be gained by using the party as a vehicle of protection to Southern institutions and as a check to oppressions upon Southern rights?

Perhaps the best measure of the effectiveness of Southern attempts to maintain political parties "on broad, national Republican principles" is found in the electoral vote cast by states for President at four-year intervals. The decade of the forties is typical. It was opened by a wild uproarious

[85] Speech in the House, June 12, 1848. *Congressional Globe,* 30 Cong., 1 sess., 826.
[86] Edward A. Pollard, *Lost Cause,* 62.
[87] *Letter of Hon. Langdon Cheves to Editors of the Charleston Mercury,* pamphlet, 4. "The Whig party of the South," declared David Outlaw of North Carolina in the House on June 10, 1852, "have, at the expense of having their motives aspersed and misconstrued by their friends, relations, and neighbors, arrested sectionalism at home. They have stood by the Constitution, and by the rights of all sections." *Appendix to the Congressional Globe,* 32 Cong., 1 sess., 678.

campaign — the first of its kind in history — in which the Democratic candidate Van Buren and the Whig candidate William H. Harrison were vying with each other for national support. The former was acclaimed as "the Northern Man with Southern Principles," the latter as "the Southern Man with American Principles." [88] In that election, Illinois, New Hampshire, and South Carolina were aligned for Van Buren, against Connecticut, Mississippi, and Michigan for Harrison. Four years later, Georgia, Louisiana, New Hampshire, and New York supported James K. Polk of Tennessee; while Massachusetts, Ohio, Maryland, and North Carolina were for Henry Clay of Kentucky.[89] In 1848, Alabama and Mississippi voted with Iowa and Maine for Lewis Cass of Michigan, while Florida and Tennessee united with Rhode Island and Vermont on Zachary Taylor of Louisiana.

The sectional distribution of the popular vote in this last campaign became a subject of special interest to Edward Stanly, representative from North Carolina, who compiled the returns in order to show that the South still retained an effective source of protection in the Union and hence was not at that time justified in resorting to drastic measures. These are his figures:

IN WHAT ARE CALLED THE FREE STATES

Taylor received	925,646 votes
Cass "	812,855 "
Van Buren "	291,678 "

2,030,179

---

[88] *The Northern Man with Southern Principles, and the Southern Man with American Principles,* pamphlet. See also, Thomas Ritchie, *Address of the Democratic Central Committee to the Voters of Virginia,* October 24, 1840. Reprinted in *John P. Branch Historical Papers,* June, 1911. III, no. 3, pp. 263-270.

[89] For an illuminating insight into party conditions in Virginia in this campaign, see the letters reprinted under the caption "Virginia and Texas, 1844" in *John P. Branch Historical Papers,* June, 1913. IV, no. 1, pp. 116-137.

PRINCIPLE OF THE CONCURRENT VOICE

IN THE SLAVEHOLDING STATES

Taylor and Fillmore received	....	435,378
Cass and Butler "	....	409,436
Van Buren "	....	299

845,113

From these facts, Stanly then pointed out that the Whig candidate, Zachary Taylor, a Louisiana planter, "reported to be the owner of two hundred slaves," received in the free states over a hundred thousand more votes than did the Democratic candidate Lewis Cass of Michigan "who is reported to have said he thanked God he never owned a slave — said he never would, and prayed for the abolition of slavery!" [90]

This was the goal towards which the Southern members of both political parties were consciously working. Looking forward to the presidential campaign of 1848, Jefferson Davis expressed the hope that the forthcoming convention of the national Democratic party "representing every section of the Union, and elevated above local jealousy and factious strife, may proceed to select candidates, whose principles, patriotism, judgment, and decision indicate men fit for the time and the occasion." [91] Another appeal representing a more advanced stage of campaign oratory came from the pen of Robert J. Walker, an adopted son of Mississippi, whose greatest contribution to the theories of Southern protection was his insistence upon the acquisition of more slave-territory from other nations to the south. In a public letter intended for the voters at the election of 1856, Walker

[90] *Appendix to the Congressional Globe,* 31 Cong., 1 sess., 340. "So strong was party feeling with some gentlemen from the non-slaveholding States, that when the issue was a northern or a southern Speaker, they refused to vote for a northern Speaker." *Ibid.,* 339.
For the effect of national parties in keeping the South divided over the subject of the Wilmot Proviso in this campaign and after, see the letter of William L. Marcy to Thomas Ritchie, November 29, 1849. C. H. Ambler, ed., "Ritchie Letters," *John P. Branch Historical Papers,* June, 1915. IV, no. 3, pp. 406-407.
[91] Letter to C. J. Searles, September 19, 1847. Dunbar Rowland, ed., *Davis, Constitutionalist,* I, 95.

made this characteristic campaign plea: "Come with the farewell warnings of Washington on your lips, and imprinted on your hearts — not in sectional array of the North against the South — but in the glorious panoply of our whole country, from North to South, from East to West! let the thirty-one columns wheel into line, and with the same inspiring battle-cry, pealing from rank to rank, re-echoing from State to State, THE UNION TO THE RESCUE! let us together march to the polls, as our fathers did, in the hour of peril, to the music and flag of the Union." [92]

Political leaders in the South proudly recognized their success in establishing this concurrent voice in the machinery of the national government. Clingman in 1847 pointed with pride to the fact that there were "in almost every State and district of the Union large and powerful minorities of one or the other party, embracing men of every variety of occupation and standing socially. And in looking back for more than a dozen years to the exciting elections which the country has gone through, it will be found that, in the national contests, the candidate who triumphed received majorities in both of the great sections of the Union. Owing to these circumstances, the country has experienced no serious evils from the great political excitement it has at times undergone. Neighbors, friends, and relatives, being divided thus, they have been tolerant towards each other." [93]

[92] Robert J. Walker, *An Appeal for the Union*, pamphlet, 15.

[93] Speech in the House, December 22, 1847. *Appendix to the Congressional Globe*, 30 Cong., 1 sess., 46.

An interesting example of local division between parties was created by the two leading newspapers in Richmond, Virginia. During the later forties, the *Richmond Whig*, a powerful Whig organ that had for years held undisputed sway over local politics, discovered a close rival in the *Richmond Daily Examiner*, a Democratic paper, edited by the able John Moncure Daniel. So intense did the friendly rivalry become between the parties in Richmond that in common parlance such distinguishing titles were used as "Our friend, Democrat" or "Our enemy, Whig." A. N. Wilkinson, "John Moncure Daniel," *Richmond College Historical Papers*, June, 1915. I, no. 1, 75. Another striking instance of national party alignment is found in Tennessee. "Our State," wrote Cave Johnson, February 15, 1851, "is the most nearly balanced in the Union, success depending mainly on the organization and activity of the party; the party out being generally successful because the more active." St. George L. Sioussat, "Tennessee and National Politi-

PRINCIPLE OF THE CONCURRENT VOICE

In his farewell address on March 4, 1850, Calhoun, though he had long since lost faith in the party as a means of Southern protection, was, nevertheless, willing to admit that those "who know the strength of party ties will readily appreciate the immense force which this cause exerted against agitation and in favor of preserving quiet." In reviewing the events of the middle decades, Calhoun further explained: "The great mass of the people of the South were divided, as in the other section, into Whigs and Democrats. The leaders and the presses of both parties in the South were very solicitous to prevent excitement and to preserve quiet; because it was seen that the effects of the former would necessarily tend to weaken, if not destroy, the political ties which united them with their respective parties in the other section." [94]

But at that moment, no one knew better than Calhoun himself that this source of protection was rapidly losing its significance; for the increasing importance of the negro slave as an issue in national politics was baffling even the "superior and consummate skill" of Southern politicians intent upon maintaining political divisions "on broad, national Republican principles." In 1848, James M. Mason brought into the Senate a manifesto of the Utica, or Free Soil, Convention from which he read these lines: "The old issues, which for the last twenty years have divided them [the parties], are now settled or set aside; a new issue has been presented, in which all minor differences — and in which differences that, under other circumstances, would be important — are

cal Parties," American Historical Association, *Annual Report*, 1914, I, 246. The author of this monograph finds that between 1840 and 1850 the successful candidate for governor in Tennessee never received a majority of over 4000 votes out of a total of over 100,000 votes cast at each election. P. 256.

Reference is made to the valuable service of national political parties in saving the Union during the decades of the forties and fifties in Allen Johnson, "The Nationalizing Influence of Party," *Yale Review*, November, 1906. XV, 287-288.

[94] *Congressional Globe*, 31 Cong., 1 sess., 451.

merged and swallowed up." [95]   Calhoun himself had written to J. H. Means in 1849 that "the prospect is as things now stand, that before four years have elapsed, the Union will be divided into two great hostile sectional parties." [96] By 1850, a Virginia pamphleteer found that the Northern vote in Congress on the slavery issue "is almost unanimous, without distinction of parties, against the South." [97]

Herein was the application of a theory of parties which Calhoun had earlier advanced, not as ideal, to be sure, but as inevitable. "In a country of such vast extent and diversity of interests as ours," so he wrote, "parties, in all their stages, must partake . . . more or less of a sectional character. The laws which control their formation, necessarily lead to this.   Distance . . . always weakens, and proximity — where there is no counteracting cause — always strengthens the social and sympathetic feelings. Sameness of interests and similarity of habits and character, make it more easy for those who are contiguous to associate together and form a party than for those who are remote. . . . as party violence increases, and party efforts sink down into a mere struggle to obtain the honors and emoluments of government, the tendency to appeal to local feelings, local interests, and local prejudices will become stronger and stronger, — until, ultimately, parties must assume a decidedly sectional character." [98]

Other Southern leaders, however, were not ready with Calhoun to abandon the political party as a source of protection, for in the early fifties when the old national party alignments were breaking down, Alexander H. Stephens, Howell Cobb, and Robert Toombs, the triumvirate from Georgia,

[95] Speech in the Senate, July 6, 1848. *Appendix to the Congressional Globe*, 30 Cong., 1 sess., 887.
[96] J. F. Jameson, ed., *Correspondence of Calhoun*, American Historical Association, *Annual Report*, 1899, II, 765.

[97] A Citizen of Virginia [Muscoe R. H. Garnett] *The Union, Past and Future: How It Works and How to Save It*, pamphlet, 6.
[98] *Discourse on the Constitution*, R. K. Crallé, ed., *Works of Calhoun*, I, 306-307.

worked for a national reorganization of parties that would retain the concurrent principle for the South. During the meetings of the Nashville Convention of 1850, they even launched a new party, the Constitutional Union Party, which they hoped would assume a distinctly national character.[99]

On February 15, 1851, Robert Toombs wrote to a committee for organizing a Constitutional Union Celebration at Macon, Georgia, these lines: "The Whigs and Democrats of New York and Ohio are thoroughly denationalized. Indeed there is no non-slaveholding state in which the free-soil Whigs do not control the Whig organization, and none in which the Democratic free-soilers do not control it, except N. Jersey, Pennsylvania, Indiana, Illinois, and Iowa. Our safety, and the safety of the country, therefore, lies in refusing all coöperation with either the Whig or Democratic parties of the North, and a thorough union with the sound men of both these parties into a united National party. If this is impracticable, we ought to stand aloof from both and support none but a sound National candidate." [100]

In the following year, Alexander H. Stephens declared before the House that if neither of the parties should come out on national principles to support the Constitution and the Compromise of 1850, he hoped the people of the United States would "rise in their majesty, vindicate their rights, repudiate the action of both conventions, and put forward a national man upon national principles, and call upon the good men and true of all sections . . . to rally to their standard." [101] Referring again to reorganization on broad national Republican principles, Stephens maintained in 1854 that "there is nothing that will tend so much to a

---

[99] U. B. Phillips, *Life of Toombs*, 99. R. P. Brooks maintains that Cobb was not interested in a national reorganization of parties: "Howell Cobb and the Crisis of 1850," *Mississippi Valley Historical Review*, December, 1917, Vol. IV, no. 3, p. 294.

[100] U. B. Phillips, *Life of Toombs*, 101.

[101] Speech on April 27, 1852. *Appendix to the Congressional Globe*, 32 Cong., 1 sess., 464.

speedy pacification of both parties North as a resolute purpose on our part to adhere to this course." [102]

But the sectional break in political parties that had been brewing for years under the minor party captions of "Liberty Party" in 1844, "Free Soil Party" in 1848, and the "Free Democracy Party" in 1852, came definitely in 1856 with the organization of the new Republican Party.[103] The Southern reaction was immediate. On July 28, scarcely a month after the first Republican national convention had assembled in Philadelphia and selected its first slate of nominees for the Presidency and Vice-presidency, James F. Dowdell of Alabama noted the recent party transformation with these words: "A few, a very few, short months ago, two great and proud parties contended for the mastery in this Government. They both were national and patriotic. The men of the South and the men of the North, irrespective of State lines or geographical affinities, rallied under their banners. . . . Like links of steel, they bound together the different sections of this Union; and, embracing in their liberal policy the interests of every part, kept alive those sentiments of affection and feelings of fraternal sympathy which constitute the true bonds of union, and in the absence of which all forms of government fail, and constitutions are powerless for good. But the spoilers came." [104]

On the following September 30, Robert J. Walker, in his appeal for national support of the Democratic Party at the forthcoming election, disclosed how the warnings of Washington, Jackson, Clay, and Webster against geographical parties had at last been disregarded: "For the first time in

[102] Letter to Wm. M. Burwell, June 26, 27, 1854, as quoted from Stephens' manuscript in A. C. Cole, *Whig Party in the South,* 307. For the nationalizing influence of parties during the crisis of 1850, see the valuable article by Robert P. Brooks, "Howell Cobb and the Crisis of 1850," *Mississippi Valley Historical Review,* December, 1917. IV, no. 3, 279-298.

[103] See the platforms of these minor parties in K. H. Porter, ed., *National Party Platforms,* 7, 22, 32.

[104] Speech in the House, July 28, 1856, *Appendix to the Congressional Globe,* 34 Cong., 1 sess., 1057.

our history, such a geographical party is now formed. It is composed exclusively of the States of the North, and is arrayed in violent hostility against the Southern section of the Confederacy. It draws a line, clear and distinct, between the North and the South, and wars upon the people and institutions of the latter." [105]

Finally, in 1860, under the eminent probability of seeing this new geographic party assume the reins of government, Samuel J. Tilden, who contributed to the Southern theory of ideal party combinations, felt constrained to follow his theoretical contributions with a lamentable account of their misapplication: "In the practical working of this beautiful but complex system, the Republican party is a phenomenon new and startling. It is the first instance in which any partisan organization has been able to compete, with any prospect of success, for ascendency in our federative government, without being national in its structure, without being composed of majorities — or of minorities able to compete effectively with majorities — in all the states of both great sections of the Union. The Republican party has no practical existence in all the fifteen Southern States." Then looking forward to the general November elections which were to come within a fortnight, Tilden added: "If such an organization as the Republican party should acquire complete possession of the federative government, what sort of a system would it be? To the people of the fifteen states it would be a foreign government . . . None of their citizens would have concurred in bringing the Administration into existence; none of their public opinion would be represented in that Administration." [106] The actual fulfilment of this hy-

[105] Robert J. Walker, *An Appeal for the Union*, pamphlet, 2.

[106] Letter to William Kent, dated October 26, 1860. John Bigelow, *Writings and Speeches of Samuel J. Tilden*, I, 291, 292. See also Thomas G. Pratt and James A. Pearce, Senators from Maryland, Letter to

their constituents entitled "The Triumph of Sectionalism the Death Knell of the Union," *An Appeal for the Union*, pamphlet, 3.

For the "doorsill" doctrine of protection against sectional parties, see Robert Toombs, Letter to T. W. Thomas, Decem-

pothesis at the November election established beyond question the futility of all attempts at applying the concurrent
voice to political parties. But in this respect, the results of
the election are of little consequence, for the South had
wisely abandoned this highway of protection, a decade earlier, as hopeless.

ber 4, 1859. U. B. Phillips, ed., *Cor-
respondence of Toombs, Stephens, and*   *Cobb,* American Historical Association, *Annual Report,* 1911, II, 450.

CHAPTER V

THE PRINCIPLE OF CONSTITUTIONAL GUARANTEES

"IF it be true, as some allege, that there is a large majority of the people of the North who are unwilling to stand by the constitutional guarantee [the rendition of fugitive slaves] . . . I, for one, am for tearing asunder every bond that binds us together. . . . Any people capable of defending themselves, who would continue their allegiance to a Government which should deny them a clear, unquestionable, constitutional right of the magnitude and importance of this to the people of the South, would deserve to be stigmatized as poltroons." [1] The words are from a new champion of a new cause: Alexander H. Stephens was speaking on April 27, 1852, before the House of Representatives in defense of the principle of constitutionalism. The development within the South of this means of defense involved a consideration of the fundamental nature and character of a constitution, a study of the means of insuring constitutional limitations, and an application of the explicit provisions of the constitution to the pressing problems of the day; for in these factors lay the strength of the constitutional principle as a source of protection to a Southern minority during the decade of the fifties.

THE FUNCTIONS OF A CONSTITUTION

"Why do we want constitutions?" asked Robert Toombs, a leading statesman of Georgia, in addressing the Senate on July 30, 1856. "Because we know that majorities are

[1] *Appendix to the Congressional Globe,* 32 Cong., 1 sess., 460.

unjust. . . . The Constitution is based on the idea, that where the interests of particular localities are at stake men are not to be trusted; majorities are not to be relied upon; they are unjust; they will take advantage." [2]

Whence the formation of these selfish majorities? Calhoun had an answer for this fundamental question in 1848: "a struggle will take place between the various interests to obtain a majority, in order to control the government. If no one interest be strong enough, of itself, to obtain it, a combination will be formed between those whose interests are most alike; — each conceding something to the others, until a sufficient number is obtained to make a majority. The process may be slow, and much time may be required before a compact, organized majority can be thus formed; but . . . once formed, the community will be divided into two great parties, — the major and minor, — between which there will be incessant struggles on the one side to retain, and on the other to obtain the majority, — and, thereby, the control of the government and the advantages it confers." [3] It was upon this basic conflict between a majority with power and a minority without power, that the South founded its philosophy of constitutionalism. Calhoun himself declared that the means by which the oppression of the one upon the other is prevented "by whatever name called, is what is meant by CONSTITUTION, in its most comprehensive sense, when applied to GOVERNMENT." [4]

The support of this concept of a constitution as an instrument of minorities was widespread throughout the South. "A constitution," once declared John A. Quitman, who was taking an active stand for constitutionalism in the fifties, "is intended . . . for the benefit of the minority, to protect

[2] *Appendix to the Congressional Globe,* 34 Cong., 1 sess., 1052.
[3] *Disquisition on Government,* R. K Crallé,

ed., *Works of Calhoun,* I, 16.
[4] *Ibid.,* 7.

them against the action of the majority; to protect the weak against the strong, the poor and infirm against the rich and powerful." [5] Calhoun reached the same conclusion when he wrote in his Fort Hill Letter, 1832: "the Constitution will be viewed by the majority . . . as shackles on their power. To them it will have no value as the means of protection. As a majority they require none. Their number and strength, and not the Constitution, are their protection." [6]

But this abstract philosophy of constitutionalism was designed for a definite purpose; for when applied to the conditions in the Union, the Federal Constitution became an instrument for the protection of the Southern minority against the encroachment of the Northern majority. William L. Yancey, perhaps the most energetic devotee of the Southern cause that Alabama ever produced, presented this application of the theory in unquestionable language during an address at Washington, D. C., in 1860: "It is easy for the North, with its majority in the millions, to say they are for this Union . . . Because with no Constitution at all the people of the North can protect themselves by a predominant vote. How is it with the minority — the minority States? How is it with the South? . . . Minorities, gentlemen, are the true friends of our Constitution, because that Constitution is their shield and their protection against the unchecked and unlicensed power of the majority." [7]

This application of abstract constitutional principles to concrete conditions in the Union became strikingly important to Southern political thinkers about 1850; and in this

[5] An address to the electors of Adams County, 1832. J. F. H. Claiborne, *Life and Correspondence of Quitman*, I, 118.
[6] Letter to Governor Hamilton, August 28, 1832. R. K. Crallé, ed., *Works of Calhoun*, VI, 187.
"The Constitution," declared William L. Yancey, "was an assurance to the man who had property that he would not be robbed of it, an assurance to the minority that the majority would in all things be governed by the written law and not by the higher law." Speech in New York City, October 10, 1860. E. D. Fite, *Presidential Campaign of 1860*, Appendix D, p. 321. Reprinted from the *New York Herald*, October 11, 1860.
[7] J. W. DuBose, *Life and Times of Yancey*, 497.

renewed interest there is a certain indication that the South was at that time laying the foundation for a shift to constitutional guarantees as a source of protection within the Union. On October 6, 1848, Jefferson Davis thus wrote to a relative: "We of the South are the minority and such we must remain; our property, our security in the Union depends upon the power of the constitutional curb with which we check the otherwise, unbridled will of the majority." [8] On December 12, 1849, Henry W. Hilliard declared in Congress: "In our Government we are protected against the tyranny of a popular majority — the worst of all tyrannies — by the provisions of the Constitution." [9] And on April 4, 1850, James S. Green of Virginia declared on the same floor that the Constitution "was especially designed to protect the minority, situated as the southern States now are." [10]

THE ENFORCEMENT OF CONSTITUTIONAL LIMITATIONS: A GLANCE IN RETROSPECT

If constitutions are instruments of minorities for limiting the sway of the majority, it appears to follow that the minority in order to be protected effectively should exercise a determining voice in establishing and maintaining constitutional limitations; for otherwise, a constitution moulded at the will of a numerical majority would afford no protection whatever to a minority, aside from such limitations upon power as the majority was willing to impose upon itself. In the South it was contended that the fathers of the Constitution were themselves aware of this necessity, and

[8] Dunbar Rowland, ed., *Davis, Constitutionalist*, I, 214.
[9] *Appendix to the Congressional Globe*, 31 Cong., 1 sess., 34. On January 3, 1851, Hilliard restated his position in an address at Philadelphia: "The Constitution — not the will of a majority — is the supreme law of the United States. A more disastrous political condition could not be imagined than that to which we should be exposed if the restraints which the Constitution imposes were withdrawn." H. W. Hilliard, *Speeches and Addresses*, 365.
[10] *Appendix to the Congressional Globe*, 31 Cong., 1 sess., 426.

that they had provided adequate minority protection in the fifth article of the Federal Constitution. To be sure, the authority originally granted to the national government was acceptable to the Southern states; otherwise they never would have ratified the Constitution. But of far more consequence than an enumeration of the powers originally delegated to the national government was the provision for adding new powers after that government had been put into operation.

Presumably, the addition of new powers to the central government depended solely upon the amending clause, which is Article V of the Constitution.[11] The extra-majority vote therein required for expanding national powers gave to the South as a substantial minority an adequate guarantee for the maintenance of constitutional limitations. During the debates of the Convention on the slave-trade, for example, James Madison later wrote that "the earnestness of S. Carolina & Georgia was further manifested by their insisting on the security in the V article, against any amendment to the Constitution affecting the right reserved to them."[12] And Calhoun once pointed out that "it was proposed in the Convention to increase the confederative power, . . . by vesting two thirds of the States with the right of amendment, so as to require more than a third, instead of a fourth, to withhold power. The proposition was rejected, and three fourths unanimously adopted."[13] The Southern states entered the Union apparently confident that, so long as they constituted more than one-fourth of the total num-

---

[11] "The Congress, whenever two thirds of both houses shall deem it necessary, shall propose Amendments to this Constitution, or, on the Application of the Legislatures of two thirds of the several States, shall call a Convention for proposing Amendments, which, in either Case, shall be valid to all Intents and Purposes, as Part of this Constitution, when ratified by the Legislatures of three fourths of the several States, or by Conventions in three fourths thereof, as the one or the other Mode of Ratification may be proposed by the Congress." U. S. Constitution, Art. V.

[12] Letter to Robert Walsh, November 27, 1819. Gaillard Hunt, ed., *Writings of Madison*, IX, 2.

[13] The Fort Hill Letter to Governor Hamilton, August 28, 1832. R. K. Crallé, ed., *Works of Calhoun*, VI, 178.

ber of states in the Union, their power of enforcing constitutional limitations was absolute.

This concept of the original purpose of Article V provides the key to all subsequent political theories for establishing effective constitutional limitations upon numerical majority rule. One of the most pertinent statements is found in the twenty-second number of Turnbull's *The Crisis:* "Should it so happen, that there may be an object, for which the Constitution has not provided, . . . an amendment to the Constitution, may, at any time, be proposed, and if the new power asked for, be necessary to war, foreign negotiation and commerce . . . there is no fear, but what three-fourths of the States will agree to the amendment. . . . If the assent of three-fourths of the State Legislatures, for this purpose, cannot be obtained, it would prove that the power ought not to be exercised." [14] Thirty-three years later, Robert J. Turnbull wrote: "To the *honest* expositor of the constitution, it is sufficient that a law is subversive of the vital interests of seven States out of the twenty-four, to be convinced that it is not based upon that constitution." [15]

Calhoun considered the principle at greater length. Under the Articles of Confederation, as he pointed out, the demand for local protection was so great that any new grant of power to the central government *"required the consent of all the States, while to withhold power the dissent of a single State was sufficient."* But under the Federal Consti-

---

[14] R. J. Turnbull, *The Crisis*, no. 22, p. 111.

[15] R. J. Turnbull, *Observations on State Sovereignty, Federal Usurpations, and State Interposition*, 107.

Similar views were expressed by John Taylor, who restated the principle of the fifth article by insisting that in theory "the people of the States had a right to make the Federal constitution, and to prohibit its alteration, except with the concurrence of three-fourths of the legislatures of the several States." *Tyranny Unmasked*, 343.

St. George Tucker wrote in 1803 that the Federal Constitution "can not be controlled, or altered without the express consent of the body politic of three fourths of the states in the union, or, of the people, of an equal number of the states." *Blackstone's Commentaries*, I, Appendix, 171.

See further, Thomas Jefferson, Letter to William Johnson, June 12, 1823. P. L. Ford, ed., *Writings of Jefferson*, X, 232, note; and especially, Felix Grundy, speech in the Senate, March 1, 1830. *Register of Debates in Congress*, 21 Cong., 1 sess., 214.

tution, this extreme concession to the states was somewhat
modified "so that three fourths of the States may now grant
power; and, consequently it requires more than one fourth
to withhold." This extra-majority requirement of the fifth
article was inserted, so he thought, "clearly with a view of
interposing a barrier against this strong instinctive appetite
of the Government for the acquisition of power"; and since
by that article a three-fourths majority was required for the
addition of new powers, Calhoun was convinced "that it was
not intended that the States should be more united than the
will of one fourth of them, or, rather, one more than a
fourth, would permit." [16]

But this method of enforcing constitutional limitations
upon a numerical majority lost its effectiveness as soon as
that majority in control of the national government devised
means of expanding its powers without resorting to the
process of constitutional amendment. An unexpected and
fatal weakness in the scheme for constitutional limitations
developed under the doctrine of implied powers, as expressed
in Marshall's opinion in *McCulloch* v. *Maryland.* "A new
mode of amending the Constitution has been added to the
ample ones provided in that instrument," wrote Spencer
Roane in 1819, "and the strongest checks established in it
have been made to yield to the force of precedents! The
time will soon arrive, if it is not already at hand, when the
Constitution may be expounded without ever looking into
it! — by merely reading the acts of a renegade Congress.
. . ." "That man must be a deplorable idiot," so Roane
concluded, "who does not see that there is no earthly difference between an *unlimited* grant of power and a grant
limited in its terms, but accompanied with *unlimited* means
of carrying it into execution." [17] John Randolph restated

[16] The Fort Hill Letter to Governor Hamilton, August 28, 1832. R. K. Crallé, ed.,
Works of Calhoun, VI, 177, 189, 178.
[17] "Hampden" Letter no. 1. *Richmond En-*
quirer, June 11, 1819, as quoted in *John P.*
Branch Historical Papers, June, 1905, II,
79, 80.

the idea in 1824 when, in quoting from an eminent statesman, he said that "it is not, perhaps, so much by the assumption of unlawful powers, as by the unwise and unwarrantable use of those which are most legal, that governments
oppose their true end and object." [18]

Needless to say, this use of implied powers, endorsed by
the Supreme Court, which was exercising the functions of
a constitutional interpreter, completely destroyed the efficacy of the extra-majority principle in the fifth article.
"Give to a majority of the States the right of amendment,"
asserted Calhoun, "and the arresting power, on the part
of the State, would, in fact, be annulled. The amending
power and the powers of the Government would, in that
case, be, in reality, in the same hands. The same majority
that controlled the one would the other, — and the power
arrested, as not granted, would be immediately restored in
the shape of a grant." [19]

A few decades of national expansion without once invoking the process of constitutional amendment convinced those
who would still use the Constitution as a source of protec-

[18] Speech in the House, April 15, 1824,
Annals of Congress, 18 Cong., 1 sess., 2361.
Both Randolph and Roane had probably
read the Virginia Report of 1800, wherein
at that early date Madison had written:
"it must be wholly immaterial whether unlimited powers be exercised under the name
of unlimited powers, or be exercised under
the name of unlimited means of carrying
into execution limited powers." Gaillard
Hunt, ed., *Writings of Madison,* VI, 284.
[19] The Fort Hill Letter of Governor Hamilton, August 28, 1832. R. K. Crallé, ed.,
Works of Calhoun, VI, 176.
Against the unwarranted extension of national powers by the Executive and Congress, the Judiciary afforded no remedy.
"In vain would the oppressed minority of
the people of the United States look to
the judicial department of the federal government for relief from unconstitutional
laws," wrote Robert J. Turnbull. "The
members of this department represent the

interests of the majority of the people of
the United States, and are appointed with
the advice and consent of this majority
in the Senate; and should they prove,
from conscientious motives, otherwise than
easy tools for the accomplishment of the
views of that majority, their removal by
impeachment, and the re-appointment of
others better adapted to the purposes of a
corrupt majority, is both easy and certain.
"A bare majority of both houses of Congress, and a President who always represents the interests of the majority of the
people of the United States, is fully adequate to the re-organization of the federal
courts, in such a manner as would most
cherish the interests of that *majority,* to
the annihilation of the constitutional rights
of the *minority.*" R. J. Turnbull, *Observations on State Sovereignty, Federal Usurpations, and State Interposition,* (1850),
105.

tion to minority interests that this instrument must prevent "unlimited means" as well as "unlimited powers" and prohibit not only the "assumption of unlawful powers" but also the "unwise and unwarrantable use of those that are most legal." Yet for this purpose the amending process was least adapted, for it had been designed to permit expansion of national powers, not to demand restriction upon those already exercised. And while any minority of over one-fourth had the power to withhold permission, only a majority of at least three-fourths could demand restriction. "Let us examine the case," wrote Calhoun. "The disease is, that a majority of the States, through the General Government, by construction, usurp powers not delegated, and by their exercise, increase their wealth and authority at the expense of the minority. How absurd, then, to expect the injured States to attempt a remedy by proposing an amendment to be ratified by three fourths of the States, when, by supposition, there is a majority opposed to them? Nor would it be less absurd to expect the General Government to propose amendments, unless compelled to that course by the acts of a State. The Government can have no inducement. It has a more summary mode, — the assumption of power by construction. The consequence is clear; — neither would resort to the amending power; — the one because it would be useless, — and the other, because it could effect its purpose without it; — and thus the highest power known to the Constitution . . . would become in practice obsolete. . . ." [20]

Such was the constitutional dilemma from which the South in the middle decades escaped through the door of "a concurrent voice in making and executing the laws." Though a majority within the South were ready to exclaim, "A fig for the Constitution! when the scorpion's sting is probing

[20] "The South Carolina Exposition" — drafted by Calhoun and adopted by the South Carolina Legislature on December 19, 1828. R. K. Crallé, ed., *Works of Calhoun*, VI, 50-51.

us to the quick, shall we stop to chop logic?" yet Calhoun and a small group of his followers were willing to remain constitutional logic-choppers in order to attempt the restoration of the original power of a minority to enforce constitutional limitations.[21]

This small group of logic-choppers rested the foundation of their constitutional structure upon the illogic of governmental interpretation of its own powers. "According to this theory," asserted Robert Y. Hayne, Calhoun's right-hand man, "the States have a right to exercise just so much power (and no more,) as the Federal Government may think proper to leave them, and we are presented with the strange anomaly of 'the *creature* elevated above its creator, the servants above their masters.' "[22] But if the national government cannot logically interpret the instrument which created it and defined its powers, still less may any one department of that government logically do so. "The Supreme Court," said Spencer Roane, "is but a department of the general government. A department is not competent to do that to which the whole government is inadequate. The general government cannot decide this controversy, and much less can one of its departments. They cannot do it, unless we tread under foot the principle which forbids a party to decide his own cause."[23]

To Calhoun and his followers, the only logical solution

[21] The quotation is from John Randolph, speech in the House, April 15, 1824. *Annals of Congress*, 18 Cong., 1 sess., 2361. Though Calhoun became perhaps the greatest constitutional logic-chopper of all time, he once declared that he "was no advocate for refined arguments on the Constitution. The instrument was not intended as a thesis for the logician to exercise his ingenuity on." Speech in the House, February 4, 1817. *Ibid.*, 14 Cong., 2 sess., 855.

[22] Address before the State Rights Celebration at Charleston, South Carolina, July 1, 1830. *Proceedings of the State Rights Celebration,* pamphlet, 11. "Now if . . . the Federal Government 'are the exclusive judges of the extent of their own powers,' and the States are bound in all cases, no matter how gross or palpable the usurpation, implicitly to submit . . . then it is as clear as the sun at noon day, that THE STATES HAVE NO RIGHTS, or theirs are *rights* without *remedies*, which we all know amount to no rights at all." *Hayne's Fourth of July Oration, 1831*, pamphlet, 26. [23] "Hampden" Letter in the *Richmond Enquirer*, June 22, 1819, as quoted in *John P. Branch Historical Papers*, June, 1905. II, no. 1, p. 119.

was a reversion to the original principle of having the Constitution interpreted by those who made it, as provided in the fifth article by calling "into action, on all important disputed questions, this highest power of the system, — to whose controlling authority no one can object, and under whose operation all controversies between the States and General Government would be adjusted, and the Constitution gradually acquire all the perfection of which it is susceptible." "It is thus," Calhoun added, "that the *creating* becomes the *preserving* power; and we may rest assured it is no less true in politics than in theology, that the power which creates can alone preserve, — and that preservation is perpetual creation." [24]

Calhoun's method of invoking the amending process to decide constitutional issues gave to a single state the power of initiative — a power, which, as Jefferson Davis later explained, "was a temporary expedient, intended to restrain action until the question at issue could be submitted to a convention of the States." [25] The whole process is thus outlined by Felix Grundy, senator from Tennessee, in a speech on March 1, 1830: "Let the injured and oppressed State, then, assume its highest political attitude — a convention in the State, for the purpose of deciding whether the great fundamental law, which unites and binds the States together, has been violated, by Congress having exercised power reserved to the States, and not delegated to the General Government." If the aggrieved state decides this question affirmatively, "the necessary consequence is, that the act of Congress must cease to operate in the State; and Congress must acquiesce, by abandoning the power, or obtain an express grant from the great source from which all its powers are drawn." Not wishing to abandon the disputed power, Con-

---

[24] The South Carolina Exposition, 1828. R. K. Crallé, ed., *Works of Calhoun*, VI, 51.

[25] Jefferson Davis, *Rise and Fall of the Confederate Government*, I, 184.

gress may submit the issue in the form of an amendment to the states, and if "three-fourths of the States shall not concur in admitting the contested power, or shall not pronounce that it already exists, Congress will be constrained to abandon the exercise of it, in as much as no new power can be granted without such concurrence." [26]

In requiring the constant support of a three-fourths majority for the validity of national action, Calhoun's theory of nullification — for such it was called — was a logical deduction from the provisions of Article V, James Madison and his other opponents to the contrary notwithstanding. When Madison asserted in 1830 that Calhoun's doctrine "puts it in the power of the smallest fraction over $\frac{1}{4}$ of the U. S. — that is, of 7 States out of 24 — to give the law and even the Const^n. to 17 States," or when he maintained in 1835 that "any State which could obtain the concurrence of six others, might abrogate any law of the U. S. constructively whatever, and give to the Constitution any shape they please, in opposition to the construction and will of the other seventeen," [27] Madison was in effect supporting Calhoun's theoretical position that the fathers of the Constitution intended the states to be united only to that degree permitted by the concurrence of three-fourths of their number. Calhoun's contention to which Madison objected, that the extra-majority principle of Article V gave to a substantial minority a controlling voice over a numerical majority, was obviously sound as to all new powers to be granted to the national government; and, in theory, Calhoun thought it equally logical to conclude that whatever power required

[26] *Register of Debates in Congress*, 21 Cong., 1 sess., 214.

[27] Letter to Edward Everett, August 28, 1830. Notes on Nullification, 1835. Gaillard Hunt, *Writings of Madison*, IX, 399, 588. See also the resolutions of the Union and States Rights Convention in South Carolina, 1832, in J. P. Carson, *Life, Letters, and Speeches of James L. Pettigru*,

92-93. Calhoun answered his critics in his South Carolina Exposition and in his Fort Hill Letter. R. K. Crallé, ed., *Works of Calhoun*, VI, 48, 176-177. A reply to Madison's objections to nullification is found in R. J. Turnbull, *Observations on State Sovereignty, Federal Usurpations, and State Interposition*, 107, 109-110.

the support of three-fourths of the states
in the first instance should likewise require t
of that three-fourths majority for its con
Only in this way could the efficacy of the
principle be retained, and he could find no more
justification for violating this principle in the one instance
than in the other.[28]

As for objections to the method of applying the theory
of nullification — the costs, the delays, the time involved —
Calhoun might have modified his application to meet those
objections by having the states file their formal protests
with the national secretary of state until the number of states
requisite to deny the exercise of the contested power — that
is, one-fourth plus one — had done so; whereupon the
further exercise of the power would have become unconstitutional automatically without the necessity for further
procedure.

Constitutionally, in permitting a single state to initiate
amendments, Calhoun's theory of nullification was decidedly
unsound; for the initiation of amendments by a minority is
nowhere expressly provided for within the bounds of the
Constitution. Nor can minority initiation be reasonably —
not to say necessarily — inferred from any provision of that
instrument, since the express language of the fifth article is
directly to the contrary. For constitutional support Calhoun
and his followers were forced to contend that nullification
was "according to the philosophy of the government and
the true spirit of the compact." [29] They could assert that
Congress *should* take the requisite steps to determine

[28] To take the current issue over prohibition as an example, Calhoun would note that the national government gained jurisdiction over this subject only after receiving the concurrence of three-fourths of the states through an appropriate constitutional amendment; and he would insist that as soon as this three-fourths majority in support of national control over prohibition was lost, the power would have to be abandoned, since the object of Article V was to reserve all powers receiving the support of less than the required three-fourths majority to the control of the states.
[29] "Address to the People of South Carolina," South Carolina Convention, 1832, *Reports, Ordinances, and Addresses of the People of South Carolina,* 11.

hether a doubtful power had the backing of three-fourths of the states; but in order to *require* Congress to do so, except upon a two-thirds vote, they had to fall back upon theories of state sovereignty, the contractual character of the Constitution, or the constitutional limitations upon judicial power. In this respect Calhoun and his followers were as much at sea as were any of their predecessors: Jefferson in 1799 in the second Kentucky Resolutions; Roane in 1819 and 1821 in his limitations upon judicial power; and Taylor in 1822 in his theory of the concurrent state veto.[30] Nullification was not warranted by the Constitution, and for that reason the South, engaged in pursuing with Calhoun another source of protection, turned a cold shoulder to their leader's so-called second method of establishing a concurrent voice — a veto upon the execution of the laws.

So when in 1850 the South was forced to fall back upon constitutionalism as a last resort for protection within the Union, it could not then support Calhoun's position — however essential to the effective guarantee of constitutional limitations — without departing from an adherence to the letter of the Constitution. For to accept nullification was to denounce the express constitutional method of initiating amendments — a position clearly inconsistent with the demand for a strict enforcement of other clauses of the Constitution favorable to negro slavery. Indeed, had the theory of nullification been of undoubted constitutionality, and even in actual operation during the decade of the fifties, it might well have met with strong Southern opposition. For the South was then demanding that the national government take positive action under express constitutional provisions to protect the institution of negro slavery from growing attacks upon it by the Northern states. Needless to say, the

[30] Thomas Jefferson, Second Kentucky Resolutions, William MacDonald, ed., *Documentary Source Book*, (3 ed.), 276-278; Spencer Roane, letters to the *Richmond Enquirer*, 1819 and 1821 copied in *John P. Branch Historical Papers*, II, no. 1, pp. 51-122; II, no. 2, pp. 78-183; John Taylor, *Tyranny Unmasked*, 262 et seq.

probability of retaining constantly the required three-fourths majority of states in support of any constitutional provision favorable to negro slavery, in the light of the Northern attitude towards this institution in the decade of the fifties, was at best a remote one. In 1843, Henry St. George Tucker clearly foresaw the probable consequences of having Calhoun's theory of nullification turned against the very people that it was intended to protect. In condemnation of the theory, Tucker wrote: "If the surrender of our runaway slaves, or of the negro-stealers, who carry them off is evaded, against the plain words of the constitution, we must wait for redress until three fourths of the states shall decide that the act of our northern brethren is not justified by the compact." [31]

THE SWING TO CONSTITUTIONALISM: AN EXPLANATION

Why the South, deprived of its effective weapon of enforcing constitutional limitations by the amending process, was still willing to rely for protection upon the guarantees of the Federal Constitution appears at first puzzling; for, as we have seen, the leaders of Southern thought had long since come to believe with John S. Barbour that the value of a constitutional guarantee "resolves itself at last into the will of the majority, who may make it mean what they please, or strike it out altogether at pleasure." [32] Certainly by 1850, the South was willing to agree with Abel P. Upshur that no "paper guarantee was ever yet worth any thing, unless the whole, or at least a majority of the community, were interested in maintaining it." [33]

Yet, despite these denunciations of constitutional guarantees, the swing to constitutionalism in 1850 was justified, so it was contended, by the formal position of the North

[31] Henry St. George Tucker, *Lectures on Constitutional Law*, 196.
[32] *Debates of the Virginia Constitutional Convention, 1829-1830*, 136-137.
[33] *Ibid.*, 76.

upon the question of negro slavery — now the vital issue in the movement for Southern protection. While neither the word *negro* nor the word *slave* appears in the Constitution, the South was satisfied, as James M. Mason explained in Congress on July 6, 1848,[34] that the institution of negro slavery had been unquestionably recognized and adequately protected in four separate provisions of that instrument. The most important of these provisions, at least in the decade of the fifties, was that found in Article IV, Section 2: "No Person held to Service or Labour in one State, under the Laws thereof, escaping into another, shall, in Consequence of any Law or Regulation therein, be discharged from such Service or Labour, but shall be delivered up on Claim of the Party to whom such Service or Labour may be due." [35]

In line with these constitutional provisions, the formal position of the national government upon the subject of negro slavery appears in resolutions enacted from time to time by the two houses of Congress. As early as March 23, 1790, the House of Representatives of the first Congress passed resolutions in Committee of the Whole, after a heated sectional debate, stating that "Congress have no authority to interfere in the emancipation of slaves, or in the treatment of them within any of the States; it remaining with the several States alone to provide any regulations therein, which humanity and true policy may require." [36] Again on May 25, 1836, the House resolved by a vote of 182 to 9 that "Congress possesses no constitutional authority to interfere in any way with the institution of slavery in

[34] *Appendix to the Congressional Globe,* 30 Cong., 1 sess., 883.
[35] The other pertinent sections of the Constitution are Art. I, sec. 2, on the apportionment for representation and direct taxes; Art. I, sec. 9, on the free importation of negroes before 1808; and a clause in Art. V prohibiting before 1808 any amendment to the Constitution affecting the clause on the free importation "of such Persons as any of the States now existing may think proper to admit." A five-column article on the slavery clauses of the Constitution appears on the editorial page of the *Richmond Enquirer* for October 29, 1860.
[36] *Annals of Congress,* 1 Cong., 2 sess., 1474. Adopted, 29-25.

any of the States of this confederacy." [37]   In the following year, on December 21, 1837, it resolved to lay on the table "all petitions, memorials, and papers, touching the abolition of slavery"; [38] and on December 11, 1838, it adopted resolutions that "by the Constitution of the United States, Congress has no jurisdiction whatever over the institution of slavery in the several States of the Confederacy." Of the two hundred and four votes cast on this last resolution, only six were opposed to its adoption.[39]

The position of the Senate is equally strong for the protection of slavery under the Federal Constitution. Between January 3 and January 12, 1838 (inclusive), the Senate adopted by decisive majorities five resolutions which Thomas H. Benton asserted "were framed to declare the whole power of Congress upon the subject, and were presented for a 'test' vote, and as a future *'platform'* and *'permanent settlement'* of the law on the slavery question." [40] These resolutions in part assert: "it is the solemn duty of the Government to resist, to the extent of its constitutional power, all attempts by one portion of the Union to use it [the government] as an instrument to attack the domestic institutions of another, or to weaken or destroy such institutions." The resolutions then refer to slavery "existing at the adoption of the Constitution, by which it is recognized," and of attacks on this institution as "a manifest breach of faith, and a violation of the most solemn obligations." [41]

Nor had the Congress stopped short with formal resolutions: it had enacted favorable legislation in pursuance of the Constitution for the rendition of fugitive slaves. In "An Act Respecting Fugitives from Justice, and Persons Escaping from the Service of Their Masters" approved on

---

[37] *Register of Debates in Congress*, 24 Cong., 1 sess., 4031.
[38] *Congressional Globe*, 25 Cong., 2 sess., 45. Adopted, 122-74.
[39] *Congressional Globe*, 25 Cong., 3 sess., 23, 25.

[40] Thomas H. Benton, *Abridgment of Debates in Congress*, XIII, (1835-1839), p. 568, note.
[41] *Congressional Globe*, 25 Cong., 2 sess., 73-98. The resolutions are found on p. 98.

February 12, 1793, the South certainly received all that it could reasonably expect, for therein it was provided in substance that a master or his agent might recover a fugitive by taking him before a federal judge or local magistrate, who, solely upon the basis of oral testimony or by affidavit, was to determine the question of ownership.[42]

And if the South in 1850 was forced to abandon its last stronghold of the concurrent voice, it received in return, and within a fortnight from the admission of California, a drastically reinforced fugitive slave act permitting special federal commissioners, with the aid of United States marshals and their deputies, to decide to their own satisfaction the identity of the asserted slave by *ex parte* evidence, without allowing the negro whose freedom was at stake an opportunity to be heard. The commissioners were to receive twice the amount in fees for returning a suspected fugitive as for discharging him; and the decisions of the commissioners were in all cases final. Even the citizens were subjected to heavy penalties for refusing to help enforce the law upon request, or for aiding the fugitive to escape.[43]

If further evidence of good faith by Congress were needed, there was, as Benjamin F. Perry pointed out in a speech before the South Carolina Legislature, December 11, 1850, the case of the District of Columbia with 50,000 inhabitants and only 2000 slaves, wherein for "the last sixty years, ever since the Union was formed, Congress has had the power, the Constitutional power . . . to abolish slavery." Yet, said he, a bill to that end introduced into the last Senate received only seven or eight votes.[44]

[42] *United States Statutes at Large,* I, 302-305. The act is summarized in J. S. Bassett, *The Federalist System,* 189.
[43] *United States Statutes at Large,* IX, 462-465. The act is summarized in T. C. Smith, *Parties and Slavery,* 15. See also M. G. McDougal, *Fugitive Slaves, 1619-1865.* Immediately after the passage of this measure, the Attorney General John J. Crittenden declared the act to be constitutional. This opinion, as well as the law itself is found in M. W. Cluskey, ed., *Political Text Book* (12 ed.), 241-245.
[44] *Speech of Hon. B. F. Perry . . . ,* pamphlet, 16.

Furthermore, if the value of constitutional guarantees depended ultimately upon the interpretation by the courts, they too had supported the slavery provisions of the Constitution, and the laws of Congress enacted in accordance with them. "Fortunately for the south," wrote Henry St. George Tucker, in offering an alternative to Calhoun's theory of nullification, "a shorter and surer remedy was offered by the decision of the supreme court of the United States in the case of *Prigg* v. *State of Pennsylvania,* in which the laws for the protection of fugitive slaves, and giving to them a jury trial when demanded by their masters, was declared unconstitutional and void." [45]

With the sectional equilibrium hanging in the balance, Daniel F. Dickinson of New York pointed out to the Southern members of the Senate on August 26, 1850, the above cited case and other instances of support for the Southern cause at the hands of the Supreme Court and even in some cases at the hands of judges of Northern state courts. Dickinson quoted Judge Nelson in the Supreme Court of New York, who considered that "it is peremptory and unqualified that he [the slave] 'shall be delivered up' "; Chancellor Walworth of the New York Court of Errors, who declared, "the constitutional provision is imperative that *he shall be delivered up";* Joseph Story in the Prigg Case who held that the fugitive slave clause "contemplates the existence of a positive, unqualified right on the part of the owner of the slave, which *no State can in any way qualify, regulate, control, or restrain";* and Justice McLean, who, in the same case, asserted that "a positive duty is enjoined on them [the states] to deliver him up, 'on claim of the party to whom his service may be due.' " [46]

---

[45] Henry St. George Tucker, *Lectures on Constitutional Law,* 196.
[46] *Congressional Globe,* 31 Cong., 1 sess., 1660. The definite reaction against nationalism that came in 1836 with the appoint- ment of Roger B. Taney to succeed John Marshall as Chief Justice is described in Charles Warren, *The Supreme Court in United States History* (rev. ed.), Vol. II. Of this reaction, Hampton L. Carson wrote

Upon these records, the South was willing in 1850 to invoke the protection of the Federal Constitution even in the hands of a Northern majority as the chief source of reliance for maintaining the institution of negro slavery. To a degree, James F. Dowdell was correct in designating this swing to constitutionalism "a return to the original State-rights theory of non-interference with local and domestic concerns"; [47] but, unlike the earlier principle of local self-government, the application of the principle of constitutional guarantees in the fifties was directed almost solely to the protection of American negro slavery.

Southern sentiment in 1850 leaves no doubt of a complete transition during that year from the principle of the concurrent voice to the principle of constitutionalism. On February 27, Robert Toombs, in the course of one of his many speeches on the admission of California, after perceiving that even the abolitionists "admit some at least of the constitutional obligations to protect slavery," declared in behalf of the South that Northern majorities in both Houses of Congress "have brought us to the point where we are to test the sufficiency of written constitutions to protect the rights of a minority against a majority of the people." "Our security, under the Constitution," he said, "is based solely upon good faith. There is nothing in its structure which makes aggression permanently impossible. . . . In this emergency our duty is clear; it is to stand by the Constitution and laws, to observe in good faith all of its requirements, until . . . demonstrated that the Constitution is powerless for our protection." [48]

in his *The Supreme Court of the United States,* at page 337: "the triumvirate which corresponded with that of Marshall, Washington and Story, was composed of Taney, Nelson and Campbell." Quoted in G. W. Duncan, "John Archibald Campbell," Alabama Historical Society, *Transactions,* 1904, V, 113. A brief summary with citations to cases favorable to the states after 1835 is found in W. W. Willoughby, *Constitutional Law of the United States* (2 ed.), I, 134-135.

[47] Speech in the House, July 28, 1856. *Appendix to the Congressional Globe,* 34 Cong., 1 sess., 1060.

[48] *Appendix to the Congressional Globe,*

Private correspondence of the year supported the opinions expressed in Congress. On August 18, within a week after the Senate had passed the bill to admit California, L. W. Tazewell wrote R. M. T. Hunter: "These states have long accustomed themselves to regard the Senate of the U. S. as the only body upon which any reliance could be placed for the conservation of their political rights and interests. They will now see, I suppose, that this was mere delusion." [49] On the following November 7, Jefferson Davis, in a letter to S. Cobun and others, expressed the wish that "the union of the South and the sober sense of the North produce a return of that sense of justice, and faithful observance of the principles of our federal compact which will enable a minority to live as equals in the confederacy." [50]

Conventions of the year expressed the swing to constitutionalism in formal resolutions. The November session of the Nashville Convention adopted this position: "We stand upon the defensive. We invoke the spirit of the Constitution, and claim its guarantees. Our rights — our independence — the peace and existence of our families, depend upon the issue." [51] And on December 10, the State Convention of Georgia included in its "Georgia Platform" a plank stating "That it is the deliberate opinion of this Convention that upon the faithful execution of the fugitive slave bill by the proper authorities depends the preservation of our much loved Union." [52] Beyond question, the South was now ready

---

31 Cong., 1 sess., 199, 198, 201. John C. Calhoun, always in advance of his time, was ready to make the change three years earlier. These words are from his speech in the Senate on February 19, 1847: "I see my way in the Constitution. I cannot in a compromise. A compromise is but an act of Congress. It may be overruled at any time. It gives us no security. But the Constitution is stable. It is a rock. On it we can stand. It is a firm and stable ground, on which we can better stand in opposition to fanaticism, than on the shifting sands of compromise. Let us be done with compromises. Let us go back and stand upon the Constitution!" *Congressional Globe*, 29 Cong., 2 sess., 454.

[49] C. H. Ambler, ed., *Correspondence of Hunter*, American Historical Association, *Annual Report*, 1916, II, 117-118.

[50] Dunbar Rowland, ed., *Davis, Constitutionalist*, I, 595.

[51] M. W. Cluskey, ed., *Political Text Book*, (12 ed.) (1860), 597.

[52] *Ibid.*, 600.

with Alexander H. Stephens to "look to the security which rests upon principle, rather than upon numbers," believing, as did he, that the "citadel of our defense is principle sustained by reason, truth, honor, and justice." [53]

THE CONSTITUTIONAL DISPUTE CONCERNING THE TERRITORIES

In developing this new principle of protection, the South launched a great constitutional campaign for the protection of negro slavery in the territories. Addressing the House on February 17, 1854, Alexander H. Stephens, always in the thick of the territorial dispute, fixed the exact date of the opening of this campaign as June 15, 1850: "When the North had again, and again, and again, for three years, refused to abide by it [the Missouri Compromise Line], the South, driven to the wall upon it, was thrown back *upon her original rights under the Constitution.* Her next position was, that territorial restriction by Congress should be *totally abandoned,* not only south of 36° 30', but north of that line, too! Upon this ground she planted herself on the 15th day of June." [54]

If in the territorial dispute, the landslide to constitutionalism came on June 15, 1850, the way, as Stephens himself intimates, had been well prepared during the preceding three years by the opposition of the South both to the Wilmot Proviso, designed to prohibit slavery in the new territories, regardless of their location, and to the doctrine of squatter-sovereignty directed to the settlement of the slavery question in the territories by the inhabitants thereof. In attacking the Wilmot Proviso, Calhoun may be said to have first formally presented the new Southern position respecting the territories in a set of resolutions which he laid before the

[53] Speech in the House, February 12, 1859. *Appendix to the Congressional Globe,* 35 Cong., 2 sess., 124.

[54] *Appendix to the Congressional Globe,* 33 Cong., 1 sess., 195.

Senate on February 19, 1847.[55] Within a month, the Virginia Legislature had unanimously adopted Calhoun's new position in resolutions henceforth generally known as the "Platform of the South." The second of these resolutions asserted that "all territory which may be acquired by the arms of the United States, or yielded by treaty with any foreign power, belongs to the several states of this union, as their joint and common property, in which each and all have equal rights, and that the enactment by the federal government of any law which should directly or by its effects prevent the citizens of any state from emigrating with their property of whatever description into such territory would make a discrimination unwarranted by and in violation of the constitution and the rights of the states from which such citizens emigrated, and in derogation of that perfect equality that belongs to the several states as members of this Union, and would tend directly to subvert the Union itself." [56] So satisfactory was this statement of the Southern position that it was adopted in substance by the Legislature of Alabama in December, 1847, by the Texas Legislature in March, 1848, and again by the Virginia Assembly in January, 1849.[57]

In condemnation of the doctrine of squatter-sovereignty, it was the Alabama Democratic Convention which showed the way by the adoption of the "Alabama Platform of 1848." This platform, the work of the vigilant William L. Yancey, denied that the people of a territory could "lawfully or constitutionally prevent any citizen of any such States from removing to or settling in such Territory with his property, be it slave property or other." [58] Like the Virginia resolutions of the previous year, this platform received wide endorsement in other Southern states: it was supported offi-

[55] *Congressional Globe*, 29 Cong., 2 sess., 455.
[56] H. V. Ames, ed., *State Documents on Federal Relations*, 246.
[57] *Ibid.*, 244-245, notes.
[58] J. W. DuBose, *Life and Times of Yancey*, 213.

cially by conventions in Florida and in Virginia, and by the legislatures of Georgia and of Alabama.

In 1849 Robert Toombs went a step farther in declaring it to be the duty of the central government towards the territories "to remove all impediments to their free enjoyment by all sections and people of the Union, the slaveholder and the non-slaveholder" [59] — a position substantially taken by the Nashville Convention of 1850 in one of its June Resolutions which makes it the "duty of the federal government plainly to recognize and firmly to maintain the equal rights of the citizens of the several states in the territories of the United States." [60]

The decade of the fifties was largely devoted to a constitutional justification of the Southern position on the territorial question.[61] No one in the decade, however, better presented the negative arguments to the contention in Congress for unlimited national authority in the territories than did Calhoun before the Senate on February 24, 1849. "Then the simple question is," he asked, "does the Constitution extend to the territories, or does it not extend to them? Why, the Constitution interprets itself. It pronounces itself to be the supreme law of the land. . . . the Territories of the United States are a part of the land. It is the supreme law, not within the limits of the States of this Union merely, but wherever our flag waves — wherever our authority goes, the Constitution in part goes, not all its provisions certainly, but all its suitable provisions. Why, can we have any authority beyond the Constitution? . . . if the Constitution does not go there, how are we to have any authority or juris-

[59] Speech in the House, December 13, 1849. *Congressional Globe,* 31 Cong., 1 sess., 28. See also T. L. Clingman, speech in the House, December 22, 1847, *Appendix to the Congressional Globe,* 30 Cong., 1 sess., 41-48, and his letter to Foote, November 13, 1849, in his *Speeches and Writings,* 231.
[60] M. W. Cluskey, ed., *Political Text Book* (12 ed.), 596. See also the "Georgia Platform" at page 600.

[61] Of course, this new position involved a repudiation of the Missouri Compromise Line as unconstitutional. See the opinion of Chief Justice Taney in the Dred Scott Case, United States Supreme Court Reports, 19 Howard 393; and also James M. Mason, speech in the Senate, March 15, 1858. *Appendix to the Congressional Globe,* 35 Cong., 1 sess., 77.

diction whatever? Is not Congress the creature of the Constitution? . . . And shall we, the creature of the Constitution, pretend that we have authority beyond the reach of the Constitution?" [62]

Once granted that the Constitution extends to the territories, the question was then raised as to the authority over the territories which that instrument delegated to Congress. From a consideration of the most pertinent constitutional provision, John A. Quitman found a satisfactory answer to present to the House in 1856: "the authority 'to dispose of and make all needful rules and regulations for the territory and other property of the United States,' was not intended to convey to Congress the right of legislation over the Territories as subsequently constituted. This is clear. The context itself shows that the word 'territory' was palpably used in the sense of property, for the disposal of which Congress, the common agent of the States, was to make the 'needful rules and regulations,' such as to survey the lands, and to provide for their sale. . . . under the power to 'admit' [states into the Union], Congress possesses the right of paving the way for that act — of making the preliminary arrangements for the important change of the political condition of a Territory." Then reverting to the application of his theory, Quitman continued: "From the principles I have laid down, Mr. Speaker, the inference clearly follows, that Congress, possessing merely the power of municipal legislation to prepare the Territories for admission into the Union, has no power to exclude or abolish slavery in the Territories. Much less have the inhabitants of a Territory, possessing no inherent sovereignty, and having no political powers except those derived from Congress, this right." [63]

[62] *Appendix to the Congressional Globe,* 30 Cong., 2 sess., 273.
[63] *Appendix to the Congressional Globe,* 34 Cong., 3 sess., 121. For a similar analysis see J. H. Hammond, speech in the Senate, March 4, 1858. *Congressional Globe,* 35 Cong., 1 sess., 959-962.

But if the territories derive their powers from Congress, and Congress under the Constitution is limited to the preparation of a territory for statehood, where lies the final authority to govern? Alexander H. Stephens gave an answer to the House on January 6, 1857: "This resides in the people of the separate States, as part of that residuum of powers not delegated by them in the Constitution, and which in that instrument are expressly reserved 'to the States respectively or the people,' and passes out of them only in the mode provided for in the Constitution, which is on the admission of new States." [64] Stephens believed that Congress in holding the territories was acting only as a trustee for the states, who were members of a public corporation. In an earlier discussion, he brought to his support quotations from the original acts of cession of the public domain by the states to the national government, concluding from a review of these acts that "the *leading object* in all of them was to create *a common fund for the use and benefit of all the States* of the Union (the ceding State included) and for no *other use* or *purpose whatever.*" [65]

This corporation theory of the trusteeship of the territories, carried to its logical conclusion, would not only prevent Congress, the trustee, from denying equal rights to the states as members of the corporation, but it would also prevent, according to Stephens, any group of members of the corporation from denying to the other members equal rights to the common property of the corporation in the territories. To lend authority to this theory, Stephens in 1850 cited in the House the following passage from the writings of the Swiss jurist, Emeric de Vattel: "All members of a corpora-

---

[64] *Appendix to the Congressional Globe,* 34 Cong., 3 sess., 133. Also J. H. Hammond, speech in the Senate, March 4, 1858. *Congressional Globe,* 35 Cong., 1 sess., 960.
[65] Speech in the House, May 10, 1852. *Congressional Globe,* 32 Cong., 1 sess., 1314. See also the Partial Report from the Committee on Federal Relations in the Virginia Convention, April 4, 1861. *Journal of the Virginia Convention of 1861,* Appendix. Also, Journal of the Committee of the Whole, 24.

tion have *an equal right* to the *use of the common property.*
. . . They have not a right to *exclude any one of the members, or to make a distinction to his disadvantage, by assigning him a less share than that of the others."* [66]

Why was the South so insistent upon spinning out fine constitutional theories for the protection of slavery in the territories? Was it not aware that the western territories were ill adapted to slave labor? Alexander H. Stephens had himself so admitted to the House in 1857: "When I looked out upon our vast Territories of the West and Northwest, I did not then, [1850] nor do I now, consider that there was or is much prospect of many of them, particularly the latter, becoming slave States. Besides the laws of climate, soil, and productions, there is . . . the law of population." [67] Six months earlier, the aging Josiah J. Evans, senator from South Carolina, had spoken to the same effect in the opposite wing of the Capitol: "Everybody knows that slavery will not do for a farming country merely," he said. "It is of no value in a graining country; it is of no value in the mechanic arts; it can only be used to advantage in the cultivation of the great staples. There is no pretense that any one of the great staples that constitute the great material of our foreign commerce, can be cultivated anywhere within the limits of these Territories outside of the Territory of Kansas." [68] Stephens did not believe that the strength of constitutionalism as a source of Southern protection depended for its success upon the addition of slave states, for in addressing the people of Georgia in 1859, he maintained that by adhering to the constitutional principle of non-

[66] Speech on August 9, 1850. *Appendix to the Congressional Globe*, 31 Cong., 1 sess., 1084, citing Vattel's *Law of Nations*, Book I, Chapter 20, p. 113. Chief Justice Taney gave this theory legal sanction in his opinion in the Dred Scott Case, (1857), United States Supreme Court Reports, 19 Howard, 393.

[67] Speech in the House, January 6, 1857. *Appendix to the Congressional Globe*, 34 Cong., 3 sess., 134.
[68] Speech in the Senate, June 23, 1856. *Ibid.*, 34 Cong., 1 sess., 703. Also see *Speech of Joseph Segar . . . Delivered in the House of Delegates of Virginia, March 30, 1861*, pamphlet, 18.

intervention "one slave State alone, by herself, would be perfectly secure against encroachments or aggressions on her domestic internal policy, though all the rest were free." [69] Then why a decade of insistence upon the preservation of constitutional guarantees to negro slavery in the territories?

The territorial dispute was evidently only a means to an end. It was developed to determine the value of Southern reliance upon constitutional guarantees for the protection of negro slavery in the existing Southern states. "Why should we care whether they [the slaves] go into other Territories or not?" queried Jefferson Davis in the Senate, February 8, 1858: "Simply because of the war that is made against our institutions; simply because of the want of security which results from the action of our opponents in the northern States." [70] In 1857, Stephens declared in the House that if "the slightest encroachments of power are permitted or submitted to in the Territories, they may reach the States ultimately"; [71] and, two years later, Lucius Q. C. Lamar, lawyer, professor, and politician from Mississippi, thus addressed the Northern faction upon the same floor: "I ask you if you do not know that when you strike slavery from the territories you have taken the initial and most decisive step towards the destruction of slavery in the States. You know that that is your policy. . . ." [72]

That the territorial dispute was only a means to an end was a common understanding in the South during the three years that plans were materializing for a swing to constitutionalism in the fall of 1850. In 1848, Fitzwilliam Byrdsall presented Calhoun with this question: "If the Southern

[69] Farewell address as a representative in Congress, delivered July 2, 1859, at Augusta, Georgia. Henry Cleveland, ed., *Stephens in Public and Private with Letters and Speeches*, 647.
[70] *Congressional Globe*, 35 Cong., 1 sess., 619.

[71] *Appendix to the Congressional Globe*, 34 Cong., 3 sess., 134.
[72] Speech in the House, December 7, 1859. *Congressional Globe*, 36 Cong., 1 sess., 45. Also see speech of M. R. H. Garnett, representative from Virginia, on the same day, pp. 43-44.

people cannot maintain their equal rights as to their settling in new territory, what other rights under the Constitution can they maintain?" [73] The following year Calhoun received a similar letter from H. M. Judge insisting that the masses be made to see beyond their noses since "they do not see and feel that the necessary consequence of allowing all the out-posts of Slavery to be carried, involves a certain destruction of the Citadel' itself." [74] Calhoun himself declared, in his farewell address to the Senate on March 4, 1850, that the agitation in Congress for the restriction of slavery in the territories had been evoked "expressly with the view to the final abolition of slavery in the States." [75] When the South in the fall of 1850 fell back upon the principle of constitutional guarantees, it did so frankly resolved to test the strength of its new source of protection by an application of its principles to the territorial dispute. Only for this purpose were the efforts of Southern political thinkers centered upon the territories during the decade of the fifties.

The "Irrepressible Conflict" and the "Higher Law"

But whatever the real issue between the sections in the territorial dispute, there was no doubt, in the South at least, of the sectional objectives in defending or in opposing two new theories developed at the North during the decade of the fifties. These were the theories of the "irrepressible conflict" and of the "higher law." Both were considered by the South to be incompatible with the existence of negro slavery in the states; consequently, both were soundly denounced as

[73] J. F. Jameson, ed., *Correspondence of Calhoun*, American Historical Association, *Annual Report*, 1899, II, 1181.
[74] *Ibid.*, 1196.
[75] *Congressional Globe*, 31 Cong., 1 sess., 453. To the same effect were the Resolutions of the House adopted December 12, 1838. *Ibid.*, 25 Cong., 3 sess., 23, 27;

the remarks of Kenneth Rayner of North Carolina in the House on June 15, 1841. *Appendix to the Congressional Globe*, 27 Cong., 1 sess., 49; and the address of Jefferson Davis at Aberdeen, Mississippi, May 26, 1851. Dunbar Rowland, ed., *Davis, Constitutionalist*, II, 70-82.

a direct infringement of the principle of constitutional guarantees.

The theory of the "irrepressible conflict" was the joint product of Abraham Lincoln's address before the Republican State Convention of Illinois, delivered on June 16, 1858, and of William H. Seward's "Irrepressible Conflict" speech delivered at Rochester, New York, October 25, 1858. It was the opinion of the latter, however, which first attracted attention; for Lincoln, despite his activities in Illinois, was a relatively obscure national figure until the sixties. Seward, on the other hand, already at the height of his political prestige, made himself the target of immediate bombardment when he asserted: "It is an irrepressible conflict between opposing and enduring forces, and it means that the United States must and will, sooner or later, become either entirely a slaveholding nation, or entirely a free-labor nation. Either the cotton and rice fields of South Carolina and the sugar plantations of Louisiana will ultimately be tilled by free labor, . . . or else the rye-fields and wheat-fields of Massachusetts and New York must again be surrendered by their farmers to slave culture and to the production of slaves. . . ." [76]

By the sixties, Lincoln had stepped into the limelight, and then his words of 1858 were scattered throughout the South along with those of Seward. Lincoln's most pertinent remarks were these: " 'A house divided against itself cannot stand.' I believe this government cannot endure permanently half slave and half free. I do not expect the Union to be dissolved — I do not expect the house to fall — but I do expect it will cease to be divided. It will become all one thing, or all the other. Either the opponents of slavery will arrest the further spread of it, and place it where the public mind shall rest in the belief that it is in the course of ulti-

[76] W. H. Seward, *The Irrepressible Conflict*, pamphlet, 2.

mate extinction; or its advocates will push it forward till it shall become alike lawful in all the States, old as well as new, North as well as South." [77]

This theory was denounced by every legitimate agency in the South from county assemblies to state conventions. On December 2, 1859, the General Assembly of Tennessee resolved "that we recognize in the recent outbreak at Harper's Ferry the natural prints of this treasonable, '*irrepressible conflict*' doctrine put forth by the great head of the Black Republican party and echoed by his subordinates." [78] In the fall of 1860, several county assemblies in Georgia sent resolutions to the state legislature bitterly denouncing the theory for recognizing the equality of the black and white races, and for influencing Northern men to seek the establishment of such racial equality in the South. [79]

In December, 1860, the South Carolina Convention placed in its declaration of the immediate causes of secession, extracts from Lincoln's address to show beyond doubt that the application of the theory would inevitably lead to the subversion of all constitutional protection to slavery in the states. [80] In the Alabama Convention of 1861, William L. Yancey, long since despairing of constitutional protection, asserted: "No guarantees — no amendments of the Constitution — no compromises patched up to secure to the North the benefits of Union yet a little longer, can reëducate that people on the slavery issue, so as to induce them, having the majority, to withhold the exercise of its power in aid of that 'irrepressible conflict.' " [81]

[77] J. G. Nicolay and John Hay, *Complete Works of Abraham Lincoln*, I, 240. This passage is quoted in *Letter of the Hon. Howell Cobb to the People of Georgia* (December 6, 1860), pamphlet, 5; and most of it, along with other extracts from Lincoln's writings, is again repeated by T. J. Wharton, Commissioner from Mississippi to Tennessee, in his address to the Tennessee Legislature, January, 1861. *Journal of the Mississippi Convention of 1861*, Appendix, Document A, pp. 155-156.

[78] H. V. Ames, ed., *State Documents on Federal Relations*, 308.

[79] A. D. Candler, ed., *Confederate Record of Georgia*, I, 58-156.

[80] *Journal of the South Carolina Convention of 1860-1-2*, 465.

[81] W. R. Smith, *Debates of the Alabama Convention of 1861*, 142. See the *Letter*

The second of these new theories — the theory of the higher law — was in origin much older than the first, though its leading champion was also William H. Seward of New York. This theory doubtless sprang from the ranks of the abolitionists in the later thirties, for as early as June 15, 1841, Representative Kenneth Rayner of North Carolina attacked the position of John Quincy Adams on the slavery question because he "has thrown aside law and Constitution, and has dared to put the issue of this question upon the high and impregnable ground of the Divine law" — a position which Rayner declared "sweeps away every thing like human compact and rests the mutual rights of men on what the imagination of fanaticism may picture to itself as a Divine requirement." [82] In 1850, John A. Quitman wrote that nine-tenths of the Northern people were sparing no exertion to abolish negro slavery, "and, when the Constitution fails them, they appeal to 'the higher law.'" [83] In February, 1851, Robert Toombs discovered that a "great question is rising up before us [to] become a 'fixed fact' in American politics. It is . . . sometimes called the higher law, in antagonism to our constitutional compact. If the first [i. e., the higher law] succeeds, we have no other safety except in secession; if the latter [i. e., the constitutional compact], 'liberty and Union, may be forever one and inseparable.'" [84]

Before the end of the following year, the "fixed fact" had found definite expression from the pen of William Hosmer in a volume of some two hundred pages entitled, *The Higher Law*. Within those pages the author makes the following

---

of *Howell Cobb to the People of Georgia*, (December 6, 1860), pamphlet, 7; and S. D. Moore, "The Irrepressible Conflict and Impending Crisis," *DeBow's Review*, May, 1860. XXVIII, 531-551.

[82] *Appendix to the Congressional Globe*, 27 Cong., 1 sess., 48.

[83] J. F. H. Claiborne, *Life and Correspondence of Quitman*, II, 260.

[84] Letter to A. H. Chappell and Others, February 15, 1851. U. B. Phillips, ed., *Correspondence of Toombs, Stephens, and Cobb*, American Historical Association, *Annual Report*, 1911, II, 229.

contention: "Men have no right to make a constitution which sanctions slavery, and it is the imperative duty of all good men to break it, when made. . . . The fact that a law is constitutional amounts to nothing, unless it is also pure; it must harmonize with the law of God, or be set at naught by all upright men." If the constitution requires the return of fugitive slaves, he wrote, "our duty is to spurn the infamous requirement . . . we are under the most solemn obligations to amend the compact or renounce it forever." [85]

The field had already been prepared, therefore, when William H. Seward essayed to champion the free labor system that "conforms to the divine law of equality, which is written in the hearts and consciences of men." [86] It was against Seward and his followers that the South directed its "higher law" attack in the later fifties. On October 19, 1858, Jefferson Davis delivered a stirring address in New York City upon this subject, and in the course of his daring denunciation of the advocates of this theory, he declared: "You have among you politicians of a philosophic turn, who preach a high morality; a system of which they are the discoverers, . . . They say, it is true the Constitution dictates this, the Bible inculcates that; but there is a higher law than those, and they call upon you to obey that higher law of which they are the inspired givers. Men who are *traitors* to the compact of their fathers — *men who have perjured the oaths they have themselves taken* . . . these are the moral law-givers who proclaim a higher law than the Bible, the Constitution, and the laws of the land. . . . *These higher law preachers should be tarred and feathered, and whipped by those they have thus instigated.* . . . The man who . . . preaches treason to the Constitution and the dic-

[85] William Hosmer, *The Higher Law*, 176, 177.
[86] W. H. Seward, *The Irrepressible Conflict*, pamphlet, 1-2. See also his speech in the Senate, March 11, 1850. *Appendix to the Congressional Globe*, 31 Cong., 1 sess., 264, 265.

tates of all human society, is a fit object for a Lynch law that would be higher than any he could urge." [87]

By the sixties, Southern opposition to the higher law had spread to the ranks of pamphleteers and the membership of state conventions. John Townsend, writing in a pamphlet entitled *The South Alone Should Govern the South,* asked: "what can a President or a party do for the security of the South, . . . when the Northeast, and North, and Northwest of these United States are hopelessly *abolitionized,* and are now working under a 'higher law' constitution of their own?" [88] Similarly, H. L. Berguin in his *Considerations Relative to a Southern Confederacy* denounced the great Northern leader William H. Seward, who, in his determination to exterminate slavery from Virginia to Texas, "calls to his aid a 'higher law' than the Constitution *he has solemnly sworn to support.*" [89] On February 18, 1861, Fulton Anderson, commissioner from Mississippi to Virginia, warned the Virginia Convention that an "infidel fanaticism, crying out for a higher law than that of the Constitution . . . has been enlisted in the strife"; [90] and in the Alabama Convention of that year L. M. Stone maintained that the "triumph of a Higher Law party, pledged to the destruction of our Constitutional Rights, forced us to dissolve our political connection with [the] hostile States." [91]

THE STRENGTH OF THE CONSTITUTIONAL APPEAL

In opposing these new theories, the South of the sixties was still relying upon the strength of its constitutional appeal. At that time, H. L. Berguin thus presented the Southern cause: "the South should never yield one atom of her

[87] Dunbar Rowland, ed., *Davis, Constitutionalist,* III, 337-338.
[88] Page 11.
[89] Pamphlet, p. 4.
[90] *Journal of the Mississippi Convention of 1861,* 217.

[91] W. R. Smith, *Debates in the Alabama Convention of 1861,* 333. See Python (pseud.), "The Secession of the South," *DeBow's Review,* April, 1860. XXVIII, 376.

full, just, and *equal* rights under the Constitution; no more compromises — no more adjustments. . . . We have lost our political power — we must depend upon our constitutional rights. . . . our only *permanent* safety is to place ourselves firmly on our equal rights, and say to the Republican party, 'destroy the Constitution! break that compact which now makes us one people, (and which alas! is almost the sole remaining link between us,) even in its slightest obligation, and we become a separate nation.' " [92]

On January 7, 1861, Robert Toombs, amid the excitement of the Senate avowed: "We will stand by the right; we will take the Constitution; we will defend it by the sword with the halter around our necks." [93] A week later, Senator J. H. Reagan of Texas joined the heated controversy with these words: "I stand here to-day to say that if there be a southern State, or a southern man even, who would demand, as a condition for remaining in this Union, anything beyond the clearly specified guarantees of the Constitution of the United States as they are, I do not know of it. . . . they have never dreamed of asking more than their constitutional rights." [94]

Meanwhile, William L. Yancey in a great two-hour speech before the National Democratic Convention at Charleston, South Carolina, was proclaiming on January 11, 1860, that "we hold up between ourselves and your advancing column of numbers that written instrument which your fathers and ours made, and by the compact of which you with your power were to respect us and our rights." [95] Alexander H.

[92] H. L. Berguin, *Considerations Relative to a Southern Confederacy,* pamphlet, 28, 29.

[93] *Congressional Globe,* 36 Cong., 2 sess., 270.

[94] *Congressional Globe,* 36 Cong., 2 sess., 391. L. Q. C. Lamar of Mississippi, later a member of the Supreme Court, during a speech in the House, December 7, 1859, declared: "That constitution is the life and soul of this great Government. . . . We stand upon it. We intend to abide by it and to maintain it, and we will submit to no persistent violation of its provisions. . . . When it is violated, persistently violated, . . . I raise then the banner of secession, and I will fight under it as long as the blood flows and ebbs in my veins." *Ibid.,* 36 Cong., 1 sess., 45.

[95] J. W. DuBose, "Yancey, A Study,"

Stephens, having voluntarily left the House of Representatives in 1859, was appealing to the Legislature of Georgia on November 14, 1860, to this effect: "If all our hopes are to be blasted, if the republic is to go down, let us be found to the last moment standing on the deck with the constitution of the United States waving over our heads." [96]

The South was now able to strengthen its constitutional appeal by demanding of the North that it accept the opinions and decisions of the Supreme Court as the final arbiter of constitutional disputes. How the two sections had reversed their positions towards the Supreme Court, Robert Toombs disclosed in addressing the Senate on January 7, 1861: "The northern doctrine was, many years ago, that the Supreme Court was the judge. . . . they declared that that court was made, by the Constitution, the ultimate and supreme arbiter. . . . The Supreme Court have decided that, by the Constitution, we have a right to go to the Territories and be protected there with our property. You say we cannot decide the compact for ourselves. Well, can the Supreme Court decide it for us? Mr. Lincoln says he does not care what the Supreme Court decides, he will turn us out anyhow. . . . He said he would vote against the decision of the Supreme Court. Then you do not accept that arbiter. . . . The Black Republican party say, 'We care not for your precedents or practices; . . . We care not for the fathers; we care not for the judges.' They have said more: their leaders on this floor have said they will get rid of the court as James II. got rid of the honest judges when they decided against the dispensing power of the Crown. . . . You declare that the decision of the Supreme Court is null, void, and no law; that there is no Constitution but the Chicago platform; yet you propose to come here and take pos-

Gulf States Historical Magazine, January, 1903. I, no. 4, p. 246.
[96] Henry Cleveland, ed., *Stephens in Public* and *Private with Letters and Speeches*, 696-697.

session of this Government, and swear to maintain the Constitution. . . ."[97] Thus by a strange transformation of circumstances, the North was now demanding strict construction of implied powers in regard to the national judiciary, opposing, in 1855, a bill to remove from the state courts to the federal courts all suits against federal officers for acts done under federal authority, and advocating in 1858, as a means of preventing appeals from the state courts to the Supreme Court, the repeal of the twenty-fifth section of the Judiciary Act of 1789![98]

Yet, in spite of express constitutional provisions, drastic fugitive slave laws, and favorable decisions of the Supreme Court, the South found itself increasingly impotent to enforce the rendition of fugitive slaves. "I hold in my hand," said Robert Toombs to the Senate, January 24, 1860, "copies and abstracts of laws and resolutions of nine States of this Union, all of which have been adopted with the direct intent to abrogate and annul this plain provision of the Constitution. . . . They are all plain, direct, undeniable violations of the oaths which the men who passed them took to support the Constitution of the United States."[99] Within a year, these abstracts received the official consideration of the State Convention of South Carolina in its declaration of the immediate causes which induce and justify Secession: "We assert that fourteen of the States have deliberately refused, for years past, to fulfil their constitutional obligations, and we refer to their own Statutes for the proof. . . . The States of Maine, New Hampshire, Vermont, Massachusetts, Connecticut, Rhode Island, New York, Pennsylvania, Illinois, Indiana, Michigan, Wisconsin and Iowa,

---

[97] *Congressional Globe,* 36 Cong., 2 sess., 269, 270.
[98] Charles Warren, *The Supreme Court in United States History,* (2 ed.) II, 264, 333. Chapters 25, 26, and 27 (pp. 206-357) present a more complete study. For a valuable study on the use of state rights

as a tool of circumstance by all sections of the Union, see A. M. Schlesinger, *New Viewpoints in American History,* pp. 220-244.
[99] *Appendix to the Congressional Globe,* 36 Cong., 1 sess., 89. See also his speech on March 7 at p. 157.

have enacted laws which either nullify the Acts of Congress or render useless any attempt to execute them. In many of these States the fugitive is discharged from the service or labor claimed, and in none of them has the State Government complied with the stipulation made in the Constitution. . . . In the State of New York even the right of transit for a slave has been denied by her tribunals; and the States of Ohio and Iowa have refused to surrender to justice fugitives charged with murder, and with inciting servile insurrection in the State of Virginia. Thus the constituted compact has been deliberately broken and disregarded by the non-slaveholding States. . . ." [100]

New Schemes for Enforcing Constitutional Guarantees

This open violation of constitutions, statutes, and judicial decisions in utter disregard of the Southern appeal had brought forth a number of interesting devices to strengthen the constitutional position of the South. As far back as 1847, Calhoun had written: "There is and can be but one remedy short of disunion, and that is to retaliate on our part, by refusing to fulfil the stipulations [of the Constitution] in their favor." [101] In the Nashville Convention of 1850, a minority favored retaliation as a method of inducing the North to comply with the terms of the Constitution; [102] and a decade later, Alexander H. Stephens, leading champion of constitutionalism in the fifties, was ready to adopt this principle: "Let your committee on the state of the republic," so he suggested to the Georgia Legislature, November 14, 1860, "make out a bill of grievances; let it be sent

---

[100] *Journal of the South Carolina Convention of 1860-1-2*, 463, 464. See the chapters on "The Attitude of Certain Northern States" in B. B. Munford, *Virginia's Attitude towards Slavery and Secession*, 201-213.

[101] Letter to a member of the Alabama Legislature. Cited in Thomas H. Benton, *Thirty Years' View*, II, 699.

[102] R. R. Russel, "Economic Aspects of Southern Sectionalism," *Illinois University Studies*, XI, 157.

by the governor to those faithless States; and if reason and argument shall be tried in vain — if all shall fail to induce them to return to their constitutional obligations, I would favor retaliatory measures." [103]

Several interesting methods of retaliation were proposed. Calhoun in his suggestions to the members of the Alabama Legislature on this point had maintained that denial of "the right of their ships and commerce to enter and depart from our ports is the most effectual, and can be enforced." [104] R. B. Rhett proposed in the South Carolina Convention of 1852 "that it should be the duty of the Legislature, by suitable and effectual provisions and penalties, to debar and exclude the citizens of those States from entering, abiding, or holding property within this State"; [105] and in the fall of 1860, Governor Joseph E. Brown of Georgia recommended to his state legislature several methods of retaliation by reprisals. He proposed first, to seize the property in Georgia belonging to citizens of the offending state in order to indemnify the injured party for the loss of his fugitive slave; second, to enact "such laws as will drive the manufactured articles of such States, as far as possible, from the markets of Georgia"; and third, in case the foregoing remedies were inadequate, to repeal "the penal code and all other laws of this State which protect the lives, liberties and property of the citizens of other States while in this State" so that the citizens "of each Free State in this Union, guilty of like bad faith to the people of Georgia, be declared *without the protection* of the laws of this State, until the States to which they respectively belong, shall have repealed their unconstitutional and obnoxious legislation, and returned to the observance of their constitutional pledges." [106]

[103] Henry Cleveland, ed., *Stephens in Public and Private with Letters and Speeches,* 707.

[104] As cited in Thomas H. Benton, *Thirty Years' View,* II, 699.

[105] *Journal of the State Convention of South Carolina of 1852,* 17.

[106] A. D. Candler, ed., *Confederate Records of Georgia,* I, 34, 36, 37, 42-43.

Another group of proposals for strengthening the constitutional position of the South called for new amendments to the Constitution expressive of the Southern interpretation of that instrument. On December 18, 1860, John J. Crittenden of Kentucky proposed to the Senate six constitutional amendments relating to slavery in the states and territories.[107] Six days later, Robert Toombs of Georgia, as a member of the Committee of Thirteen to devise means of settling the sectional controversy, reported to this Committee that, in his opinion, the full security of Southern rights depended upon the adoption of seven constitutional amendments which he then presented. Five of these seven amendments were typical Southern interpretations of the provisions of the Federal Constitution relating to negro slavery.[108] In the Georgia Convention of 1861, on the very day that an ordinance of secession was adopted, H. V. Johnson introduced a proposal containing nine "indispensable amendments" to be considered by a proposed Southern Congress at Atlanta, Georgia.[109]

All these amendments contained little that was new and nothing that was radical. They were clearly in accord with the November resolutions of Greene County, Georgia, demanding new amendments, not to secure "any rights additional to those now meant to be secured to us by the Constitution; but that we would have those rights set forth in terms, such as our Northern fellow-citizens would construe, as *we* do, the Constitution as it *is*." [110] The substance of these proposed amendments was later incorporated into the Confederate Constitution; and it is worthy of note that a proposal was advanced in the Virginia Convention of 1861 requesting the Committee on Federal Relations "to report the

[107] *Congressional Globe*, 36 Cong., 2 sess., 114.
[108] U. B. Phillips, *Life of Toombs*, 210.
[109] January 18, *Journal of the Georgia Con-* vention of 1861, 17-18.
[110] A. D. Candler, ed., *Confederate Records of Georgia*, I, 78.

Constitution of the Confederate States of the South, as Virginia's ultimatum, and that they recommend the same to the Northern States of this Confederacy." [111]

In a final attempt to restore the usefulness of the principle of constitutional guarantees as a source of protection to a Southern minority, many statesmen advocated the extreme position of temporary separation from the North. Thus in January, 1861, A. H. Handy, Commissioner from Mississippi, in urging the Governor of Maryland to take steps towards separation, defended his position on these grounds: "Secession is not intended to break up the present government, but to perpetuate it . . . we go out for the purpose of getting further guarantees and security for our rights . . . our plan is for the Southern States to withdraw from the Union for the present, to allow amendments to the Constitution to be made, guaranteeing our just rights." [112] T. R. R. Cobb of Georgia was another who urged that "We can make better terms out of the Union than in it"; [113] while Alexander H. Stephens wrote after the war in regard to the position of Georgia: "Two-thirds, at least, of those who voted for the Ordinance of Secession, did so, I have but little doubt, with a view to a more certain Re-formation of the Union . . . they acted under the impression and belief that the whole object . . . could better be accomplished by the States being out of the Union, than in it." [114]

THE END OF THE CONSTITUTIONAL ROAD

Meanwhile, a growing realization that the North through the control of a necessary majority of free states would soon be able to mould the Constitution at its will was rapidly undermining Southern reliance upon the principle of constitu-

---

[111] *Journal of the Virginia Convention of 1861*, 109.
[112] George Lunt, *Origin of the Late War*, 441, citing Schaffner's *Secession War*.
[113] From an address to the Georgia Legislature, November 12, 1860, as quoted in A. H. Stephens, *War between the States*, II, 321.
[114] *Ibid*. See also, Albert Pike, *State or Province, Bond or Free*, pamphlet, 36-37.

tional guarantees. As long as the South maintained express provisions in the Constitution concerning negro slavery — provisions that could not be removed without Southern consent — there remained the possibility that those provisions might ultimately be enforced to the satisfaction of the Southern states. But now the South was facing the possibility (and it thought the probability) of losing even those express constitutional guarantees by the irrefutable, *constitutional* means of the amending process!

John C. Calhoun with his usual prophetic insight had uttered this note of warning in the Southern Address of 1849: "If fanaticism and the love of power should, contrary to their nature, for once respect constitutional barriers, . . . there would be still left one certain way to accomplish their object, if the determination avowed by the North to monopolize all the territories, to the exclusion of the South, should be carried into effect. That of itself would, at no distant day, add to the North a sufficient number of States to give her three fourths of the whole; when, under the cover of an amendment of the Constitution, she would emancipate our slaves. . . ." [115]

Accepting the stated intention of the Republican Party to abolish slavery as soon as it had the power, Josiah E. Evans, Senator from South Carolina, on June 23, 1856, entered into an elaborate speculation on the future safety of the institution of negro slavery in the United States: "Whenever you have sixty States in this Union, three fourths of them can alter the Constitution, and abolish slavery everywhere. You have thirty-one now; you want only twenty-nine. Where are they to come from? Kansas and Nebraska can make six; New Mexico will make half as

---

[115] R. K. Crallé, ed., *Works of Calhoun,* VI, 308-309. For an earlier statement of Southern security against this danger, see Charles F. Mercer, speech in the Virginia Constitutional Convention, November 5, 1829. *Proceedings and Debates of the Virginia Convention of 1829-1830,* 186-187.

many; California may be well divided into three States; and there is no doubt of the fact, I venture to say, that within the next forty or fifty years it will be accomplished — that the Indians will be driven out, and those large territories, extending from the Atlantic to the Pacific, will be divided into States of this Union." [116]

But to a Virginian writing only four years later on the "Issues of 1860," this menace of a constitutional overthrow of slavery was a much more immediate one. Finding that the relative strength in states and population between the North and the South had already given "the first *forty* and the latter *twenty-eight* senators, and the first *one hundred and forty-nine* and the latter *eighty-nine* representatives," the author who signed the pen-name "Python" ventured the astounding prediction "that *in ten years,* the North will hold, sectionally, the requisite constitutional number of States, senators and representatives, to enable them to propose and adopt amendments to the Constitution as they may please." [117]

How widespread this latter sentiment had become in the sixties we may gather from the words of Stephen A. Douglas of Illinois uttered in the Senate on March 2, 1861: "How often have I heard it from one to the other of the Southern States declared that it was the fixed purpose of the North, as soon as they obtained a majority of three-fourths, to change the Constitution so that we would have authority to abolish slavery in the States by an act of Congress! Sir, I have heard it in these Halls, as well as upon the stump." [118]

The South had now come to the end of the constitutional

[116] *Appendix to the Congressional Globe,* 34 Cong., 1 sess., 703. The Nashville Convention of 1850 at its June session also estimated in its "Address" that in fifty years the non-slaveholding states would have the required two-thirds majority in Congress and the three-fourths majority of the states necessary to abolish slavery by constitutional amendment. Edward Channing, *History of the United States,* VI, 80, citing the *Resolutions, Address and Journal.*
[117] Letter dated December 9, 1859, and published in *DeBow's Review* for March, 1860. XXVIII, 258.
[118] *Congressional Globe,* 36 Cong., 2 sess., 1388.

road. "Moral philosophy and constitutional law," reflected Henry A. Wise of Virginia in his *Seven Decades of the Union,* published soon after the Civil War, "had fallen before steam and telegraphs and railroads and territorial acquisitions and unprecedented immigration. Free Soil was a majority, and a majority brooked no limitations to its will. . . . Slavery of the colored race would be destroyed, and the freedom of the white race would lose all its guarantees against the abuses of a majority." [119] Another chronicler of these decades, John W. Draper, one time professor of chemistry in New York University, distinguished as scholar and writer in several fields, wrote in his *History of the American Civil War* (1867): "There is a political force in ideas which silently renders protestations, promises and guarantees, no matter in what good faith they may have been given, of no avail, and which makes constitutions obsolete. Against the uncontrollable growth of the antislavery idea the South was forced to contend." [120] Whether the trend away from the principle of constitutional guarantees was inevitable, it came; and *when* and *how* and *why,* we shall seek to discover in the following chapter.

[119] Page 248.   [120] Vol. I, p. 25.

CHAPTER VI

THE PRINCIPLE OF SOUTHERN INDEPENDENCE

"ALL my aims and objects are to cast before the people of the South as great a mass of wrongs committed on them, injuries and insults that have been done, as I possibly can. One thing will catch our eye here and determine our hearts; another thing elsewhere; all united, may yet produce spirit enough to lead us forward, to call forth a Lexington, to fight a Bunker's Hill, to drive the foe from the city of our rights."[1] Here once more are the words of a new leader in a new cause: William L. Yancey was speaking in 1858 before the Southern Commercial Convention in Montgomery, Alabama; and his words are none the less significant if expressed two years before the cause that they represent came into its own. For here was another signpost on a new highway of protection to Southern minority interests. Down the highways of local self-government, of the concurrent voice, and of constitutional guarantees, in the order named, Southern political philosophers had already journeyed; but in every case they had come to the end of the road short of the goal of satisfactory protection to the South. All three of these roads had lain within the Union; the only one left — that of Southern independence — lay outside; but what did that matter if it led to the goal?

THE RISE OF THE SECESSIONISTS PER SE

On December 17, 1860, John P. Kennedy, writing in a pamphlet entitled *The Border States,* made the assertion

[1] J. W. DuBose, *Life and Times of Yancey,* 362.

"that the secession movement is not the suddenly inspired project of the present day; that it does not grow out of the events of the recent canvass and election, nor even primarily out of that agitation of slavery, which constitutes the flagrant cause of disturbance in the Border States." After developing this thesis at some length, the author concluded with this statement: "The agitation of slavery, therefore, notwithstanding its engrossment of the country and the odious prominence it has assumed, is, after all, but a parade of idle and mischievous debate." [2]

If these assertions are at all startling to the present-day historian, they were a matter of common belief among a number of contemporary writers who were subjected to the trying experiences of the fifties and sixties. Edward A. Pollard, Virginia historian, in his volume, *The Lost Cause* (1867), takes the position that the sectional dispute over the institution of negro slavery was only incidental to the desires of "a political North and a political South" to dominate the central government. In support of his position, he pointed out that the early part of the political history of slavery "is scarcely more than an enumeration of dates and measures, which were taken as matters of course, and passed without dispute." Pollard believed that only with the "jealousy of Southern domination came the slavery agitation; proving clearly enough its subordination to the main question." [3]

Of a similar opinion was W. C. Fowler, author of *The Sectional Controversy,* published in 1862. In this volume, Fowler contended that, after the first Missouri Compromise had been adopted, the North still refused to admit Missouri, under the pretext that the state was excluding free negroes and mulattoes from its borders, but in reality because of *"the desire to retain political power."* [4] And Jefferson Davis

[2] *Op. cit.,* pp. 14, 37.
[3] *Op. cit.,* pp. 47-48.
[4] *Op. cit.,* pp. 80-83.

in his *Rise and Fall of the Confederate Government* (1881) clearly implied that the basis of the sectional controversy lay in a so-called balance-of-power theory between the North and the South rather than in the issue of negro slavery.[5]

Of all these contemporary impressions, the most vivid is found in the preface to a volume by Sidney George Fisher on *The Law of the Territories.* Writing on November 12, 1859, within a month after John Brown's raid at Harper's Ferry, to which he made reference, Fisher thus presented the struggle for power between the two sections: "The South rules the President, and Congress, and the Supreme Court. It has all kinds of influence, social, commercial, political. It dictates to Tammany Halls and to Empire Clubs. . . . But, like Achilles, the South has a vulnerable point which its enemies have found out. They have aimed at this point a weak shaft by a feeble hand, and, suddenly, the whole ingenious armament of the Southern politicians, obedient Presidents, submissive Congress, a pliant judiciary, responsive Tammany Halls, and active rowdy clubs, have become useless as the guns of a ship that has sprung a leak." [6]

There is more than passing evidence to support these impressions. Indeed, strong argument may be advanced to prove that the Southern states originally entered the Union with the expectation of dominating the national government

---

[5] *Op. cit.,* I, 11-14. See also his letter to S. Cobun, November 7, 1850. Dunbar Rowland, ed., *Davis, Constitutionalist,* I, 592-596.

[6] S. J. Fisher, *The Law of the Territories,* preface, xix-xx. Of particular interest in this connection are the views of two English writers. After touring America in 1857-1858, Charles Mackay in his *Life and Liberty in America* (1859) wrote: "The struggle between the North and South, of which the negro is made the pretext, is, as all the world knows by this time, a struggle for political power and ascendency — for the patronage of the Republic, and of the several Commonwealths which compose it." Vol. II, pp. 48-49. Another Englishman, James Spence, writing in 1861, asserted that "many of the aggressive and most reprehensible acts of the South . . . have not had the extension of Slavery as an object of desire, as an end, but simply as a means by which to maintain its political position, in face of the rapidly increasing population of the Northern power." *The American Union,* 84. Further information may be found in the numerous extracts compiled in S. D. Carpenter, *Logic of History* (1864), p. 24 *et seq.*

through a rapid growth of population in the South. Even before the Federal Convention had assembled, James Madison, discussing the prospects of a stronger Union with a legislature based upon population, wrote Edmund Randolph on April 8, 1787, that the "northern States will be reconciled to it by the *actual* superiority of its populousness; the Southern by their *expected* superiority on this point." [7]

This possibility of the future control of the national government by the South may be used to explain certain sectional discrepancies in the Federal Convention of 1787 on the issue of local self-government. How else may one better account for so many Southern proposals to enlarge the sphere of the national government — proposals which were defeated with the assistance of a Northern vote? Charles Pinckney, for example, favored giving Congress the power to establish a university and to assume the debts of the states; James Madison would have permitted Congress to grant charters of incorporation wherever the authority of a single state was incompetent; and both of these men worked diligently for the power in the national government to negative state laws. Even the obstinate George Mason, whose subsequent persistence in opposing the Constitution was equalled only by that of Patrick Henry, twice proposed in the Federal Convention to give Congress the power "to enact sumptuary laws." [8] Particularly enlightening is Mason's stand, coming, as it does, after his support of the prohibition on export taxes, wherein he "hoped the Northern States did not mean to deny the Southern this security. It would hereafter be as desirable to the former, when the latter should become the most populous." [9]

In both the Virginia and the South Carolina ratifying conventions, the advocates and opponents of the Federal

[7] Gaillard Hunt, ed., *Writings of Madison*, II, 340.
[8] These defeated proposals in the Federal Constitutional Convention are collected in W. M. Meigs, *The Growth of the Constitution*, 305-316.
[9] Jonathan Elliot, ed., *Debates* (2 ed.), V, 432.

Constitution took issue on the future development of the population of the South, as if ratification of the Constitution should depend upon the possibility of future domination of the central government. In the Virginia Convention, George Nicholas, speaking for ratification, used this argument: "But the influence of New England and the other Northern States is dreaded; there are apprehensions of their combining against us . . . it must be supposed that our population will, in a short period, exceed theirs, as their country is well settled, and we have very extensive uncultivated tracts. We shall soon outnumber them in as great a degree as they do us at this time: therefore this government . . . will be very shortly in our favor." [10] But to the contrary, George Mason, who had apparently changed his mind on the future growth of the South, ridiculed the argument of Nicholas. "A very sound argument indeed," said Mason, "that we should cheerfully burn ourselves to death in hopes of a joyful and happy resurrection!" [11]

A similar debate ensued in the South Carolina Convention. There Edmund Rutledge was for ratification and Rawlings Lowndes against it. "The Constitution had provided for a census of the people," Rutledge explained on January 16, 1788, "and the number of representatives was to be directed by the number of the people in the several states; this clause was highly favorable to the southern interest. Several of the Northern States were already full of people: it was otherwise with us; the migrations to the south were immense, and we should, in the course of a few years, rise high in our representation, whilst other states would keep their present position. Gentlemen should carry their views into futurity, and not confine themselves to the narrow limits of a day, when contemplating a subject of such vast importance." [12] But two days later, Lowndes declared to the

[10] *Ibid.*, III, 102.
[11] *Ibid.*, III, 267.

[12] *Ibid.*, IV, 276-277.

contrary that with "respect to migration from the Eastern States to the Southern ones, he did not believe that people would ever flock here in such considerable numbers, because our country had generally proved so uncomfortable, from the excessive heats, that our acquaintance, during the heats, is rather shunned than solicited." [13] In the North Carolina Convention, James Iredell, a leading advocate of ratification, maintained that the "Northern States have been much longer settled, and are much fuller of people, than the Southern, but have not land in equal proportion, nor scarcely any slaves. . . . In twenty years, there will probably be a great alteration. . . ." [14]

Outside the halls of the ratifying conventions, the possibility of Southern control of the central government was projected as a leading argument for adopting the Constitution; for David Ramsay in his "Address to the Freemen of South Carolina" set forth the following contention: "It must be known to many of you, that the Southern states, from their vast extent of uncultivated country, are daily receiving new settlers; but in New England their country is so small, and their land so poor, that their inhabitants are constantly emigrating. As the rule of representation in Congress is to vary with the number of inhabitants, our influence in the general government will be constantly increasing. In fifty years, it is probable that the Southern states will have a great ascendency over the Eastern." [15]

In like manner it may be said that the uncertainty of the future was responsible for the opposition to the Constitution in the Northern states. Some of the most ardent supporters

[13] *Ibid.*, IV, 309.
[14] *Ibid.*, IV, 178. During the discussion in the Virginia Convention over the control of navigation on the Mississippi, William Grayson declared: "This contest of the Mississippi involves this great national contest; that is, whether one part of the continent shall govern the other. The Northern States have the majority, and will endeavor to retain it. This is, therefore, a contest for dominion — for empire." *Ibid.*, III, 365. See also pp. 292, 343.
[15] P. L. Ford, ed., *Pamphlets on the Constitution*, 375.

of local autonomy and constitutional limitations in America were found in the Northern ratifying conventions.[16] It was the return of the first census of 1790, coupled with the experience in actual control of the government, that allayed Northern fears for the future, and hence justified the demands of the Northern party, the Federalists, for a stronger and more active central government. Observing this new party attitude towards national powers, Thomas Jefferson, on May 23, 1792, wrote President Washington that the "Monarchical federalists . . . have themselves adopted the very constructions of the constitution, of which, when advocating it's acceptance before the tribunal of the people, they declared it insusceptible." [17]

After the first decades of the Union, there were further evidences of a sectional conflict directed primarily towards the domination of the central government. During the dispute over Missouri, the *National Intelligencer*, a leading paper at the seat of the Government, in an editorial for January 29, 1820, found that the "truth is, and it is in vain to shut our eyes to the fact, that there are considerations of deeper interest at the bottom of this question. The balance of power vibrates; and the feelings of our politicians vibrate in sympathy." [18]

[16] See Jonathan Elliot, ed., *Debates*, (2 ed.), II.

[17] P. L. Ford, ed., *Writings of Jefferson*, VI, 5. During the discussion of the bank bill in the House on February 8, 1791, James Madison accused Elbridge Gerry of contending that Congress had an unlimited power under the sweeping clauses of the Constitution, whereas, continued Madison, "recurring to the opinion of that gentleman in 1787, he said the powers of the Constitution were then dark, inexplicable, and dangerous; but now, perhaps as a result of experience, they are clear and luminous!" *Annals of Congress*, 1 Cong., 1 sess., 1958. But after 1800, when the Republicans under Jefferson and Madison gained control of the government, there arose considerable agitation within the Northern states for separation from the South. Nor was this agitation confined to the New England discontent culminating in the Hartford Convention of 1814. See Hezekiah Niles, *Things As They Are, or Federalism Turned Inside Out!!*, pamphlet, 48, 49, 50, 51. For two interesting letters from North Carolina on the New England situation in 1814, see A. D. Murphy, letter to Thomas Ruffin, November 24, 1814, W. H. Hoyt, ed., *Papers of Archibald D. Murphy*, I, 76; and W. R. Davie, letter to Landsford, November 29, 1814. J. G. R. Hamilton, "William Richardson Davie: A Memoir Followed by His Letters and Notes by Kemp Battle," *John Sprunt Historical Monographs*, no. 7, pp. 71-72.

[18] *National Intelligencer*, January 29, 1820. "The idea of a balance of power between

THE SOUTH AS A CONSCIOUS MINORITY

After a study of the Missouri question, David L. Yulee, in 1850, explained that, if "the South were permitted to monopolize the Louisiana Purchase, there was danger, as the North supposed, that her growth would overwhelm, in time, the northern power. . . . the real interest which gave momentum to the issue, was the balance of political power between the slave and non-slaveholding States." [19] James M. Mason believed in 1858 that "it was then frankly avowed, that the condition sought to be imposed on Missouri, was to prevent the expansion of political power in the South, by the constitutional right of slave representation." [20]

The Missouri conflict was only an indication that the sectional battle for the domination of the national government in the middle decades was to be shifted to the winning of the West. With the Missouri dispute still unsettled, Spencer Roane wrote James Monroe on February 16, 1820: "Let us cherish, also, the western people, they have an identity of interests with us, and they also hold the Keys of the Mississippi. If driven to it, we can yet form with them a great nation. The influence of a southern sun has given to them a justice and generosity of character, which we look for in

two combinations of states, and not the existence of slavery, gave rise to this unfortunate . . . absurd controversy." John Taylor, *Construction Construed*, (1820), 291. In 1821 Calhoun did "not in the least doubt, but that the Missouri question was got up by a few designing politicians in order to extend their influence and power"; but he did not think that the people of the North "entered into their views, or that even the leaders were actuated by a hatred to the South." "Letters from John C. Calhoun to Charles Tait," *Gulf States Historical Magazine*, September 2, 1902, I, no. 2, p. 103.

[19] Speech in the Senate, August 6, 1850. *Appendix to the Congressional Globe*, 31 Cong., 1 sess., 1164.

[20] Speech in the Senate, March 15, 1858. *Ibid.*, 35 Cong., 1 sess., 75. During the congressional debates over the Missouri question, William Plumer, Jr., representative from New Hampshire, wrote that the South was throwing out many threats of disunion designed to frighten the North out of its purpose of strengthening its control of the national government. Against this Southern design, Plumer wrote his father, February 20, 1820: "We have now a clear majority [in the House] & nothing but firmness is necessary to give us all the success, on which we have ever calculated, that is to say, getting Maine, & keeping Missouri out." E. S. Brown, ed., *The Missouri Compromises and Presidential Politics, 1820-1825, From the Letters of William Plumer, Jr.*, 12. For an example of the threats to which Plumer referred, see Charles Pinckney, speech in the House, February 14, 1820. *Annals of Congress*, 16 Cong., 1 sess., 1310-1329. Meanwhile, a member of the North Carolina state

vain, among the northern Yankies." [21] That this battle for
the West was still going on apace in the forties was the
conclusion of William Allen of Ohio, who, disgusted at the
failure of western settlers to obtain protection from the national government, found an explanation in the fact that "it
was the two wings overshadowing the new centre . . . It
was a question of balance of power. The old North and the
old South dreaded the power of the new centre." [22]

In the decade of the fifties, the Southern advocates of a
controlling power in government, shut off from the west,
were reaching out to the southward for other worlds to con-
quer. "We must *reinforce the powers of slavery as an element of political control,*" maintained the *Richmond Enquirer,* "and this can only be done by the *annexation of
Cuba.*" [23] About the same time, the *Southern Standard* published at Charleston, South Carolina, insisted that "With
Cuba and St. Domingo, we could control the productions of
the tropics, and, with them, the commerce of the world, and
with that, the power of the world"; and then added: "Our

senate, one Plummer of Warren County,
had in 1815 advanced a proposal for
selecting presidential electors on a general
ticket because of the sectional advantage
that would accrue therefrom. "It is also
known," he said, "that our Sister States
to the Eastward, who generally differ from
us in political opinion, from an early period
of the Government so fixed their mode of
electing Electors as to throw the whole
weight of their electorial vote into one
scale, whilst this State, and a few others,
by electing our Electors by districts, have
so divided our votes in the Electorial College, that one of the smallest of the Eastern
States has had more weight in the election
of a President than the large and respectable State of North Carolina." W. H.
Hoyt, ed., *Papers of Archibald D. Murphy,*
II, 30, note.
[21] "Letters of Spencer Roane" (1788-1822),
Bulletin of the New York Public Library,
March, 1906. X, no. 3, p. 175. As early as
1805, "Curtius" [John Taylor?] foresaw

this conflict between the East and the South
for the control of the West, and predicted,
quite accurately, the outcome: "The most
active rivalries will unquestionably arise
between the southern and the western
states, while there will be no source of
jealousy between the states of the east
and those of the west. Add to this the fact
that the greater part of the population of
the western country will arise out of emi-
grations from New-England; and it will
become apparent that the power of the
western states, so far from uniting itself
with that of the southern states, will be
most apt to unite with that of the eastern."
Curtius [John Taylor?], *A Defence of the
Measures of the Administration of Thomas
Jefferson,* pamphlet, 88.
[22] Remarks in the Senate, March 3, 1847.
Congressional Globe, 29 Cong., 2. sess.,
570.
[23] As quoted in Henry C. Carey, *The North
and the South,* pamphlet, 18.

true policy is to look to Brazil as the next great slave power." [24] In 1857, William Walker of Louisiana was looking to the acquisition of Nicaragua as a matter of "immediate and vital consequence to the people of the Southern States." [25]

Finally, just as the early leaders of the formative period were appealing to this power-loving radical group to enter the Union because of the likelihood of ultimate control over the central government, so now in the sixties other leaders in Southern political thought were appealing to these radicals to remain within the Union because of the actual Southern control of the central government. The argument advanced by the conservative Alexander H. Stephens in the Georgia Secession Convention of 1861 was a fitting continuation of that of the early forefathers in the ratifying conventions of 1788 to win the support of the aggressive dominationists of that day: "We have had a majority of the Presidents chosen from the South; as well as the control and management of most of those chosen from the North. We have had sixty years of Southern Presidents to their twenty-four, thus controlling the Executive department. So of the judges of the Supreme Court, we have had eighteen from the South, and but eleven from the North; although nearly four-fifths of the judicial business has arisen in the Free States, yet a majority of the Court has always been from the South. This we have required so as to guard against any interpretation of the Constitution unfavorable to us. In like manner we have been equally watchful to guard our interests in the Legislative branch of government. In choosing the presiding

[21] *Ibid.*, 42.

[25] Letter to C. J. Jenkins, September 2, 1857. C. A. Gulick, Jr., ed., *Papers of Mirabeau Buonaparte Lamar*, IV, pt. 2, p. 48. See also, W. E. Dodd, "Robert J. Walker, Imperialist," *Bulletin of Randolph-Macon Women's College*, January, 1915, I, no. 2, pp. 3-23. John A. Campbell objected to the acquisition of Mexico because "its population would be in a great measure of the free class" and hence would result "in an increase of the strength of the non-slaveholding states and a corresponding diminution of our own." Letter to Calhoun, November 20, 1847. J. F. Jameson, ed., *Correspondence of Calhoun*, American Historical Association, *Annual Report*, 1899, II, 1140.

Presidents (*pro tem.*) of the Senate, we have had twenty-four to their eleven. Speakers of the House, we have had twenty-three and they twelve. While a majority of the Representatives, from their greater population, have always been from the North, yet we have so generally secured the Speaker, because he, to a great extent, shapes and controls the legislation of the country. Nor have we had less control in every other department of the general government. Attorney-Generals we have had fourteen, while the North have had but five. Foreign ministers we have had eighty-six, and they but fifty-four. While three-fourths of the business which demands diplomatic agents abroad is clearly from the Free States, from their greater commercial interests, yet we have had the principal embassies, so as to secure the world markets for our cotton, tobacco and sugar on the best possible terms. We have had a vast majority of the higher officers of both army and navy, while a larger proportion of the soldiers and sailors were drawn from the North. Equally so of Clerks, Auditors and Comptrollers filling the Executive department; the records show for the last fifty years, that of the three thousand thus employed, we have had more than two-thirds of the same, while we have but one-third of the white population of the Republic." [26]

Undoubtedly there had always existed in the Ante-bellum South an aggressive radical element, who, flaunting the banner of domination or rebellion, had originally entered the

[26] *Extract from a Speech by Alexander H. Stephens,* pamphlet, 2-3. Similar tactics were used to pacify the radicals during the crisis of 1850: "Out of the sixty years since the Constitution was framed, the South has had the Presidents all of the time, except twelve years and one month. . . . We have a southern Speaker. . . . A majority of the Cabinet are from slave-holding States. In the Supreme Court, we have five to four. In the army and navy, we have our full share." Edward Stanly of North Carolina, speech in the House, March 6, 1850. *Appendix to the* *Congressional Globe,* 31 Cong., 1 sess., 339. Note also these words of B. F. Perry to the South Carolina radicals of 1850: "Since the formation of the Federal Government, the Southern States have given to the Union nine Presidents out of thirteen, and have had a very large portion of all the important Federal offices. Three fourths of this time the South has been in power, and had the control of the Government!" *Speech of Hon. B. F. Perry in the House of Representatives of South Carolina on December 11, 1850,* pamphlet, 13.

Union only with the expectation of controlling the central government, and who were willing to remain in it only so long as the certainty of that control continued to exist. Consequently, as rapidly as the certainty of domination within the Union waned, the demand for separation from the Union waxed stronger and stronger. And it was out of this background that there arose, certainly by the thirties, a group of so-called secessionists *per se,* who advocated a Southern Confederacy in preference to any possible source of protection that might be granted in a Union with the Northern section.

One of the most prominent of this number was James Henry Hammond — lawyer, Congressman, Governor, Senator — already active in South Carolina politics in the early thirties. Reflecting upon his varied political experiences, he wrote on March 24, 1861: "A Southern Confederacy has been the cherished dream and hope of my life"; and again in 1862: "From the commencement of my legally political life I have worked faithfully for the dissolution of the Union often with all against me but Rhett." [27] Further evidence of such a group appeared in a letter from John H. Lumpkin to Howell Cobb in 1850: "Wm. L. Mitchell and various other prominent individuals I have met with are in favor of a dissolution of the Union *per se* . . . and newspaper editors have become bold enough to insert communications in their columns without any mark of disapprobation, openly advocating an immediate dissolution of the Union." [28]

---

[27] Elizabeth Merritt, "James Henry Hammond, 1807-1864," *Johns Hopkins University Studies,* 1923. XLI, no. 4, pp. 142, note, and 96-97.

[28] U. B. Phillips, ed., *Correspondence of Toombs, Stephens, and Cobb,* American Historical Association, *Annual Report,* 1911. II, 207. See further, U. B. Phillips, *The Literary Movement for Secession,* pamphlet. On July 4, 1851, the German philosopher, Francis Lieber, during the course of an address at Charleston, South Carolina, remarked: "There are those, even, it seems to me, who have first rashly conceived of secession as a remedy, and now adhere to it as the end and object to be attained, [even] when they are shown that it would not cure the evils complained of, but, on the contrary, would induce others, infinitely greater and infinitely more numerous." *An Address on Secession,* pamphlet, 5.

In the thirties this group was seeking to make Texas the nucleus of a separate Southern Confederacy; for, unlike the majority Southern opinion favoring annexation, the radicals preferred to have Texas remain independent. "Let Texas remain as She is," wrote Henry C. Phelps to Mirabeau B. Lamar on January 21, 1838, ". . . should the greedy an[d env]ious North *permit* the south to strike off the Texas Star can commingle with its Kindred." [29] Several months later just before Lamar became governor of Texas, J. Hamilton wrote him: "Instead of weakening yourselves & the Southern States by agitating the slave question which our adversaries will involve in the discussions of the question of *annexation,* — you will be silently building up a rock of salvation & a pillar of strength for the South in which we may stand & take refuge when driven to separation by the abolition of the North — An event which seems to be inevitable." [30]

For the most part, these secessionists, whose writings made slight impression until the sixties, were men of little prominence in the realm of Southern political thought. Of them, Gideon Welles recorded in his Diary for July 18, 1863, these words: "Many of the lesser lights — shallow political writers and small speech-makers — talked flippantly of disunion, which they supposed would enrich the South and impoverish the North." [31] And their number was proportionate to their prominence — at least, such was the opinion of J. H. Thornwell, who, in 1861, ventured this estimate in the *Southern Presbyterian Review*: "We do not believe, when the present controversy began, that the advocates of what is called disunion *per se*, men who preferred a Southern Confederacy upon the grounds of its intrinsic

[29] C. A. Gulick, Jr., ed., *Papers of Mirabeau Buonaparte Lamar*, II, 27.
[30] *Ibid.*, II, 277. "Keep to yourselves," advised A. B. Longstreet in a letter to Lamar in 1837, "and very likely, you will in time have many distracted states petitioning to be let into your confederacy." *Ibid.*, II, 4-5.
[31] *Diary of Gideon Welles*, I, 377.

superiority to the Constitutional Union of the United States, could have mustered a corporal's guard. The people of the South were loyal to the country. . . ." [32]

THE "UNITED SOUTH" AND PLANS FOR AGGRESSIVE ACTION

The movement for separation from the Union was not confined to the efforts of this scattered group of secessionists *per se;* for, indirectly, every attempt to crystallize Southern opinion upon the adoption of a concerted aggressive policy of protecting Southern interests hastened the final stroke for Southern independence. As in the rise of the secessionists, the movement for co-operation between men of all the Southern states extended back into the thirties, gained strength in the forties, reached a peak in the crisis of 1850, and then, after a temporary lull, climbed to new heights of support with the approach of the sixties, until, at length, in the fall of 1860, after the election of Abraham Lincoln to the presidency, the movement gained the unquestioned enlistment of a large majority of the Southern people.

The more radical the co-operationists shaded off in their beliefs into the ranks of the extreme secessionists, so that the border line of differences between the two groups is one in name only, depending largely upon the willingness of their members to admit or deny working for a Southern confederacy as an end in itself. John C. Calhoun, always looking ahead to new sources of protection a decade or more in advance of his time, expressed what is perhaps a typical co-operationist's attitude when he wrote on October 26, 1838: "Would to God that the whole South . . . had adopted the same course, and merged all of their local, and passed differences in one general effort for their common

---

[32] J. H. Thornwell, *The State of the Country*, reprinted from the *Southern Presbyterian Review*, pamphlet, 8.

interest." [33] R. B. Rhett, though never taking an open stand with the secessionists *per se,* nevertheless promoted their extreme doctrines when, at a meeting of the congressional representatives from the Southern states held in Washington, December 20, 1836, he proposed a resolution for the appointment of a committee of two members from each state to consider the best methods of dissolving the Union.[34]

An active co-operationist in the forties, perhaps to be classified in his political attitudes between the foregoing views of Calhoun and of Rhett, was the aging Langdon Cheves, whose words, representative of his group, are found in a letter to the *Charleston Mercury,* September 11, 1844: "Let associations be formed in every Southern, and, if possible, in every South-Western State, and let them confer together and interchange views and information; let leading men, through committees and private correspondence, collect, compare and concentrate the views of like men in the respective States, and when ripe for it, and not before, let representatives from these States meet in Convention, and, if circumstances promise success, let them *then* deliberate on the mode of resistance and the measure of redress. . . . Continue to enlighten the public mind, rouse the public feeling, excite the public shame, for the degradation to which we have been brought; let your exertions be not occasional and desultory, but organized and incessant . . . What if the unhappy event of separation shall be provoked, is to pre-

[33] Letter to Dr. Danall [?] October 26, 1838. J. F. Jameson, ed., *Correspondence of Calhoun,* American Historical Association, *Annual Report,* 1899, II, 408. See also his letter to J. H. Means at page 765. Just before his death Calhoun wrote: "The Union is doomed to dissolution, there is no mistaking the signs. . . . I fix its probable occurrence within twelve years or three Presidential terms. . . . the probability is, it will explode in a Presidential election." From a fragmentary memoranda found with J. M. Mason's papers. Virginia Mason, *Life and Correspondence of James M. Mason,* 72, 73.

[34] W. C. Fowler, *Sectional Controversy,* 124. Resolutions for concerted action by the Southern states in opposition to Northern attacks upon slavery were adopted by the Senate of South Carolina, December, 1824. See also the message of Governor John L. Wilson to the South Carolina Legislature, December 1, 1824, and the Resolutions of the General Assembly of Georgia on December 28, 1827. H. V. Ames, ed., *State Documents on Federal Relations,* 207, 205, 213.

vent us doing our own business, as we have done before, and reaping the profits which we now bestow on others, and which have made the commercial men of the North and East 'Merchant Princes'?" Though exclaiming in this letter: "Before God, we do not wish disunion," Cheves nevertheless proceeded to say that "There are worse evils than disunion, and we can hardly doubt that we have been long suffering under them." [35]

With the approach of the crisis of 1850, after the introduction of the Wilmot Proviso in 1847, proposals for concerted action became more common; and of these, Calhoun was the recipient of a number. In 1847, there came a letter from Wilson Lumpkin contending that "our great and only difficulty is to unite and consolidate the action of the Slave holding States. Attempts made by States Single-handed must fail." [36] Two years later, H. W. Conner wrote: "From all I have seen and learned, *I am more convinced than ever of the vital importance of prompt decided and efficient action on the part of the South* . . . the action should be *bold, determined* and decisive." [37]

Concerted efforts for the promotion of common principles featured the work of organized Southern groups about the year 1850. The Virginia Legislature resolved unanimously in 1847 and 1849 that the passage of the Wilmot Proviso would make it the duty of every Southern state "to take firm, united and concerted action in this emergency." From a caucus of sixty-nine Southern delegates in Congress held on December 23, 1848, there evolved an address to the Southern people praying for "unity among ourselves." Florida, on January 13, 1849, announced herself ready to join with other Southern states "for the defence of our rights, whether through a Southern Convention or otherwise";

[35] *Letter of the Hon. Langdon Cheves,* Pamphlet, 2, 3, 5, 4.
[36] J. F. Jameson, ed., *Correspondence of* Calhoun, American Historical Association, *Annual Report,* 1899, II, 1136.
[37] *Ibid.,* 1190.

Missouri on March 10, 1849, was willing "to coöperate with the slave holding States for mutual protection against Northern fanaticism"; and Mississippi on March 6, 1850, asserted that the Southern states "must prepare to act — to act with resolution, firmness and unity of purpose." [38] And of the Nashville Convention composed of 175 delegates from nine Southern states, W. O. Goode gave a true characterization when he wrote R. M. T. Hunter two months before the first meeting that it would "consist of men, for the *most part anxious to preserve the* Union, but firmly *resolved to save the South.*" [39]

The break between the two sections that might have come in 1850 was successfully evaded for another decade; but the efforts to develop Southern unity of action went on apace throughout the fifties. At a meeting of the Southern congressmen in Washington, 1850, another address to the Southern people was adopted advocating the establishment of a newspaper in Washington to promote Southern interests and to unify Southern opinion.[40] The extensive correspondence in the early fifties between Governor Seabrook of South Carolina and Governor Quitman of Mississippi disclosed that both these men favored the use of numerous state conventions and Southern congresses to maintain the sense of unity in the South.[41]

The most active agitator in the decade was the able William L. Yancey, who would make use of committees of public safety: "But if we could do as our fathers did," he

---

[38] H. V. Ames, ed., *State Documents on Federal Relations,* 244-247, 253, 256.
[39] C. H. Ambler, ed., *Correspondence of Hunter,* American Historical Association, *Annual Report,* 1916, II, 109. For a study of the work of the co-operationists during this period, see P. M. Hamer, *The Secession Movement in South Carolina, 1847-1852.*
[40] U. B. Phillips, *Life of Toombs,* 93.
[41] J. F. H. Claiborne, *Life and Correspondence of Quitman,* II, 36 *et seq.* In

1852, a Southerner wrote R. M. T. Hunter that the South should "form a treaty with England, giving her certain privileges in *the cotton trade and vast navigation, in return for which, she could stand by the South, and crush the Free Soilers between Canada and the South States.*" C. H. Ambler, ed., *Correspondence of Hunter,* American Historical Association, *Annual Report,* 1916, II, 145.

wrote in the Slaughter Letter, June 15, 1858, "organize Committees of Safety all over the cotton States (and it is only in them that we can hope for any effective movement,) we shall fire the Southern heart — instruct the Southern mind — give courage to each other, and at the proper moment, by one organized, concerted action, we can precipitate the cotton States into a revolution." [42] Earlier in the decade there had been established a League of United Southerners, which Yancey, the founder, herein commended, since in his opinion, such a league "will hold the Southern issue paramount, and will influence parties, legislatures, and statesmen." [43]

The desire for Southern unity also prompted efforts throughout the South for the establishment of railroads. To that effect, Franklin H. Elmore wrote Calhoun in 1845: "A Rail Road Communication based at Memphis in a slave region and extended direct to Charleston, passing through the most Martial portion of our people and who have, as at present situated, the least interest of all the South in Slavery, would render their relations with us at Charleston and Memphis so intimate and advantageous, that their interests and ours would be indissolubly united. They would be to us a source of strength power and safety and render the South invulnerable." [44] Twelve years later, Thomas F. Drayton of South Carolina wrote Jefferson Davis to the same effect: *"As to myself, believing that Railways are for the South, the most efficient means, both offensive & defensive, that she can have,* I have endeavored to help [?] them w[h]ere most needed." [45]

One of the strongest minority movements within the

---

[42] J. W. DuBose, *Life and Times of Yancey*, 376. Yet Yancey denied that he was a secessionist *per se*, p. 390.

[43] *Ibid.*

[44] J. F. Jameson, ed., *Correspondence of Calhoun*, American Historical Association, *Annual Report*, 1899, II, 1063.

[45] Letter dated April 9, 1858. Dunbar Rowland, ed., *Davis, Constitutionalist*, III, 217. See further, T. D. Jervey, *Robert Y. Hayne and His Times*, Book IV, 383 *et seq*, and Henry Cleveland, ed., *Stephens in Public and Private with Letters and Speeches*, 605-621.

South for aggressive concerted action came in the attempts to organize a sectional political party. Isaac E. Holmes, representative from South Carolina, expressed the wish in a letter to Howell Cobb that "the Southern Representatives would consent to act together without regard to Whig or Democrat. The Wilmot Proviso is paramount to all party." [46] Calhoun became interested in this movement before his death and worked for a "bloc" in politics to be formed from the Southern members of both parties in Congress so that the South might present a united front upon the floors of the national legislative halls. [47] In opening the State Convention of 1852, the Governor of South Carolina pleaded for a united South, heretofore "divided and distracted by the convulsive throes of party strife"; [48] and in 1856 the "League of United Southerners" asserted that a solid South "should never be sacrificed to the base behests of party expediency . . . The South must rely on herself — she cannot safely build her castles on the shifting sands of party." [49]

Here again Yancey was leading the ranks of the co-operationists. In a letter to James D. Meadows on June 16, 1859, he wrote: "The concentration of the Northern masses in favor of the principle of Abolition, . . . utterly crushing the ability of the national Democracy to protect the South, has convinced me that hereafter the South should place her reliance and confidence on herself alone. . . . In my opinion, the stern despotism, and exclusiveness and jealousies of party have contributed more to dissensions in the South on the question of her rights and remedies than any other cause, and I believe that the public mind of our section has arrived at that conclusion." [50]

[46] U. B. Phillips, *Life of Toombs*, 59. See also the farewell address of Andrew Jackson, March 4, 1837. J. D. Richardson, ed., *Messages and Papers*, III, 295.

[47] U. B. Phillips, *Life of Toombs*, 59-62.

[48] *Journal of the South Carolina Convention of 1852*, 9.

[49] "Address of the Southern League," *DeBow's Review*, March, 1859. XXVI, 346.

[50] J. W. DuBose, *Life and Times of Yan-*

THE SOUTH AS A CONSCIOUS MINORITY

The approaching election of 1860 was a golden opportunity for the advocates of aggressive concerted action. Once more they worked through legislature and convention, on the stump and in the press, to effect the unity needed to stave off the election of Lincoln, candidate of the Republican Party. From the results of the early fall elections in Ohio, Pennsylvania, and Indiana, a victory for Lincoln seemed certain to the editors of the *Richmond Enquirer*, who, on October 15, 1860, in an editorial entitled "Let Us Reason Together" made one of their final campaign pleas for unity: "Now that the fact is palpable, *can the South longer refuse to unite and present an unbroken front? Can*not some plan be devised, whereby we may yet, *unitedly and solidly, battle against our Northern foes?*" [51] Once more, the plea for unity was to be denied; but the consequences gave to the advocates of aggressive action and their more extreme friends, the secessionists *per se,* their greatest victory under the cloak of a stinging defeat.

The Appeal for Southern Independence

Behind the efforts of the secessionists as well as of an increasing number of the co-operationists lay a philosophy of sectionalism so outstanding as to preclude the possibility of ever attaining a common American nationality. "There is a question pending between the North and the South," declared R. B. Rhett in 1833, "resulting from the difference in the political, mental and social organism of the two sections, which no party measure can settle — which cannot be settled save by treaty or by revolution." [52] On March 11, 1836, J. H. Hammond wrote Beverly Tucker: "I believe disunion

---

cey, 388-389. "Let national parties and national candidates alone then for the present and strike boldly for Georgia." J. H. Lumpkin, letter to Howell Cobb, February 10, 1851. U. B. Phillips, ed., *Correspondence of Toombs, Stephens, and* *Cobb,* American Historical Association, *Annual Report,* 1911, II, 227.
[51] *Richmond Enquirer,* October 15, 1860.
[52] As quoted in J. W. DuBose, *Life and Times of Yancey,* 60.

must take place, and have long believed that the planting States under one federal head would exhibit more prosperity than the world has ever seen." [53] In 1851, the Columbus, Georgia, *Sentinel* found no hope of eliminating the sectional conflict "as long as slaveholders and abolitionists live under a common government"; [54] and about the same time there was broadcast in a "Tract for the People" this plea: "Unite, and you shall form one of the most splendid empires on which the sun ever shone, of the most homogeneous population, all of the same blood and lineage, a soil the most fruitful, and a climate the most lovely." [55]

In the sixties, this appeal to a Southern nationality as a basis for independence was even more pronounced. Typical are the questions which J. H. Thornwell presented in the *Southern Presbyterian Review:* "What is there in the circumstance of *one* Confederacy of *divided interests,* that shall secure a freer and safer development than *two Confederacies,* each representing an *undivided* interest? Are not two homogeneous Unions stronger than one that is heterogeneous? Should not the life of a Government be one?" [56] In 1861, Fulton Anderson, commissioner from the State of Mississippi to the State of Virginia, insisted before the Convention of the latter state that "all that is left us is the creation of a great and powerful Southern Union, composed of States inhabited by homogeneous populations, and having a common interest, common sympathies, common hopes, and a common destiny." [57]

As long as other sources of protection had won more gen-

[53] Elizabeth Merritt, "James Henry Hammond," *Johns Hopkins University Studies,* XLI, no. 4, p. 39.
[54] As quoted in U. B. Phillips, *Life of Toombs,* 102. In a letter to Howell Cobb, July 1, 1849, Henry L. Benning maintained that "the only safety of the South from abolition universal is to be found in an *early* dissolution of the Union." U. B. Phillips, ed., *Correspondence of Toombs, Stephens,* and Cobb, American Historical Association, *Annual Report,* 1911, II, 171.
[55] *Behind and Before, or What Is to Be Done,* pamphlet, no. 8, p. 8.
[56] J. H. Thornwell, *The State of the Country,* pamphlet, p. 29, reprinted from the *Southern Presbyterian Review.*
[57] *Journal of the Mississippi Convention of 1861,* 219.

eral support throughout the South, the appeals for independence had been as seeds fallen on barren ground. But if the ground were barren in the thirties and forties and fifties, it became intensely fertile in the fall of 1860. For the election of Abraham Lincoln to the presidency on November 6, 1860, immediately germinated those seeds of independence already sown in the ground of Southern minds everywhere. How quickly thereafter those seeds produced an abundant harvest! On November 7, with the result of the election anticipated but not confirmed, Governor Joseph E. Brown sent a special message to the Georgia Assembly recommending the immediate calling of a state convention, the appropriation of one million dollars for a military fund, and a formal appeal to arms. "To every demand for further concession or compromise of our rights," he said, "the reply ought to be, 'the argument is exhausted,' and we now 'stand by our arms.' " [58]

On receipt of the news of Lincoln's election, the South Carolina Legislature, November 13, 1860, called a convention of the people of that state; and on November 19, the Governor of Mississippi called in special session the state legislature, which, ten days later, issued a declaration justifying secession as the proper remedy for their grievances.[59] Still within a month after the election, A. B. Longstreet wrote to the *Richmond Enquirer,* in a letter dated December 6, disclosing the strength of the independence movement in South Carolina. Instead of a radical, half-hearted effort, sponsored by a minority group of designing politicians as had been acclaimed, Longstreet wrote that the great body of the people in mass "drive politicians before them like sheep. They do not wait for leaders to appoint meetings, with intent to address them. They gather in multitudes, find out

---

[58] As quoted in H. J. Pearce, *Benjamin H. Hill, Secession and Reconstruction,* 41.

[59] H. V. Ames, ed., *State Documents on Federal Relations,* 310, note.

where a speaker is, visit him, and compel him to speak." [60]

More impressive was the harvest of the Southern members of Congress in an address to the South, December 13, 1860: "The argument is exhausted. All hope of relief in the Union through the agencies of committees, Congressional legislation, or constitutional amendments, is extinguished, and we trust the South will not be deceived by appearances or the pretense of new guarantees. . . . We are satisfied the honor, safety and independence of the Southern people are to be found only in a Southern Confederacy . . . and that the sole and primary aim of each slaveholding state ought to be its speedy and absolute separation from an unnatural and hostile Union." [61] Most impressive of all were the state acts of secession themselves. Beginning with the South Carolina Ordinance on December 20, 1860, seven states had officially delivered a stroke for Southern independence by the first of the following February; [62] and, at that time, the end of the Ante-bellum Period was in sight.

To be sure, there were still the ideas of Southern men, chiefly from the border states, who were bent upon reconciliation, whether by congressional committees or peace conventions; but they were for the most part artificial ideas, and they became increasingly so. For that reason, they could retard but not prevent the movement for Southern independence. By March 2, 1861, Senator James M. Mason was

[60] *Richmond Enquirer*, December 11, 1860. On November 29, 1860, James M. Mason wrote to his sister Anne: "the dissolution of the Union is a *fixed* fact. As certain as the sun rises, South Carolina goes out as soon as the *Act of Separation* can be reduced to form, after the 17th of December, when the convention meets — *and she is right*." Virginia Mason, *Life and Correspondence of J. M. Mason*, 160. On December 10, 1860, L. Q. C. Lamar expressed this opinion: "If the formation of a Southern Confederacy, to extend from the Delaware or the Susquehanna to the western line of New Mexico, or to include

California, were adopted, I believe that a large majority of the Southern people would be rejoiced." Letter to P. F. Liddell. Edward Mayes, *L. Q. C. Lamar: His Life, Times, and Speeches*, 637.

[61] U. B. Phillips, *Life of Toombs*, 205.

[62] Mississippi, January 9; Florida, January 10; Alabama, January 11; Georgia, January 19; Louisiana, January 24; and Texas, February 1. These were followed by Virginia, April 17; Arkansas, May 6; Tennessee, May 7; and North Carolina, May 20. H. V. Ames, ed., *State Documents on Federal Relations*, 317, note, and references.

deriding the proposed constitutional amendment guaranteeing slavery in the states as a "bread pill"; while Senator
Robert W. Johnson of Arkansas was convinced the amendment "would allure and be a delusion" — nothing more.
On that day, Senator Stephen A. Douglas of Illinois, observing the Southern attitude towards all attempts at the
adjustment of the sectional difficulties, was led to remark:
"I am afraid some of our friends, who think it would be a
little better to get out of the Union than stay here, are opposing this very amendment for fear that it will pacify the
people, by showing them that the North is determined to do
them justice, and that all that we want is time. Hence they
must defeat it for fear they will get all the guarantees they
ask for." [63]

Meanwhile, in the Virginia Convention, Unionism had
been supplanted by independence. Most of the delegates
who had been returned as Union men afterwards voted for
secession.[64] And so the movement continued until eleven
Southern states had struck for Southern independence.

THE DEFENSE OF THE RIGHT OF REVOLUTION

Shortly after the election of Abraham Lincoln, Howell
Cobb, from his vantage-point on the dividing line between
two great epochs of Southern political thought, saw behind
him only "the cold formalities of a broken and violated Constitution" and before him, a decree of separation from the
North — one that "will be accepted by the South as the only
solution which gives her any promise of future peace and
safety." [65] Still peering into the future, Cobb foresaw a new
theoretical problem for the South: that of justifying the demand for a divorce from the Northern section.

This problem was already the chief object of attention

[63] *Congressional Globe*, 36 Cong., 2 sess.,
1387, 1388, 1389.
[64] Edward A. Pollard, *Lost Cause*, 94.

[65] *Letter of Hon. Howell Cobb to the People
of Georgia, December 6, 1860*, pamphlet, 15.

in the Southern political mind; for, on the day before Cobb had expressed his ideas in a public letter to the people of Georgia, two eminent Southern statesmen were debating before the United States Senate the most logical justification for separation from the Northern states. It was December 5, 1860, three days after Congress convened, and the day following the presentation of the President's general message on the state of the country. President Buchanan, a Northern man with Southern principles, had, in true compromising spirit, denied to the South the constitutional right of secession and to the North the constitutional right of coercion.[66] The message was up for consideration for the first, but not for the last time; and on it, Alfred Iverson, Senator from Georgia, took this stand: "I rather agree with the President that the secession of a State is an act of revolution . . . But, sir, while a State has no power, under the Constitution, conferred upon it to secede from the Federal Government or from the Union, each State has the right of revolution, which all admit. Whenever the burdens of the Government under which it acts become so onerous that it cannot bear them, or if anticipated evil shall be so great that the State believes it would be better off — even risking the perils of secession — out of the Union than in it, then that State, in my opinion, like all people upon earth, has the right to exercise the great fundamental principle of self-preservation, and go out of the Union." [67]

After Iverson had completed his remarks, Louis T. Wigfall, Senator from Texas, arose to make reply: "He and I do not understand the Constitution in the same way. . . . If I believed that the act of secession was one of revolution, that it was one in direct conflict with the Constitution of the United States that I am sworn to obey, I would hesitate much before I would utter such sentiments as I am in the

[66] The message is found in J. D. Richardson, ed., *Messages and Papers*, V, 626-653.

[67] *Congressional Globe*, 36 Cong., 2 sess., 10-11.

habit of uttering . . . no man who admits that the Constitution is a compact between States, to which each State acceded as a State, can deny the right to secede, whenever any State sees fit." [68]

Here were presented the two theories upon which the South now relied: the inherent right of revolution and the constitutional right of secession. Some advocates of separation supported one theory; some, another; and to make the justification for independence doubly sure, the South in 1860 and 1861 was generally supporting both. "There is no incompatibility," wrote G. W. Johnson to Jefferson Davis in 1861, "between the right of secession by a State and the right of revolution by the people. The one is a civil right founded upon the Constitution; the other is a natural right resting upon the Law of God." [69]

The advocates of the right of revolution repeatedly harked back beyond the formation of the Constitution to the words of Thomas Jefferson in the Declaration of Independence: "That whenever any Form of Government becomes destructive of these ends, [that is, the unalienable rights of life, liberty, and the pursuit of happiness] it is the Right of the People to alter or to abolish it, and to institute new Government, laying its foundation on such principles and organizing its powers in such form, as to them shall seem most likely to effect their Safety and Happiness. Prudence, indeed, will dictate that Governments long established should not be changed for light and transient causes . . . But when a long train of abuses and usurpations, pursuing invariably the same Object evinces a design to reduce them under absolute Despotism, it is their right, it is their duty, to throw off such Government, and to provide new Guards for their future security." [70]

[68] *Ibid.,* 12.
[69] *Journal of the Confederate Congress,* Senate Document 234. 58 Cong., 2 sess., I, 541.

[70] *Documents Illustrative of the Formation of the Union,* House Document no. 398, 69 Cong., 1 sess., 22. In 1788, efforts were made in Virginia to incorporate this prin-

During an address at New Orleans in October, 1860, William L. Yancey considered this inherent right of self-preservation at some length: "It is the right to save ourselves from despotism and destruction — the right to withdraw ourselves from a government which endeavors to crush us. It is the right, expressed in the Declaration of Independence, to do this thing, whenever the government under which we live becomes oppressive, and erect a new government which may promise to preserve our liberties." [71]

Further support for the right of revolution may be gleaned from the records of the session of Congress in which Iverson was speaking on December 5, 1860. Jefferson Davis declared on the following January 10 that "if the Declaration of Independence be true, (and who here gainsays it?) every community may dissolve its connection with any other community previously made." [72] On the following January 24, Albert Rust, representative from Arkansas, maintained that though he did not believe in the "legal, constitutional right of secession," he was convinced that the six Southern states which had already separated themselves from the Union had done so "in the exercise of a right inherent in every freeman — the right to resist injustice; to avenge and retaliate wrong; to repel aggression; the rights, above and superior to all other rights, of self-defense and self-preservation." [73]

This theory of the right of revolution found its way into Southern state conventions and their declarations of secession. Charles E. Hooker, official representative from the State of Mississippi, thus explained the theory in the South Carolina Convention: "There is, however, a great principle

---

ciple into the Federal Constitution, for a committee of the state ratifying convention proposed as a constitutional amendment, "that the doctrine of non-resistance against arbitrary power and oppression is absurd, slavish, and destructive to the good and happiness of mankind." Jonathan Elliot, ed., *Debates* (2 ed.), III, 657.

[71] J. W. DuBose, *Life and Times of Yancey,* 533-534.

[72] *Congressional Globe,* 36 Cong., 2 sess., 309.

[73] *Appendix to the Congressional Globe.* 36 Cong., 2 sess., 97.

underlying all constitutions and governments — I mean
. . . that it is the right of the people to alter, to change, to
amend, aye, to abolish the form of government whenever to
them it shall seem proper. That . . . is the great principle
which underlies not only your federal constitution, but which
lies at the basis of all your State constitutions — the right of
the people, the power of the people, aye, the duty of the
people, to resume the powers of government with which
they have intrusted their agents whenever those agents have
proven and manifested themselves to be unfaithful in the
discharge of the trust." [74]

The theory received official sanction in the South Carolina
declaration of the immediate causes justifying secession,
wherein it is contended that one of the two great principles
established by the colonies in gaining their independence was
"the right of a people to abolish a Government when it becomes destructive of the ends for which it was instituted." [75]
Finally, after a Southern Confederacy had been formed, the
accredited commissioners from the Confederate Government to the Federal Government maintained that seven
states had withdrawn from the Union "in the exercise of
the inherent right of every free people to change or reform
their Political Institutions." [76]

Problems in the application of the theory concerned the
South very little. Howell Cobb thought that the exercise
of the right of revolution "depends for its maintenance upon
the stout hearts and strong arms of a free people"; [77] and
Alfred Iverson admitted that those who exercised the right
did so at their own peril and at the risk of having to take the
consequences. [78] But Jefferson Davis believed that the opera-

---

[74] *Journal of the Mississippi Convention of
1861,* 166.
[75] *Journal of the South Carolina Convention of 1860-1-2,* 462. The other great
principle was "the right of a State to
govern itself."
[76] A. H. Stephens, *War between the States,*
II, 736.

[77] Letter to John Rutherford and others,
August 12, 1851. U. B. Phillips, ed.,
*Correspondence of Toombs, Stephens, and
Cobb,* American Historical Association
Annual Report, 1911, II, 258.
[78] *Congressional Globe,* 36 Cong., 2 sess.,
11.

tions of revolutions under the Declaration of Independence involved no further obligations than breaking the alliance between the states, for, said he, "could any man reasoning *a priori* come to the conclusion that the men who fought the battles of the Revolution for community independence — that the men who struggled against the then greatest military Power on the face of the globe in order that they might possess those inalienable rights which they had declared — terminated their great efforts by transmitting posterity to a condition in which they could only gain those rights by force?" [79]

On the relationship between revolutions and constitutions, the Southern doctrine apparently was that the latter were subordinate to the former. William L. Yancey, in discussing the sectional conflict, pointed to a law transcending the Constitution when he declared in a speech at Columbus, Georgia, in 1855, that the "laws of nature in their majesty stand out from the issue more imperative than the obligations due to national parties, or even to Constitutions." [80]

The leading exponent of constitutionalism in the fifties, Alexander H. Stephens, in a moment of despondency or loss of faith in his cause, pronounced in 1859 that there was above the Constitution a higher law that might be said to justify in certain instances the application of the extreme right of revolution even in violation of express constitutional provisions. "Many," he said, "seem to be not only aston-

---

[79] Speech in the Senate, January 10, 1861. *Ibid.*, 309.
[80] J. W. DuBose, *Life and Times of Yancey*, 300. In the Virginia Convention of 1861, delegates from the western counties, who were extreme Union men, attempted to force the secessionists into a difficult position by advocating resolutions favoring the "extra and ultra constitutional right" of separation, which they defined as "an appeal from the cancelled obligations of the Constitutional Compact to the original rights and the law of self-preservation."

The secessionists refused to accept these resolutions, though the justification for secession finally adopted leaned towards the revolutionary rather than the constitutional theory. *Journal of the Virginia Convention of 1861*, Appendix, resolutions submitted by James Burley on March 16, 1861, resolution 3, pp. 2-3. Also the partial report of the committee on federal relations submitted on March 9, resolution 8. See further the Journal of the Committee of the Whole, April 6, pp. 61, 63, 66, 68.

ished, but offended, at the 'higher law' doctrine of the senator from New York (Mr. Seward). "I, too, believe in the higher law — the law of the Creator, as manifested in his works and his revelation. Upon this, our cause eminently rests. I claim nothing barely upon the ground that 'thus it is nominated in the bond.' I recognize to the fullest extent, the doctrine that all human laws and constitutions must be founded upon the Divine law. And if there is any right secured, or any obligation imposed in our constitution, inconsistent with this law, underlieing and overruling all others, such right and such obligation must be yielded. I would not swear to support any constitution inconsistent with this higher law. . . . We must stand on the higher law, as well as upon the constitution. The latter must be subordinate to the former." [81]

The Defense of the Right of Secession

Writing to an editor of the *Richmond Enquirer* on November 23, 1860, scarcely more than a fortnight after the election of Lincoln, James M. Mason, then serving his fourteenth consecutive year in the Senate, made this suggestive statement concerning the right of secession as a justification for separation from the Union: "Fortunately for the occasion and its consequences, this is not an open question in Virginia. Our honored State has ever maintained that our Federal system was a confederation of sovereign powers, not a consolidation of States into one people, and, as a consequence, whenever a State considered the compact broken, and in a manner to endanger her safety, such State stood remitted, as in sovereign right, to determine for herself, and under no responsibility, save to the opinion of the civilized world, both the mode and measure of redress." [82]

[81] Speech at Augusta, Georgia, July 2, 1859. Henry Cleveland, ed., *Stephens in Public and Private with Letters and Speeches*, 649.

[82] Virginia Mason, *Life and Correspondence of James M. Mason*, 158-159.

PRINCIPLE OF SOUTHERN INDEPENDENCE

Unlike the right of revolution which had lain dormant since officially proclaimed in the Declaration of Independence, the dispute over the nature of the Union had never been allowed to die in any decade since the new government was put into operation. Oddly enough, the first official statement of what came in 1860-1861 to be the accepted Southern doctrine on this point, was also drafted by the sage of Monticello and adopted in the very month and year in which James M. Mason was born. For Mason was less than two weeks old when the Kentucky Legislature on November 16, 1798, passed resolutions written by Jefferson asserting "that the several States composing the United States of America, are not united on the principle of unlimited submission to their general government; but that by compact under the style and title of a Constitution for the United States and of amendments thereto, . . . that to this compact each State acceded as a State, and is an integral party, its co-States forming, as to itself, the other party: . . . that as in all other cases of compact among parties having no common Judge, each party has an equal right to judge for itself, as well of infractions as of the mode and measure of redress." [83]

Beginning with this early concept of the nature of the Union as a justification for opposing the Alien and Sedition Acts, there had come out of the South, and within the span of a single lifetime, a most remarkable succession of ideas for minority protection, strengthened by, if not dependent upon, the doctrine of state sovereignty and its concomitant attributes. There was no necessary connection between the doctrine of state sovereignty as used in the sixties to justify independence and the doctrine of state rights as advanced during the first three decades of the Union in behalf of local self-government; yet in the early period state sovereignty was repeatedly used to support state rights.

[83] William MacDonald, ed., *Documentary Source Book* (3 ed.), 268.

THE SOUTH AS A CONSCIOUS MINORITY

In 1803, St. George Tucker of Virginia attached to his *Blackstone's Commentaries* an appendix of 237 pages entitled "View of the Constitution of the United States," in which he held that "the union is in fact, as well as in theory, an association of states, or, a confederacy"; and from this Tucker deduced the conclusion that each member "is still a perfect state, still sovereign, still independent, and still capable, should the occasion require, to resume the exercise of it's functions, as such, in the most unlimited extent." [84]

In 1819 and again in 1821, Spencer Roane in both of his series of articles to the *Richmond Enquirer* devoted by far the greater portion of his attack upon John Marshall and the Supreme Court to a concept of Union resting primarily upon "the States themselves in their highest political and sovereign authority." [85] Roane's loyal co-laborer, John Taylor, not only erected the structure of his concurrent state veto, as presented in the latter half of his *Tyranny Unmasked*, upon the foundation of state sovereignty, but he devoted his entire last volume, *A New View of the Constitution*, to the subject of state sovereignty as a logical basis for his other theories.

In the middle decades, the issue of state sovereignty was kept alive largely by the necessity of resorting to this doctrine as a justification for applying the theory of nullification. The congressional debates of the thirties, opening with the great contest between Daniel Webster and Robert Y. Hayne, abounded with arguments on the nature of the Union; and in view of the general constitutional opposition to the theory of nullification, it is somewhat surprising to find the Senate on January 12, 1838, resolving, in a consid-

[84] St. George Tucker, ed., *Blackstone's Commentaries*, I, Appendix, 141, 187. Of Tucker's view on state sovereignty, Alexander H. Stephens wrote that a "clearer or truer exposition of this feature of the Constitution of the United States was never made in fewer words." *A Constitutional View of the Late War between the States*, I, 505.

[85] The quotation is from the *Richmond Enquirer*, March 20, 1819, as found in *John P. Branch Historical Papers*, June, 1905, II, no. 1, 54.

eration of the slavery issue, that, "in the adoption of the Federal Constitution, the States adopting the same acted, severally, as free, independent, and sovereign States; and that each, for itself, by its own voluntary assent, entered the Union with the view to its increased security against all dangers." [86]

While Daniel Webster was facing Robert Y. Hayne and John C. Calhoun on the floors of Congress, Joseph Story was opposing Abel P. Upshur and Henry St. George Tucker in the workshop of the authors. In 1833, Joseph Story, then a professor in the Harvard Law School, had written his *Commentaries on the Constitution,* the main body of which was preceded by a discourse on the nature of the Union, historically considered. In reply to Story's nationalistic concepts, Abel P. Upshur came out in 1840 with a remarkable volume entitled, *Brief Enquiry into the True Nature and Character of Our Federal Government Being a Review of Judge Story's Commentaries on the Constitution of the United States.* It is perhaps the strongest historical analysis for the support of state sovereignty that has ever been written.

Three years after Upshur's work appeared, Henry St. George Tucker, a law professor, as was his father, St. George Tucker, at the University of Virginia, published his *Lectures on Constitutional Law for the Use of Law Classes at the University of Virginia* — an invaluable work, since, in addition to the author's own contributions, it presents copious extracts from the most pertinent contentions of Story and of Upshur. Calhoun, in the last years before his death, found time to restate his own ideas on the nature of the Union in his comprehensive *Discourse on the Constitution of the United States.*

The crisis of 1850 was particularly rich in its reiterations of the principle of state sovereignty; and though this crisis,

[86] *Congressional Globe,* 25 Cong., 2 sess., 98.

which might have led to separation, was averted by an appeal to the principle of constitutional guarantees, as a source of protection, the South Carolina Convention of 1852 restated the position which in substance a former convention in the State had taken just twenty years earlier, in these words: *"We, the people of the State of South Carolina, in Convention assembled, do declare and ordain, and it is hereby declared and ordained,* That South Carolina, in the exercise of her sovereign will, as an independent State, acceded to the Federal Union, known as the United States of America; and that in the exercise of the same sovereign will, it is her right, without let, hindrance, or molestation from any power whatsoever, to secede from the said Federal Union; and that for the sufficiency of the causes which may impel her to such separation, she is responsible alone, under God, to the tribunal of public opinion among the nations of the earth."[87]

Throughout the decade of the fifties — the era of constitutionalism — state sovereignty became the foundation-stone in the theory of the trusteeship of the territories, as advanced by Stephens, Quitman, and others. One of the strongest references to this foundation-stone is found in the words of Quitman on December 18, 1856: "The States of this Union are *States,* in every sense. I refer not only to the usual American sense of that word, but to the acceptation of the term as used by writers on the law of nations. They are separate political existences, each retaining within itself the entirety of its political sovereignty, and exercising the powers of government, in part, separately through its State government, and, in part, jointly with the other States, through

[87] *Journal of the State Convention of South Carolina of 1852,* 18-19. See also, Address to the people of South Carolina by their delegates in convention, *Journal of the South Carolina Convention of 1832,* 55. For numerous brief quotations and references on the subject of state sovereignty and the right of secession taken principally from the newspapers of this period, consult, A. C. Cole, "The South and the Right of Secession in the Early Fifties," *Mississippi Valley Historical Review,* December, 1914. I, 376-399.

the Federal Government, but all exercising their highest sovereign power only in convention, or such other mode as their constitution or organic law shall prescribe." [88]

Certainly, the South of the sixties was not advancing any new theory when it contended that there existed a constitutional right of secession based on the nature and character of the Federal Union. But even if Southern libraries, public and private, had not contained the works of Taylor, Upshur, Calhoun, and the Tuckers, the number of pamphlets issued in 1860-1861 alone would have sufficed to spread the doctrine of secession by the time the South was ready to make use of it in the stroke for Southern independence.

Among the pamphlets devoted to a study of the nature of the Union, there were the following: a thirty-two page pamphlet containing the *Speech of Louis T. Wigfall on the Pending Political Issues, Delivered at Tyler, Smith County, Texas, on September 3, 1860;* the twenty-four page pamphlet by W. D. Porter, entitled *State Sovereignty and the Doctrine of Coercion;* the ten-page pamphlet by "States" on *The Right to Secede;* the sixteen-page pamphlet under the caption *Address of the Hon. Charles L. Scott of California, to His Constituents on the Constitutional Right of Secession;* and still another by Albert Pike, *State or Province? Bond or Free? Addressed Particularly to the People of Arkansas.* In addition to these pamphlets, there were public letters, newspaper materials, prepared addresses, and almost constant debate in Congress after December 3, 1860, — all devoted largely to the constitutional implications of the stroke for independence.

Summarily considered, the constitutional justification for secession was directed in the first place to proving beyond question that the states were sovereign. Throughout the Ante-bellum Period, and especially in the sixties, this end had been accomplished to the satisfaction of the South by show-

[88] *Appendix to the Congressional Globe,* 34 Cong., 3 sess., 120.

ing in the words of Upshur "that the people of the several States, while in a colonial condition, were not 'one people' in any political sense of the terms; that they did not become so by the declaration of independence, but that each State became a complete and perfect sovereignty within its own limits; that the revolutionary government, prior to the establishment of the confederation, was, emphatically, a government of the States as such, through congress, as their common agent and representative, and that, by the articles of confederation, each State expressly reserved its entire sovereignty and independence . . . that the [present] Constitution is federative, in the power which framed it; federative in the power which adopted and ratified it; federative in the power which sustains and keeps it alive; federative in the power by which alone it can be altered or amended; and federative in the structure of all its departments." [89]

Strong as these early historical arguments in support of state sovereignty are — and in the opinion of the author they clearly outweigh the contentions of Story, Everett, and the other nationalists — to reproduce them here is entirely beyond the scope of this work; but it is significant that three of these historical arguments were included in the "Declaration of the Immediate Causes which Induce and Justify the Secession of South Carolina from the Federal Union." They were: first, that on July 4, 1776, the Declaration of Independence declared that the colonies "are, and of right ought to be, FREE AND INDEPENDENT STATES"; second, that on September 3, 1783, "His Britannic Majesty acknowledges the said United States, viz: New Hampshire, Massachusetts Bay, Rhode Island and Providence Plantations, Connecticut, New York, New Jersey, Pennsylvania, Delaware, Maryland, Virginia, North Carolina, South Carolina, and Georgia, to be FREE, SOVEREIGN AND INDEPENDENT

[89] A. P. Upshur, *Brief Inquiry into the Character of the Federal Government*   (1863 reprint), 54, 78.

STATES; that he treats with them as such"; third, that in 1788-1789, the existing Constitution was ratified by the states as states since any one of them by remaining outside might unquestionably have retained its separate sovereignty.[90]

Since it was well understood by the sixties that sovereignty represented supreme, indivisible, unlimited power in the state, the South might have been content, with L. M. Stone in the Alabama Convention of 1861, to rest its case on the fact that the right of secession "constitutes the very essence of State sovereignty, and is inseparable from it."[91] But in the hope of developing stronger *constitutional* arguments for secession, the Southern political philosopher of the sixties did evolve from the fundamental premise of state sovereignty, two concepts of the nature of the Union, depending upon the character of the Constitution: the international-law concept and the business-partnership concept. Under the first, the Constitution became a treaty; under the second, a compact; and in either case the right of secession was equally legitimate.

Senator Louis T. Wigfall thoroughly discussed the international-law concept, both in his address on September 3, 1860, at Tyler, Texas, and in his speech before the Senate on December 5, 1860. In the course of the latter, he said: "The United States Government can this day revoke the ratification of any treaty between her and Great Britain. If she does revoke the ratification of that treaty, that treaty ceases to be binding between the United States and Great Britain, and every citizen of the United States is released from any obligation to obey any single stipulation or article in that treaty. . . . When, then, one of these States revokes the treaty, as it is called in our platform — because the second Kentucky resolution says that it is a compact

---

[90] *Journal of the South Carolina Convention of 1860-1-2*, 461, 462.

[91] W. R. Smith, *Debates of the Alabama Convention of 1861*, 59.

under the style and title of a Constitution for the United States, to which each State acceded as a State, and a compact between nations is a treaty — if, then, one of these States shall revoke that treaty, resume all the powers which she had delegated to the Federal Government, and vest them in her own State government, that very instant, I say, the State is, by operation of law, out of the Union; her citizens cease to owe obedience to the laws of the United States; and she is, to all intents and purposes, a foreign Power." [92] In his former address, Wigfall declared that even though "the right to secede had not been reserved, it yet would have existed because *the States* are States, and because the right to make and revoke treaties, to form alliances, and dissolve them, to enter into compacts and to break them, is *an incident* that *belongs* to all *political communities*." [93]

But this international-law concept of the Constitution subjected the party or parties revoking the "treaty" to a declaration of war by the other party or parties to the "treaty" whenever, in the opinion of the latter, the excuse for revocation was not adequate. [94] The South of the sixties, therefore, followed its leaders of former decades by directing its energies chiefly to a development of the business-partnership theory of the nature of the Union, wherein the Constitution becomes a compact or business agreement between the states as partners for the promotion of the common welfare of all the members of the partnership. "The Federal Government," explained S. F. Hale, commissioner from Alabama to the Governor of Kentucky, "results from a Compact entered into between separate sovereign and independent States, called the Constitution of the United States, and

[92] *Congressional Globe,* 36 Cong., 2 sess., 13.

[93] *Speech of Louis T. Wigfall on the Pending Political Issues,* pamphlet, 17.

[94] "If the States feel justly offended because the seceding State has withdrawn from their alliance, they can treat her as a hostile neighbor, a nation with whom they have cause of war, and may follow her with all the means that the law of nations points out in cases of public war." "Langdon," "The Right of Peaceful Secession,"*1860 Association Tract no. 5,* pamphlet, 16.

Amendments thereto . . . Each State is bound in good faith to observe and keep, on her part, all the stipulations and covenants inserted for the benefit of other States in the Constitutional Compact — the only bond of Union by which the several States are bound together." [95]

To the support of the compact-theory, Albert Pike brought the words of James Madison, a father of the Constitution, as written to Spencer Roane in a letter dated June 29, 1821: "Our governmental system is established by a *compact,* not between the Government of the United States and the State *Governments,* but between THE STATES AS SOVEREIGN COMMUNITIES, *stipulating* EACH *with* THE OTHER a surrender of certain portions of their respective authorities, to be exercised by a common Government, and a reservation for *their* own exercise, of all the other authorities." [96] From this compact-theory of the Union, there developed at least five distinct justifications for the right of secession:

(1) Since there is no common arbiter to settle disputes between the partners to the compact — the government being only an agent of the parties or states — each partner must decide for himself when his interests have been so violated as to justify withdrawal from the partnership. "Our doctrine is . . . ," wrote W. D. Porter in 1860, "that inasmuch as the covenant or compact was between sovereigns, and there is no umpire or common interpreter between them, each has the right to judge for itself of infractions of the contract, and to determine for itself the mode and measure of redress." [97] Howell Cobb held the same view, though he best stated his opinions a decade earlier in the following

---

[95] W. R. Smith, *Debates of the Alabama Convention of 1861,* 375.
[96] As quoted in Albert Pike, *State or Province? Bond or Free?,* pamphlet, 16-17. The letter is found in Gaillard Hunt, ed., *Writings of Madison,* IX, 66. On the distinction between the federal compact and the social compact by which the states themselves were established, see St. George Tucker, ed., *Blackstone's Commentaries,* Appendix, I, 145.
[97] W. D. Porter, *State Sovereignty and the Doctrine of Coercion,* pamphlet, 6.

words: "Being a party to the compact, which the constitution forms, she [a state] has the right which all other parties to a compact possess to determine for herself when, where and how the provisions of that compact have been violated. It is equally clear that the other parties to the compact possess a corresponding right to judge for themselves, and there being no common arbiter to decide between them, each must depend for the justification of their course upon the justice of their cause, the correctness of their judgment and their power and ability to maintain their decision." [98]

(2) The failure of any member of the partnership to live up to the terms of the compact releases all the other members from the compact. "We maintain that in every compact between two or more parties," ran the South Carolina declaration of the immediate causes justifying secession, "the obligation is mutual; that the failure of one of the contracting parties to perform a material part of the agreement, entirely releases the obligation of the other; and that where no arbiter is provided, each party is remitted to his own judgment to determine the fact of failure, with all its consequences." [99] S. F. Hale explained to the Governor of Kentucky that the compact "when persistently violated by one party to the prejudice of her sister States, ceases to be obligatory on the States so aggrieved, and they may rightfully declare the compact broken, [and] the Union thereby formed, dissolved." [100]

Strangely enough, it was Daniel Webster, the great Northern expounder of the Constitution and defender of the

---

[98] U. B. Phillips, ed., *Correspondence of Toombs, Stephens, and Cobb,* American Historical Association, *Annual Report,* 1911, II, 257. This was a public letter to John Rutherford and others, dated August 12, 1850. See also the letter of William Rutherford, Jr. to Howell Cobb, April 16, 1850, II, 190; and the general letter of R. M. T. Hunter to James R. Micou and others, November 24, 1860, published in the *Richmond Enquirer,* December 12, 1860.
[99] *Journal of the South Carolina Convention of 1860-1-2,* 463.
[100] W. R. Smith, *Debates of the Alabama Convention of 1861,* 375.

Union, who contributed the most striking analysis of this second justification for secession under the compact-theory. Speaking in defense of the compromise measures of 1850, at Capon Springs, Virginia, Webster in 1851, the year before his death, uttered words which became a boomerang for his cause when used to advantage by the Southern secessionists of the sixties: "How absurd it is to suppose that, when different parties enter into a compact for certain purposes, either can disregard any one provision, and expect, nevertheless, the other to observe the rest! . . . I have not hesitated to say, and I repeat, that, if the Northern States refuse, willfully and deliberately, to carry into effect that part of the Constitution which respects the restoration of fugitive slaves, and Congress provide no remedy, the South would no longer be bound to observe the compact. A bargain can not be broken on one side, and still bind the other side." [101]

(3) The Federal Compact never had any legal existence since the parties did not agree upon its nature or its meaning. This "meeting of the minds" analogy to the business contract was the pet hobby of Albert Pike, who wrote in his pamphlet as follows: "If seven men agree to go into business together, and make a contract to that effect, and three of them hold that it is an ordinary partnership they have established, while the other four hold that it is a corporation — if such were the different understandings of the parties in framing the contract, perhaps on the principle that there is no contract unless the wills of the contracting parties agree, there would be *no* contract between them at all. It clearly could not be a mere partnership for part, and a corporation for part, of them. . . . This is precisely the case with the Union which is now being dissolved." [102]

[101] As quoted in Jefferson Davis, *Rise and Fall of the Confederate Government*, I, 167. Also quoted in R. M. T. Hunter, letter to James R. Micou and others, November 24, 1860. *Richmond Enquirer*, December 12, 1860.

[102] Albert Pike, *State or Province? Bond or Free?*, pamphlet, 6-7.

(4) A party may withdraw from the compact if reservations were made to that end at the time of acceptance. Here was a position widely supported in the sixties, and its chief sponsor was Louis T. Wigfall who first developed the idea in his speech at Tyler, Texas: "Virginia reserves the right to secede, or resume, whenever the granted powers are *perverted* to her *injury or oppression.* New York, and Rhode Island, *whenever it shall become necessary to their happiness;* whether there has been any *perversion* to their injury and oppression OR NOT. The right of secession is therefore as clearly a legal, peaceable, constitutional right, *as if it had been contained in the body of the Constitution itself,* in express words. Any conditions which one of the parties to a contract, may annex to it, at the time of its execution, become a part of it as fully as if they had been *originally written in the body of it,* and these conditions inure, not solely to the benefit of the party inserting them, but equally to all the others." [103]

Further discussing the principles of law involved, while addressing the Senate on December 5, Wigfall asked: "If a partnership is about to be entered into by individuals, and they refer it to an attorney, who is to draw up the articles of agreement, and when they come to sign it, and after it has been signed by some, one of the parties inserts above his signature an additional qualification, is there a court of justice in a civilized nation that will not hold that that new stipulation is as much a part of the compact as if it had been inserted in the body of it? Does it not inure to the benefit

<hr />

[103] *Speech of Louis T. Wigfall on the Pending Political Issues,* pamphlet, 15. The reservations of Virginia, New York, and Rhode Island, to which Wigfall refers may be found in Jonathan Elliot, ed., *Debates,* or in *Documents Illustrative of the Formation of the Union,* House Document no. 398, 69 Cong., 1 sess. Virginia: "We the delegates . . . declare and make known that the powers granted under the Constitution being derived from the People of the United States may be resumed by them whensoever the same shall be perverted to their injury" — p. 1027; New York: "We the Delegates . . . Do declare and make known . . . That the Powers of Government may be reassumed by the People, whensoever it shall become necessary to their Happiness" — p. 1034; Rhode Island (same as New York) — p. 1052.

of the party who has inserted it? . . . Does it not inure to the benefit of every other party who has signed that compact?" Then drawing the analogy, Wigfall pointed out that as soon as the ratifying convention of New York "in the very articles of ratification declared explicitly and expressly that they reserved to themselves the right to reassume the powers therein delegated whenever it should be necessary to their happiness," the right of secession immediately "became a perfect constitutional right on the part of New York, and it became also a perfect constitutional right on the part of every other State which, either previously or subsequently to that time, became a party to the compact." [104]

(5) The right to withdraw from the partnership is reserved in the tenth amendment to the compact itself. "It is nowhere made an offense against the new government for the State to resume its delegated powers," ran an 1860 Association Tract on *The Right of Peaceful Secession.* "Finding, then, neither grant by the States, nor prohibition to them, of their sovereign power to secede . . . it may well be deemed, this power remains in the people of the State. . . ." [105] A clearer exposition was presented by Jefferson Davis to the Senate, January 10, 1861: "All that is not granted in the Constitution belongs to the States; and nothing but what is granted in the Constitution belongs to the Federal Government; . . . where among the provisions of the Constitution do you find any prohibition on the part of a State to withdraw; and if you find [no such provision] . . . must not this power be in that great depository, the reserved rights of the States? How was it ever taken out of that source of all power to the Federal Government? It was not delegated to the Federal Government; it was not prohibited to the States; it necessarily remains, then, among the reserved powers of the States." [106]

[104] *Congressional Globe,* 36 Cong., 2 sess., 13.

[105] Tract no. 5, pamphlet, p. 15.
[106] *Congressional Globe,* 36 Cong., 2 sess.,

THE SOUTH AS A CONSCIOUS MINORITY

THE DEFENSE OF THE RIGHT OF NON-COERCION

To facilitate the stroke for independence, the Southern philosopher developed one other theory derived from the nature of the Union: the theory of non-coercion. Few principles of government have ever received more intensive consideration from every rank of society and in every walk of life than did this one during the six months immediately following the election of Abraham Lincoln in November, 1860. It was well that it should be so; for coercion applied to the South meant war, and war brought havoc and destruction in its train.

Sensing the impending crisis upon this issue, President Buchanan essayed to settle the controversy once for all in his general message to Congress on December 4, 1860. Unfortunately, he was to be as unsuccessful as Chief Justice Taney had been in his attempt to settle the slavery controversy through his opinion in the Dred Scott Case. Perhaps, too, the President was to be unsuccessful for the same reason; for Buchanan, like Taney, had taken the extreme South-

308. "I believe that it contravenes no provision of the Constitution, for one or more of the States to secede from the Union; not by virtue of any power conferred upon them by that instrument, but in consequence of the States never having surrendered it to the General Government: the Constitution declares that 'the powers not delegated to the United States by the Constitution are reserved to the States respectively, or the people.' I apprehend that it will be admitted that the States may exercise any or all of their reserved powers without a violation of the Constitution. If, then, they have never parted with their right to resume their original sovereignty, when, in their opinion, the Government becomes destructive of the ends for which it was instituted, it is no violation of the Constitution for them to secede." R. M. T. Hunter, January 15, 1861, as quoted in W. C. Fowler, *The Sectional Controversy,* 219. See further, Jno. S. Millson of Virginia, speech in the House, January 21, 1861. *Appendix to the Congressional Globe,* 36 Cong., 2 sess., 78; and R. M. T. Hunter, general letter to James R. Micou and others, November 24, 1860. *Richmond Enquirer,* December 12, 1860. The best discussion on this reserved rights theory of secession took place in the Virginia Convention of 1861. On March 9, the Committee on Federal Relations reported that unless Virginia received a satisfactory response to her requests, "she will feel compelled to resume the powers granted by her under the Constitution of the United States, and to throw herself upon her reserved rights." This part of the report was debated on April 9, and despite attempts to strike it out, the clause on reserved rights was adopted substantially as reported, by a vote of 81-41. *Journal of the Virginia Convention of 1861,* Appendix. Partial Report of the Committee on Federal Relations, p. 8, and Journal of the Committee of the Whole, pp. 72-81.

ern viewpoint, so that his interpretation of the doctrine of non-coercion could hardly have been expected to have met the acceptance of the Northern majority.

"Has the Constitution delegated to Congress the power to coerce a State into submission which is attempting to withdraw or has actually withdrawn from the Confederacy?" asked Buchanan. "If answered in the affirmative, it must be on the principle that the power has been conferred upon Congress to declare and to make war against a State. . . . It is manifest upon an inspection of the Constitution that this is not among the specific and enumerated powers granted to Congress, and it is equally apparent that its exercise is not 'necessary and proper for carrying into execution' any one of these powers. So far from this power having been delegated to Congress, it was expressly refused by the Convention which framed the Constitution." After further consideration, the President added: "Without descending to particulars, it may be safely asserted that the power to make war against a State is at variance with the whole spirit and intent of the Constitution." [107]

In its reference to the Federal Convention, this message provided the major clue for the defense of the right of non-coercion — a clue that led back to the opinions of the "fathers," who, let it be said here, were never permitted to sleep while the Constitution which they created and the Union which they established rocked upon the angry sea of secession. Time after time during the winter of 1860-1861, the ghostly forms of these noble men of 1787 stalked across the floors of Congress, while some diligent "savior of the South" re-uttered for them their words in the Federal Convention. Thus, Madison and Mason and Ellsworth and Hamilton paraded the aisles of the halls of Congress at the bidding of Senator Judah P. Benjamin of Louisiana on December 31, 1860; and they repeated their march for the

[107] J. D. Richardson, ed., *Messages and Papers*, V, 635, 636.

benefit of Representative John H. Reagan of Texas on January 15, 1861.[108]

As taken from Madison's Notes, these are in part the words of the fathers re-uttered in the Congress of 1860-1861 through the medium of Senator Benjamin: James Madison — "The use of force against a State would look more like a declaration of war than an infliction of punishment, and would probably be considered by the party attacked as a dissolution of all previous compacts by which it might be bound"; George Mason — "The most jarring elements of nature, fire and water, themselves, are not more incompatible than such a mixture of civil liberty and military execution. . . . Will not the citizens of the invaded State assist one another, till they rise as one man, and shake off the Union altogether?"; Oliver Ellsworth — "This Constitution does not attempt to coerce sovereign bodies, States, in their political capacity"; and Alexander Hamilton — "It has been observed, to coerce the States is one of the maddest projects that was ever devised. A failure of compliance will never be confined to a single State. . . . Can any reasonable man be well disposed toward a Government which makes war and carnage the only means of supporting itself — a Government that can exist only by the sword?" [109]

Aside from their work in Congress, these ghosts of the fathers were otherwise occupied in visiting the offices of editors, the desks of writers, the platforms of orators, the halls of state legislatures, and the floors of state conventions. Here are the resolutions introduced in the spirit of the fathers during the sessions of the Virginia Convention on a single day, February 16, 1861: (1) Resolved, "That since the decision of the Supreme Court of the United States in the

---

[108] *Congressional Globe,* 36 Cong., 2 sess., 212-217; 392-401.
[109] Speech in the Senate, December 31, 1860. *Ibid.,* 213, 214. But of the opinions of the "fathers" on slavery, Louis T.

Wigfall declared in the Senate, April 11, 1860: "It is twaddle to talk about the wisdom of our ancestors, and every man knows it." *Ibid.,* 36 Cong., 1 sess., 1658.

case of Chisholm *vs.* the State of Georgia, and the adoption of the eleventh amendment to the Constitution, we are at a loss to understand how the impression that the Federal Government possessed the power to coerce a State could have gained credence"; (2) Resolved, that if the United States undertakes to recapture the forts taken over by the seceding states, "Virginia will regard such acts as an invasion of the rights of sovereign States"; (3) Resolved, "That we will resist the coercion of the States which have so withdrawn, because there is no rightful power to use force against them under present circumstances." [110]

As an alternative to the use of force, Buchanan had suggested common consent and mutual goodwill as the only legitimate basis of a permanent Union. "The fact is," said the President, "that our Union rests upon public opinion, and can never be cemented by the blood of its citizens shed in civil war. If it can not live in the affections of the people, it must one day perish." [111] Here again the South was willing to follow the leadership of the President. Jefferson Davis, for example, maintained in the Senate, a few days after the President's message was delivered, that, in the absence of patriotism and affection as a bond of union between the sections, it would be "far better, instead of attempting to preserve a forced and therefore fruitless Union, that we should peacefully part and each pursue his separate course." [112] Everywhere the South displayed the slogan of consent to offset the Northern slogan of coercion. "The permanence and security of our Government," asserted L. M.

[110] *Journal of the Virginia Convention of 1861,* 45, 46. See also, pp. 51, 54, 62, 84, 85, 86, 100.
[111] J. D. Richardson, ed., *Messages and Papers,* V, 636. Interesting are the following words of Andrew Jackson coming after his experiences with South Carolina: "But the Constitution can not be maintained nor the Union preserved, in opposition to public

feeling, by the mere exertion of the coercive powers confided to the General Government. The foundations must be laid in the affections of the people." Farewell Address as President, March 4, 1837. *Ibid.,* III, 297.
[112] Speech on December 10, 1860. *Congressional Globe,* 36 Cong., 2 sess., 29.

Stone in the Alabama Convention, "depend alone upon the principle of common affection and common interest." [113]

The time came, however, when the mantle of leadership that Buchanan had thrown upon himself was to pass to other shoulders; for, on January 8, 1861, the President modified his original position to permit the use of force against a state for defensive purposes.[114] Immediately, Jefferson Davis took issue with the President's new position: "What power has the President to use the Army and the Navy except to execute process? . . . Are we to have sergeants sent over the land instead of civil magistrates? . . . when we trace our history to its early foundation, under the first two Presidents of the United States, we find that this idea of using the Army and the Navy to execute the laws at the discretion of the President, was one not even entertained, still less acted upon, in any case." [115]

The mantle which Buchanan discarded fell upon the shoulders of R. M. T. Hunter, who, on January 11, 1861, elaborately discussed the constitutional justification for the slogan of consent as an essential to the maintenance of the Union: "I proceed then, Mr. President, to make good my proposition, that this Federal Government cannot be carried on within the limits and jurisdiction of a State, without the assent, the aid, and the sympathy of its people. In the first place, it depends on the Legislatures of the different States to elect members of this body. If a majority of the States, although they might represent a small minority of the people, were to refuse to send Senators here, your Government is gone; you have lost one of the most important arms of the system; you have no longer a Senate. . . . Can you administer the judicial powers of this

[113] W. R. Smith, *Debates in the Alabama Convention of 1861*, 59. See Alexander H. Stephens, letter to Abraham Lincoln, December 30, 1860. Henry Cleveland, ed., *Stephens in Public and Private with Letters and Speeches*, 153; R. M. T. Hunter, speech in the Senate, January 11, 1861, *Congressional Globe*, 36 Cong., 2 sess., 330.
[114] J. D. Richardson, ed., *Messages and Papers*, V, 656.
[115] Speech in the Senate, January 10, 1861. *Congressional Globe*, 36 Cong., 2 sess., 307.

Government within a State if that State withdraws its assent and is determined to resist that administration? . . . Suppose a State repeals the penalties for murder as against the officers of the General Government; suppose it repeals the penalties for false imprisonment as against those officers; . . . if a State were to undertake to obstruct the course of Federal justice in that way, where would the remedy be found within the constitutional power of this Government? . . .

". . . To obtain the right of exclusive legislation within dock-yards, forts, arsenals, and other needful buildings, Congress must have, first, the consent of the States. That must be given under the Constitution. Suppose a State refuses its consent. Where would be your court-houses, your forts, your custom-houses? Where would you have the *locus in quo,* from which to administer the functions and the power of this General Government? Everywhere, if they were to refuse to give you this assent, you would be under State jurisdiction; and thus it would be in the power of the State constantly to thwart, obstruct, and prevent the administration of Federal justice, or the administration of Federal power, within her limits and jurisdiction . . . Sir, the only mode in which you could protect the administration of the Federal affairs and the Federal jurisdiction within the State, would be to set aside the State government by force, and to reduce it to a territorial condition; and then what would be the result? You first coerce a State because it secedes from thirty-two other members of this Confederacy; and you turn around and secede yourselves from it by reducing it from the condition of a State to the position of a Territory!" [116]

[116] *Ibid.,* 330-331. A most interesting continuation of the discussion over the theory of non-coercion is found in a speech by Stephen A. Douglas before the Senate on March 15, 1861. *Ibid.,* 1458. The position here taken by Douglas on the application of force against a state was cited with approval by Alexander H. Stephens, *History of the United States,* 615-617. Virginia's position on coercion is well treated in B. B. Munford, *Virginia's Attitude toward Slavery and Secession,* 263-300.

THE SOUTH AS A CONSCIOUS MINORITY

Under the new leader, the defense of the right of non-coercion went on unabated until the voices of opposing factions in Congress were drowned by the sound of opposing guns upon the battlefields. It was another case of action against words: the words of the Southern theorists were answered by an appeal to arms!

CHAPTER VII

APPLICATIONS IN THE CONFEDERATE CONSTITUTION

SIMULTANEOUSLY with the stroke for Southern independence there came a movement among the seceding states for union under a new constitution. The first official acts of secession themselves provided that delegates should be sent to Montgomery, Alabama, to draft a Southern Constitution and to institute a new system of government. Accordingly, these delegates, having been duly appointed, assembled at Montgomery on February 4, hurriedly drafted a provisional constitution and inaugurated a provisional government; then five days later, they selected a committee of two from each state represented to draft a permanent constitution.

After almost three weeks of intensive study, this committee on February 26 submitted its original draft of the Constitution to the convention, and for two weeks there followed on the convention floor a discussion of the clauses in the proposed instrument. Numerous suggestions for revision and amendment were advanced, but most of them were rejected. On March 11, the Constitution was unanimously adopted by the convention and immediately submitted to the states for ratification. Acting through conventions, the states lost little time in accepting the work produced at Montgomery, though the permanent government did not supersede the provisional one until the following year.

THE MODEL OF THE NEW CONSTITUTION

Writing apparently before the opening of the Montgomery Convention, Albert Pike, whose pamphlet contributed to the separation of Arkansas from the Union, urged that the Southern states represented in this Convention would fortunately "not have to *discover* the great principles of Constitutional Government" because these "are already embodied in our present great Charter; and the experience of seventy years has developed its few defects, and shown in what respects and how it needs amendments." [1] In recommending that the old Constitution become a model for the formation of the new one, Pike was expressing an opinion generally voiced throughout the South.

Nowhere was this opinion more pronounced than in the secession conventions of the Southern states. In the Alabama Convention, C. G. Whatley was "for establishing *speedily* another Government upon the basis of the old Federal Constitution"; [2] and in the Texas Convention A. P. Wiley would follow the old Constitution so closely as to warrant the title: "The Constitution of the *Southern* United States." [3] In the Louisiana Convention, a committee, having recommended the appointment of six delegates to Montgomery, *"Resolved,* That the delegates thus chosen are hereby instructed to urge upon said Convention to enter at once upon the formation of a Federal Union for the slaveholding States, and . . . to take as their guide the Constitution of the United States, and to conform as nearly as possible to it." [4]

Still wider acceptance of the Federal Constitution appeared in the formal acts of the state conventions. The South Carolina Convention requested its commissioners appointed to the other slaveholding states "to submit, on our part, the Federal Constitution as the basis of a Provisional

[1] Albert Pike, *State or Province? Bond or Free?*, pamphlet, 39-40.
[2] W. R. Smith, *Debates of the Alabama Convention of 1861*, 137. See also speech by William L. Yancey, p. 143; and the report of the Alabama Committee of Thirteen, *Journal of the Confederate Congress,* Senate Document 234, 58 Cong., 2 sess., I, 12.
[3] *Journal of the Texas Convention of 1861,* 33. Also see pp. 50, 74, 77.
[4] *Journal of the Louisiana Convention of 1861,* 12.

THE CONFEDERATE CONSTITUTION

Government"; [5] and the Mississippi Convention resolved in its ordinance of secession that "the people of the State of Mississippi hereby consent to form a federal union . . . upon the basis of the present Constitution of the said United States, except such parts thereof as embrace other portions than such seceding States." [6]

To what extent the framers of the new Constitution followed the wishes of their constituencies may be surmised from reports upon the product of their labors. With the work of framing the Constitution completed, the Texas delegation on March 13, 1861, wrote back to its constituents that the "convention have as will be seen adopted in the main the old constitution, making such amendments as give it the interpretation claimed by the South, and a few additions which we consider decided improvements." [7] Howell Cobb, president of the Convention, presented a certified copy of the Constitution to South Carolina with these words: "It will be seen that the Convention here have conformed to the general wish of the people of these States, in adopting a Constitution upon the general principles of the Constitution of the United States." [8]

"Let every man compare the new with the old," suggested the Texas Convention in its *Address to the People of Texas,*

[5] *Journal of the South Carolina Convention of 1860-1-2,* 482-483.

[6] *Journal of the Confederate Congress,* Senate Document 234, 58 Cong., 2 sess., I, 8. Likewise the Alabama Convention incorporated into its secession ordinance a provision that "it is the desire and purpose of the people of Alabama to meet the slaveholding States, who approve of such purpose, in order to frame a provisional or a permanent government, upon the principles of the Government of the United States." *Ibid.* And the Louisiana Convention, upon the recommendation of a committee, instructed its delegates to Montgomery "to aid in forming a Provisional Government on the basis of the Constitution of the United States." *Journal*

cf the Louisiana Convention of 1861, 19.

[7] *Journal of the Texas Convention of 1861,* 208. At the first regular meeting of the Montgomery Convention, C. G. Memminger proposed the formation of a temporary government "upon the basis of the Constitution of the United States," whereupon T. R. R. Cobb suggested that the provisional constitution create "a single executive head, with the powers of the President of the United States." *Journal of the Confederate Congress,* Senate Document 234, 58 Cong., 2 sess., I, 19, 20.

[8] *Journal of the South Carolina Convention of 1860-1-2,* 186. He used the same language in transmitting the Constitution to Texas. *Journal of the Texas Convention of 1861,* 209.

"and see for himself that we still cling to the old constitution made by our fathers." [9] Such a comparison does reveal striking similarities. Both instruments follow the same form, except that the bill of rights is incorporated into the main body of the Southern Constitution rather than attached in the form of amendments. Both have the same number of articles with the subject-matter arranged in the same order of sections and clauses. Only a change in terminology, an addition or omission of a clause, or a slight modification of phraseology distinguish the two instruments.

Why were the Southern states so anxious to adopt the Federal Constitution as a model for the constitution of their own Union? Whatever may be the more fundamental explanations, *expediency* was certainly one practical answer to the question. During the crisis of 1850, William F. Gordon had written R. M. T. Hunter the following lines: "I would take our present Federal Constitution for the Southern States and put it into operation, as soon as a sufficient number of States would secede, this would simplify matters, would prevent confusion, as the officers of our *Southern Republic,* would at once understand their duties, *our Sub Treasures,* are all ready, we should . . . have our government in full and immediate Vigor without the Delay of Forming a New Constitution, which, however we might do at our leisure." [10]

This sentiment was reiterated in the South Carolina Convention of 1860, wherein the Committee on Relations with the Slaveholding States reported that the Constitution of the United States "presents a complete scheme of confederation, capable of being speedily put into operation" and

[9] *Journal of the Texas Convention of 1861,* 259. The two Constitutions are arranged in parallel columns with the innovations of the Confederate Constitution in italics, in J. L. M. Curry's *Civil History of the Confederate States,* 274-302.

[10] C. H. Ambler, ed., *Correspondence of Hunter,* American Historical Association, *Annual Report,* 1916, II, 114.

that "a speedy confederation by the South is desirable in the highest degree, which it is supposed must be temporary at first (if accomplished as soon as it should be), and no better basis than the Constitution of the United States is likely to be suggested or adopted for temporary purposes." [11] Later, the demand for popular ratification of the permanent Constitution was refused in Alabama, asserted B. H. Baker in the Alabama Convention, because the "occasion calls for action — united, prompt, resolute, determined action." [12]

The term *expediency* must also be written large in the effect upon the border states to be derived from Southern adherence to the principles of the Federal Constitution. "One great and prime obstacle to the earlier movements of the border States in favor of secession," declared William L. Yancey in the Alabama Convention, "has been a widespread belief that the Gulf States designed in seceding, to establish a Government, differing essentially from the Federal Constitution . . . A Southern Confederacy, with the Federal Constitution slightly altered to suit an entirely slave-holding community, will be an invitation to Southern States, yet in the Union, to leave it and seek for peace and security and liberty within a Union, having no enemies — no irrepressible conflicts." [13] Whether with more leisure and less external pressure the framers of the new Constitution would have produced a radically different instrument remains to be surmised from what is to follow.

[11] *Journal of the South Carolina Convention of 1861*, 481. On November 11, 1859, L. Q. C. Lamar submitted to the Mississippi Legislature a complete plan of organization for a Southern Confederacy — one designed to avoid the evils of a provisional government. "The leading feature of that plan," so he wrote in December, 1860, "is the adoption of the present government, either by a general convention of Southern States or by commissioners appointed by their authority, who shall provide that the Constitution of the United States shall remain in full force and effect among the States withdrawing." Letter to P. F. Liddell, December 10, 1860. Edward Mayes, *L. Q. C. Lamar: His Life, Times, and Speeches*, 637.

[12] W. R. Smith, *Debates of the Alabama Convention of 1861*, 360. See also the speeches of L. M. Stone, 332 *et seq.* and of William L. Yancey, 139 *et seq.*

[13] *Ibid.*, 144.

THE SOUTH AS A CONSCIOUS MINORITY

THE NATURE OF THE UNION: A CONFEDERACY

The acceptance of the Federal Constitution as a model for the seceding states silenced at once those extremists, who, even under the existing circumstances, would have favored the establishment of a consolidated system with the component states exercising only such powers as were ceded to them at the will of the central government. This extreme position had been suggested in 1849 in a letter from a secessionist *per se*, Henry L. Benning, to Howell Cobb: "I think that as a remedy for the South, dissolution is not enough, and a Southern Confederacy not enough . . . The only thing that will do when tried every way is a *consolidated* Republic formed of the Southern States. That will put slavery *under the control of those most interested* in it, and nothing else will." [14]

So distinctly in a minority was the sentiment expressed by Benning that Senator Alfred Iverson estimated in Congress in 1861 that "there is not one man in a million, as far as I know and believe, in the State of Georgia, or elsewhere in the South, who would be in favor of any such principle." [15] And against the "one man in a million," as it were, the citizens of Upson County, Georgia, had, in 1860, directed an attack through resolutions to the state legislature, asserting that "we are uncompromisingly opposed to the overthrow of our present republican form of Government and the establishment in lieu thereof of a 'Constitutional monarchy' in these Southern States, as recommended by some of the advocates of immediate disunion." [16]

Short of complete consolidation, however, and even with the aid of a Federal Constitution as a model of government, there still remained unsettled the all-important problem of

---

[14] U. B. Phillips, ed., *Correspondence of Toombs, Stephens, and Cobb,* American Historical Association, *Annual Report,* 1911, II, 171.

[15] Speech in the Senate, January 10, 1861. *Congressional Globe,* 36 Cong., 2 sess., 311.
[16] A. D. Candler, ed., *Confederate Records of Georgia,* I, 65.

the true nature and character of the proposed Southern Union. Was this to be a Union of the people of the states separately considered? Or was this to be a Union of the people of the Southern states collectively considered? It was not to be expected that the wide divergence of opinion prevalent under the Federal Constitution should now be permitted to become a thorn in the side of the new government. Whatever the solution, the element of doubt must be eliminated.

No view concerning the proposed Union was more widely held than that it should be a union of states, or a Confederacy. South Carolina, the first to attempt separation, sent to the other states commissioners "respectfully inviting their coöperation in the formation with us of a Southern Confederacy"; [17] Georgia in a single sentence resolved that "it is the right and duty of Georgia to secede from the present Union, and to co-operate with such of the other States as have or shall do the same, for the purpose of forming a Southern Confederacy"; [18] the Louisiana Convention elected its delegates to Montgomery "to form a Southern Confederacy"; [19] and in the Alabama Convention, William L. Yancey asserted that a "Permanent Government for a Southern Confederacy was looked for by the friends of secession. . . . It was a part of the plan of secession and when the people decided for secession, they decided for a Southern Confederacy." [20]

One of the first motions to be introduced in the Montgomery Convention looked to the temporary establishment of a "Confederacy of the States which have seceded"; [21] and on a subsequent motion of Alexander H. Stephens, an en-

[17] *Journal of the South Carolina Convention of 1860-1-2*, 482.

[18] *Journal of the Georgia Convention of 1861*, 15, 20-23.

[19] *Journal of the Louisiana Convention of 1861*, 19.

[20] W. R. Smith, *Debates of the Alabama Convention of 1861*, 141.

[21] *Journal of the Confederate Congress*, Senate Document 234, 58 Cong., 2 sess., I, 19.

acting clause for all bills passed by the Congress of the temporary government was adopted to read: "The Congress of the Confederate States of America do enact." [22] The drafting committee of the permanent Constitution finally accepted the title "Confederate States of America" in preference to the name "Federal Republic" which was for a while in use;[23] and throughout the debates on the Constitution in the Convention, the new government to be established was almost invariably referred to as that of "the Confederate States" or else as that of "the Confederacy."

The Constitution itself throws conclusive light upon this point, for it is entitled "The Constitution of the Confederate States of America," and in its provisions the term *Confederate States* occurs sixty-four times, while the term *Confederacy* is found in eight different places. Thus the Constitution mentions "people of the Confederate States," "Congress of the Confederate States," "authority of the Confederate States"; and it refers to "any court of the Confederacy," members "to be admitted into this Confederacy," and "Territory not belonging to, this Confederacy." [24]

The structure of the Southern Confederacy was built upon the sovereignty of the states. In his opening address as president of the Montgomery Convention, Howell Cobb asserted: "We meet as representatives of sovereign and independent States"; [25] and it was in this language that the entire work of the Convention was conducted. Even in the preamble of the provisional constitution, the principle of state sovereignty was accepted in these terms: "We, the Deputies of the Sovereign and Independent States of South Carolina, Georgia, Florida, Alabama, Mississippi, and

[22] *Ibid.*, 68.
[23] T. R. R. Cobb Notes. A. H. Hull, "The Making of the Confederate Constitution," Southern Historical Association, *Publications*, IX, 290.
[24] Constitution of the Confederate States,

Journal of the Confederate Congress, Senate Document 234, 58 Cong., 2 sess., I, 909, 910, 912, 916, 921, 914.
[25] *Journal of the Confederate Congress*, Senate Document 234, 58 Cong., 2 sess., I, 16.

Louisiana. . . ." In place of this phraseology, the drafting committee of the permanent constitution substituted: "We, the people of the Confederate States, each State acting for itself, and in its sovereign and independent character. . . ." [26] This wording of the preamble led to a lively discussion on the floors of the Convention, but in the end the preamble was left as recommended by the drafting committee except for the omission of the words "for itself." T. R. R. Cobb, in his notes on the framing of the Constitution, maintained that the "Preamble of the Confederate Constitution holds unmistakably the sovereignty of the States and declares the Constitution to be a compact between them." [27]

In the body of the Confederate Constitution are two brief additions to clauses incorporated from the Federal Constitution, which, in themselves, establish the location of sovereignty in the separate states. To the old provision in the Federal Constitution that "the enumeration in the Constitution of certain rights, shall not be construed to deny or disparage others retained by the people," the Confederate Constitution added the brief phrase "of the several States"; and, while the former Constitution provided that "powers not delegated to the United States by the Constitution, nor prohibited by it to the States, are reserved to the States respectively, or to the people," the latter reserved such power to the states or to the people "thereof." [28] The far-reaching significance of these additional words, in the light of the historic dispute which preceded and accompanied the stroke for Southern independence, is too obvious to require further explanation.

Moreover, the states in ratifying the Southern Constitu-

[26] *Ibid.*, 899, 852, 909. In the permanent Constitution the names of the states had to be omitted, since it was not known what states would come into the Confederacy.
[27] A. H. Hull, "The Making of the Confederate Constitution," *Southern Historical Association, Publications,* IX, 291.
[28] Federal Constitution, Amendments IX and X. Confederate Constitution, Art. VI, sec. 5, 6.

tion considered themselves to be acting in their sovereign and independent capacity. The Georgia resolutions of ratification specifically so state,[29] while the Texas act of ratification ran as follows: "We, the deputies of the people of Texas, representing the independent sovereignty of the State, do hereby approve, accept and ratify the said constitution." [30]

If the doctrine of state sovereignty disclosed the true character of the Southern Confederacy, did it follow that the right of secession was inherent in the very nature of state sovereignty? Under the old Constitution, the South had given an emphatic answer in the affirmative; but now, under the new Constitution, this issue was consciously evaded until some future time. In the Montgomery Convention, three distinct proposals were advanced to provide expressly in the Constitution for the right of secession from the Southern Union. W. W. Boyce of South Carolina proposed that "the right of secession of any State from this Confederacy is expressly admitted, to be exercised by any State according to its pleasure." [31] James Chesnut, Jr., from the same state offered the following: "The right of a State to secede from the Confederacy shall not be denied. And whenever any State, through a convention of its people, shall dissolve the connection between it and its confederates, it shall be the duty of the President to withdraw all forces from within the territorial limits of such State, and permit it peacefully to withdraw." [32]

The most elaborate proposal for the right of secession was an amendment introduced by B. H. Hill of Georgia in these words: "When any State shall desire to withdraw

[29] *Journal of the Georgia Convention of 1861,* 188.
[30] *Journal of the Texas Convention of 1861,* 234. See also, L. Q. C. Lamar, address on "The State of the Country, at Home and Abroad," delivered on April 14, 1864, in the Atheneum, Atlanta, Georgia. Edward

Mayes, *L. Q. C. Lamar: His Life, Times, and Speeches,* 652.
[31] *Journal of the Confederate Congress,* Senate Document 234, 58 Cong., 2 sess., I, 873.
[32] *Ibid.,* 877.

from this Confederation, such desire shall be communicated to the Congress of the Confederate States, through a convention of the people of such State, specifically setting forth the causes of such desire to withdraw. Congress shall consider of such alleged grievances, and, on failure to redress or accommodate the same, to the satisfaction of the complaining State and of the Confederate States, shall arrange with such State an equitable division of the public property, and a peaceable withdrawal from the Confederation." Upon withdrawing from the Confederacy, each state was "to pay a due proportion of the public debt existing at the time of such withdrawal," and also "to account with the Confederate States for all expenditures made, or liabilities incurred by the Confederate States, in acquiring, securing, fortifying or defending the territory or jurisdiction of such State." [33]

In spite of these proposals, the Confederate Constitution contains no provision on the right of secession. Indeed, so far as the records show, no one of the three propositions was even discussed by the other members of the Convention. If secession were a right, it was left to be implied from the recognition of state sovereignty. This implication, which did not satisfy certain members of the Montgomery Convention, likewise was considered inadequate by a minority element in the state ratifying conventions. In the Louisiana Convention, Joseph A. Razier introduced a resolution, reading in part: "to prevent misunderstandings, and to secure harmony in future: *It is further ordained by the People of the State of Louisiana in Convention assembled,* That in adopting the Constitution of the Confederate States of America, the sovereign State of Louisiana does expressly reserve to herself the right, peaceably to withdraw from the Union created by that Constitution, whenever, in the judgment of her citizens, her paramount interest may require

[33] *Ibid.,* 877.

it." [34] In the North Carolina Convention, a similar motion was introduced expressing the right of a state to secede whenever in her opinion the powers conferred on the Confederate States should be perverted to her injury; [35] and in the South Carolina Convention, J. I. Middleton proposed to add to the reserved power clause of the Constitution these words: "all the powers hereinbefore delegated to the Confederate States, may, at any time, be resumed by any one of them." [36] All of these measures met a similar fate: the Louisiana motion was tabled by a vote of 92-11; the North Carolina proposal received only 26 favorable votes from a total of 114 votes cast; and by the overwhelming majority of 114-12, the South Carolina proposal was tabled.

Elsewhere in the Southern state conventions, the right of secession was apparently presupposed; for, on that basis, both the provisional and the permanent constitutions were attacked. Thus, S. McD. Moore in the Virginia Convention opposed the provisional Constitution of the Confederacy because the right of secession at pleasure "makes the government formed by the wisest and best men the world ever saw, a mere rope of sand." [37] In the Alabama Convention, A. Kimball raised similar objections: "if the old Government so formed, was a failure, where is the additional guarantee that this one is not also a failure? Is this stronger than the older one? This Government claimed the right of separate State secession, and by that process, dissolved the old one; then here is the precedent, and any State of this new Government may, with a less reason, destroy the present at pleasure." [38] Between the critics fearing the danger of secession and the critics demanding the express right of secession, the South assumed a position of neutrality, preferring

[34] *Journal of the Louisiana Convention of 1861*, 75.
[35] K. P. Battle, "Legislation of the Convention of 1861," *James Sprunt Historical Monographs*, no. 1, pp. 102, 103.
[36] *Journal of the South Carolina Convention of 1860-1-2*, 260.
[37] *Speech in the Convention*, pamphlet, 18.
[38] W. R. Smith, *Debates of the Alabama Convention of 1861*, 326.

to await future developments for a solution of this problem.

Again, if the states were sovereign, what importance must be attached to the phrase in the preamble "in order to form a permanent federal government," or what is to be considered the significance of the clause on the supremacy of national laws, copied verbatim from the old Federal Constitution?[39] No record has come down of any discussion whatever in the Montgomery Convention on the significance of the permanent federal government idea. Either it was disregarded because of its place in the preamble, or else it was conceded that the permanence of the federal government depended upon good-will among the states as the bond of union, in contrast to the exercise of force against a state. The doctrine of non-coercion did receive some attention in the Convention, for C. G. Memminger there offered the following amendment to the original draft of the Constitution: "Upon the demand of the convention of any State, all troops under the authority of the Confederate States which may be within any fort or ceded place within such State shall forthwith be removed, except when the Confederate States are in actual war with a foreign power."[40] There also B. H. Hill of Georgia proposed as an alternative to the use of force against a recalcitrant state that "if any State shall fail or refuse to conform to a decision of the court . . . the Congress of the Confederate States may withdraw from such States all or any portion of the privileges and benefits of this Confederation, without releasing such State from the duties and obligations thereof."[41] Neither of these propositions was accepted: like the right of secession, the right of non-coercion was left unsettled. The govern-

[39] "This Constitution, and the Laws of the United States which shall be made in Pursuance thereof; and all Treaties made, or which shall be made, under the Authority of the United States, shall be the supreme Law of the Land; and the Judges in every State shall be bound thereby, any Thing in the Constitution or Laws of any State to the Contrary notwithstanding." Article VI, both Constitutions.

[40] *Journal of the Confederate Congress,* Senate Document 234, 58 Cong., 2 sess., I, 873.

[41] *Ibid.,* 877.

ment was to be permanent, but, by what process, the future was to determine.

On the clause recognizing the supremacy of national laws, the interpretation of the "fathers" is left equally in doubt. John Gregg of Texas proposed to the Convention some detailed change in the clause, but the alteration did not modify the strength of the provision, nor was it in any case adopted.[42] Perhaps the supremacy of national law was deemed compatible with state sovereignty inasmuch as national laws were now to be exercised over a limited range of securely protected powers not subject to abuse by the central government. This is only a suggestion, however, for the whole question of the attributes and consequences of state sovereignty was left to be determined when the occasion for their exercise should arise. And the necessity for resorting to the concomitant rights of state sovereignty depended upon adequate protection to minorities within the Southern Confederacy. Just as in the old Union, so here, this minority protection might be guaranteed through the maintenance of constitutional limitations, the establishment of a concurrent voice in the central government, or a broad application of the principle of local self-government. To these problems the framers of the Confederate Constitution turned with more frankness of conviction and certainty of purpose.

The Enforcement of Constitutional Guarantees

The last adopted source of Southern protection within the old Union — reliance upon constitutional guarantees — had failed largely for the lack of power in the hands of a Southern minority to retain the constitutional limitations originally imposed upon the Northern majority in control of the government. To render this source of minority protection effective, the framers of the Confederate Constitu-

[42] *Ibid.*, 888.

tion, interested in protecting their own minorities, sought to provide some remedy for the defects that had been disclosed in the old Union. There, as we have seen, difficulties had arisen both from the power of the majority to expand national functions indefinitely through the door of implied powers without ever resorting to the constitutional amending process, and from the impotence of the minority to initiate constitutional amendments questioning the constitutionality of "assumed" powers exercised by the national government.[43]

. In providing a remedy for these defects, the Confederate fathers began by imposing the same general principles of constitutional limitations upon national activities as had existed in the old Union under the Federal Constitution. The central government was given only the delegated powers enumerated in the Constitution, to which new powers might be added only by constitutional amendments requiring for their ratification an extra-majority vote of the member states. To be sure there were to be implied powers; but it is surprising to find the old "necessary and proper" clause incorporated verbatim into the new Constitution. This was done doubtless in the confidence that its construction, now wholly in the hands of Southern judges, would be confined to justify only those implied powers without which the delegated powers would be useless. Nevertheless, the possibility of destroying constitutional limitations through the expansion of implied powers led the separate Southern states, as possible future minorities, to seek further protection.

The proposal that a single state might remain in the Confederacy and still refuse to obey national laws did not meet with approval in the Montgomery Convention. This proposal was rejected by the drafting committee of the permanent Constitution;[44] and during the subsequent debates in

[43] *Cf. supra.*, pp. 130-141.
[44] T. R. R. Cobb Notes. A. H. Hull, "The Making of the Confederate Constitution," Southern Historical Association, *Publications*, IX, 290.

the convention, B. H. Hill introduced for adoption a definite constitutional provision that "No State, while remaining a member of this Confederation, shall nullify or refuse to obey this Constitution, or any law passed by the Congress of the Confederate States." [45] This position is not surprising, however; for not even Calhoun had maintained that a single state might remain in the Union and refuse to obey national laws, though his theory was sometimes misinterpreted in this light.

Two other interesting suggestions to provide greater security for minorities through the maintenance of constitutional limitations were presented to the Montgomery Convention. One, the proposal of W. W. Boyce of South Carolina, offered this solution: "That while a State remains in the Confederacy, the decisions of the Supreme Court of the Confederate States on constitutional questions shall be conclusive in all cases capable of decision by legal process. That in such cases as do not admit of decision by legal process, a convention of all the States shall be assembled, in which convention the decision of the majority of the States shall be conclusive, subject only to the right of secession of the State or States dissatisfied." [46] Of course the advantages to minorities in this provision depended in the first instance upon an interpretation of "cases capable of decision by legal process." But once having defined legal questions, as contrasted with political questions, the proposition did guarantee to minorities greater solemnity of procedure and better opportunity for expression of minority opinion in the final determination of political questions.

The other suggestion came from B. H. Hill of Georgia and was stated in these terms: "Any State, by a convention of the people of such State, shall have the right to demand

[45] *Journal of the Confederate Congress,* Senate Document 234, 58 Cong., 2 sess., I, 876. The proposal was not adopted. [46] *Ibid.,* 873.

an issue to try the constitutionality of any law of the Congress of the Confederate States. Such issue shall be tried in a manner to be prescribed by Congress, by a court to be composed of the judges of the Supreme Court of the Confederate States, and of the chief justice of the State demanding the issue." The decision of this special court was to be final.[47] Though offering some additional protection to minorities, neither this proposal nor the one suggested by W. W. Boyce received favor from the Convention.

Thirty years earlier, John C. Calhoun had attempted to meet this difficulty of enforcing constitutional limitations against the unwarranted expansion of implied powers by giving to the minority the power of initiating constitutional amendments involving the exercise of doubtful powers. Though the South had rejected this theory as out of harmony with its means of protection in the thirties and destructive of its reliance upon the slavery clauses of the Constitution in the fifties, the Montgomery Convention now adopted the principle, in part at least, by giving to any three states in the Confederacy the power to call a Southern convention for the consideration of constitutional amendments. The exact wording of this interesting revision of the old Federal amending clause is as follows: "Upon the demand of any three States, legally assembled in their conventions, the Congress shall summon a convention of all the States, to take into consideration such amendments to the Constitution as the said States shall concur in suggesting at the time when the said demand is made; and should any of the proposed amendments to the Constitution be agreed on by the said convention — voting by States — and the same be ratified by the legislatures of two-thirds of the several States, or by conventions in two-thirds thereof — as the one or the other mode of ratification may be proposed by the general

[47] Ibid., 877.

convention — they shall thenceforward form a part of this Constitution." [48]

While this provision did not go so far as Calhoun had suggested, the power granted to a minority of three states to initiate the amending process — both by demanding the call of a constitutional convention and by formulating the only amendments to be considered in that convention — was, nevertheless, a powerful weapon of protection not found in the old Federal Constitution, and one that was considered adequate for securing to minorities the maintenance of constitutional limitations.

The best explanation of this provision is found in an address on the Confederate Constitution by Robert H. Smith of Alabama. In the absence of an adequate account of the proceedings in the Montgomery Convention, this valuable discourse composing twenty-four finely printed pamphlet pages is decidedly the most exhaustive and authoritative source of information on the proper interpretation to be given the new clauses in the Confederate Constitution. On the amending clause in question, this address contains the following comment: "The restrictions thrown around amendments to the organic law by the Constitution of the United States proved to be a practical negation of the power to alter the instrument. Discontent, however loud or well founded, was sure to receive no heed in advance from two-thirds of both Houses of Congress, or from two-thirds of the Legislatures of the several States; and, without a concurrence of such, no body could be assembled even to consider the complaints of members of the Union. Hence, restlessness when once created, could not be allayed, and a wound once inflicted on the body of a State never healed, but festered into a chronic and incurable complaint. The

---

[48] Confederate Constitution, Art. V. All quotations from the Confederate Constitution are taken from the draft in the *Journal of the Confederate Congress*, Senate Document 234, 58 Cong., 2 sess., I, 909-923.

substituted provision imparts a wholesome flexibility to our Constitution and, at the same time, assures us against an assembling of the States for light or transient causes, or hopeless purposes, and the consultative body, when convened, will be confined to action on propositions put forth by three States." [49]

THE APPLICATION OF THE CONCURRENT VOICE

The principle of the concurrent voice in law-making and law-enforcement presented the same possibilities of application in the Confederate Constitution as in the Federal Constitution. Some changes had been made in the check-and-balance principle; but the structural organization of the three departments, with each possessing powers of restraint upon the other two, remained largely as in the American Union. There were three innovations in procedure, however, which provided additional effective minority checks upon the process of law-making. In the first place, Congress, though given the power to tax exports, could do so only "by a vote of two-thirds of both Houses." Secondly, the admission of new states into the Union required an extra-majority vote, for the constitution specified that "Other States may be admitted into this Confederacy by a vote of two-thirds of the whole House of Representatives and two-thirds of the Senate, the Senate voting by States." Finally and most important, there existed a minority check upon national appropriations set forth in the constitutional requirement that "Congress shall appropriate no money from the treasury except by a vote of two-thirds of both Houses, taken by yeas and nays." [50] Each of these three innovations gave a minority of over one-third a positive check upon action by the

[49] Address to the People of Alabama, March 30, 1860. R. H. Smith, *Address on the Constitution*, pamphlet, 14-15. Smith was a member of the Montgomery Convention from Alabama.

[50] Confederate Constitution, Art. I, sec. 9, cl. 6; Art. IV, sec. 3, cl. 1; Art. I, sec. 9, cl. 9. There were exceptions to the two-thirds vote for appropriations.

Confederate Congress, whenever the subjects named were involved in legislative consideration.

THE PRINCIPLE OF LOCAL SELF-GOVERNMENT

By far the greatest efforts for minority protection within the Southern Confederacy were directed to a broad application of the principle of local self-government. In the Confederate Constitution, as in the old Federal instrument, this application was expressed in terms of state rights. And state rights, rather than state sovereignty, was the issue openly exhausted in all of its ramifications and publicly supported with every opportunity of its application.

The constitutional provisions insuring a greater degree of local autonomy than existed in the old Federal Union were of two classes: those further restricting the activities of the central government, and those further expanding the reserved powers of the states. The provisions of the first class might well be surmised from the Southern defense of local autonomy in the old Federal Union. The vigorous attacks there ineffectively directed against the "general welfare" clauses were now effectively concluded by the exclusion of both these clauses from the terms of the Confederate Constitution. The phrase "promote the general welfare" was stricken from the preamble, and the power of the old Federal Congress "To lay and collect Taxes, Duties, Imposts and Excises, to pay the Debts and provide for the common Defence and general Welfare of the United States" became for the new Confederate Congress the power "To lay and collect taxes, duties, imposts, and excises, for revenue necessary to pay the debts, provide for the common defence, and carry on the government of the Confederate States." [51]

Internal improvements and national bounties were also now effectively restricted, where not prohibited entirely. In

[51] Art. I, sec. 8, cl. 1, both Constitutions.

the Montgomery Convention this fight for restriction or prohibition was led by Robert Toombs of Georgia and by R. B. Rhett of South Carolina. The success of these men may be measured by the clauses of the first Article of the new Constitution additional to those found in the first Article of the old Constitution. To the old congressional power over commerce was now added this important restriction: "but neither this, nor any other clause contained in this constitution, shall ever be construed to delegate the power to Congress to appropriate money for any internal improvement intended to facilitate commerce; except for the purpose of furnishing lights, beacons and buoys, and other aids to navigation upon the coasts, and the improvement of harbors and the removing of obstructions in river navigation, in all which cases, such duties shall be laid on the navigation facilitated thereby, as may seem necessary to pay the costs and expenses thereof." [52] And to the old taxing-power was added the new restriction that "no bounties shall be granted from the treasury; nor shall any duties or taxes on importations from foreign nations be laid to promote or foster any branch of industry." [53]

How accurately these provisions reflected Southern political thought in the old Union may be gathered from the explanation given by Robert H. Smith in the address already noted: "Holding steadily in view the principle that the great object of the Federal Government is to perform national functions and not to aggrandize or depress sectional, or

[52] Confederate Constitution, Art. I, sec. 8, cl. 3. Robert Toombs who had devoted a large part of his congressional career in the old Union to restrictions on appropriations, once declared: "as a fundamental principle of human justice, I will apportion all the burdens of the Government on the persons who get the benefits, as exactly and equally as I can. Though it be imperfect, if I am legislating to that point I am legislating justly; and if I depart from it I am legislating un-

justly." Speech in the Senate, May 25, 1858. *Congressional Globe*, 35 Cong., 1 sess., 2384. On this point, see Jefferson Davis, speech in the Senate, March 1, 1851. *Appendix to the Congressional Globe*, 31 Cong., 2 sess., 338-341; and Alexander H. Stephens, speech at Atlanta, Georgia, March 21, 1861. Henry Cleveland, ed., *Stephens in Public and Private with Letters and Speeches*, 719-720.

[53] Confederate Constitution, Art. I, sec. 8, cl. 1.

local, or individual interests, and adhering to and enforcing the doctrine that a people should be left to pursue and develope their individual thrift without direct aids or drawbacks from Government, and that internal improvements are best judged of, and more wisely and economically directed by the localities desiring them, even when they legitimately come within the scope of Federal action, and knowing that, as the regulation of commerce was one of the chief objects of creating the, Government, and that under this power lurked danger of sectional legislation and lavish expenditure, the Constitution denies to Congress the right to make appropriations for any internal improvement, even though intended to facilitate commerce, except for the purpose of furnishing lights, beacons, buoys and other aids to navigation upon the coasts, and the improvement of harbors and the removing of obstructions in river navigation; and the cost and expenses of even these objects must be paid by duties levied on the navigation facilitated." Through this process, added Smith, fruitful sources of discord are cut off "by abolishing the hot-house system of imparting artificial heat and growth to chosen localities, at the expense of others, through bounties, navigation and tariff and internal improvement laws." [54]

Slight variations in the phraseology of the powers of the Confederate Congress, as contrasted with those of the Federal Congress, established further limitations upon the legislative branch of the new government. Whereas, the Federal Congress had possessed "all legislative Powers herein granted," the Confederate Congress was given "all legislative powers herein delegated." And whereas the American Congress had been granted power "to establish Post Offices and post Roads," the Southern Congress was delegated power "to establish post-offices and post-routes." [55]

[54] R. H. Smith, *Address on the Constitution*, pamphlet, 11-12.

[55] Art. I, sec. 1; Art. I, sec. 8, cl. 7, both Constitutions.

Thus, in the former Union, Congress had the authority to, build roads under its power to transmit the mails, but in the Confederacy, Congress might only designate the routes over which mail was to be carried.

The Confederate judiciary was also subject to limitations not imposed upon the judicial department of the old national government; for the framers of the Confederate Constitution, in keeping with Southern demands for judicial restrictions in the old Union, refused to extend jurisdiction to the Confederate Courts in cases "between Citizens of different States." [56] The fathers did not go so far, however, as to prevent appeals from the state courts to the Supreme Court of the Confederacy. In the Texas Convention, Hays had introduced the following resolution against such appeals: "Whereas the enlargement of the powers of the federal judiciary of the late United States, so as to embrace matters purely local and properly within the cognizance of the State tribunals, was a gross abuse of the federal system, Resolved . . . that the jurisdiction of the federal courts of the Confederate States shall be so defined and restricted by law as to avoid a repetition of such abuses; and more especially . . . that said courts should not be permitted to exercise appellate jurisdiction over the State courts in any case whatever." [57]

The substance of this resolution was considered by the framers of the Confederate Constitution, with closely divided opinions. In the drafting committee, R. W. Walker of Alabama had introduced an amendment "denying to the Supreme Court appellate jurisdiction over the State Courts," but the motion had been lost there.[58] The issue was raised again on the floor of the Convention when, on March 7, C. G. Memminger of South Carolina proposed that the

[56] Art. III, sec. 2, cl. 1, both Constitutions.
[57] *Journal of the Texas Convention of 1861*, 194.
[58] T. R. R. Cobb Notes. A. H. Hull, "The Making of the Confederate Constitution," Southern Historical Association, *Publications*, IX, 289-290.

"appellate jurisdiction of the Supreme Court shall not extend to any case which shall have been adjudged in any court of a State." [59] On the final vote, which was cast by states, this amendment was lost only through a tie, although twenty-three of the forty-two individual members voting were for its adoption.[60]

Other constitutional innovations from the old federal distribution of powers expressly broadened the sphere of state rights. Whereas, under the Federal Constitution, no state without the consent of Congress was permitted to lay a duty on tonnage, the Confederate Constitution permitted the tax "on sea-going vessels, for the improvement of its rivers and harbors navigated by the said vessels." [61] The Southern Constitution makes exception to the prohibition on interstate contracts found in the National Constitution; for the Confederate Constitution provides that "when any river divides or flows through two or more States, they may enter into compacts with each other to improve the navigation thereof." [62]

A further enlargement of the sphere of state rights gave to the member states of the Confederacy a certain concurrent power of impeachment of its national officers; for, under the Confederate Constitution, the lower House of Congress did not possess the sole power of impeachment as did its counterpart in the Federal Union. Instead, the Confederate Constitution provides that "any judicial or other Federal officer, resident and acting solely within the limits of any State, may be impeached by a vote of two-thirds of both branches of the Legislature thereof." [63] In explaining this provision, Robert H. Smith asserted that the conduct of a

[59] *Journal of the Confederate Congress,* Senate Document 234, 58 Cong., 2 sess., I, 880.

[60] For the future history of this dispute in the Confederacy, see, S. D. Brummer, "The Judicial Interpretation of the Con-

federate Constitution," in *Studies in Southern History and Politics,* pp. 107-133.

[61] Art. I, sec. 10, cl. 3, both Constitutions.

[62] *Ibid.*

[63] Confederate Constitution, Art. I, sec. 2, cl. 5.

Federal officer acting wholly within a state could not be expected to fall under the observation of the nation at large. He likened this impeachment power to an inquest of a grand jury given to the states, which, he maintained, helped to prevent inferior judicial officers from becoming so independent of state and national authority as was likely under the United States Constitution.[64]

Furthermore, it should be noted that, under certain conditions, the states were now permitted to lay a tax on tonnage nor were they any longer prohibited from emitting bills of credit as in the Federal Union.[65] Through these additions to the reserved powers of the states, together with the added restrictions upon the sphere of the central government, the principle of local autonomy was presumably so thoroughly imbedded in the provisions of the Confederate Constitution as to guarantee adequate protection to minorities.

NEGRO SLAVERY: RECOGNITION, REGULATION, PROTECTION

"This was the immediate cause of the late rupture and present revolution," declared Alexander H. Stephens of negro slavery in 1861. "Jefferson in his forecast, had anticipated this, as the 'rock upon which the old Union would split.' He was right. What was conjecture with him, is now a realized fact." [66] The dominating place of the institution of negro slavery in the sectional controversy that finally led to the stroke for Southern independence may be determined from the importance attached to the recognition, control, and protection accorded this institution in the Southern Confederacy. If negro slavery were only a means to Southern independence, as was sometimes contended, then it would not matter to the South what became of the means when the

---

[64] R. H. Smith, *Address on the Constitution*, pamphlet, 21.
[65] Art. I, sec. 10, both Constitutions. For the subsequent application of local self-government, see F. L. Owsley, *State Rights in the Confederacy*.
[66] Speech at Savannah, Georgia, March 21, 1861. Henry Cleveland, ed., *Stephens in Public and Private with Letters and Speeches*, 721.

end was attained. But if adequate protection to negro slavery as the "peculiar" institution of the Southern states was the end of a political philosophy that had finally produced a justification for independence, then it was of prime importance to guarantee, through the provisions of the Confederate Constitution, that this institution should be unquestionably recognized, definitely controlled, and adequately protected.

The recognition of negro slavery in the Southern Confederacy was insured from the Southern reaction to the negro in the secession conventions of the several states. In the Alabama Convention, for instance, G. T. Yelverton, who considered slavery as a social, moral, and political blessing, demanded open recognition of the institution in these terms: "This question of Slavery is the rock upon which the Old Government split: it is the cause of secession. Let us leave it no longer doubtful, nor in a condition to bring our New Government into new troubles." [67] In its declaration of the causes of secession, the Texas Convention attacked the Northern section for proclaiming the equality of all men regardless of race or color: "We hold as undeniable truths that the governments of the various States, and of the Confederacy itself, were established exclusively by the white race, for themselves, and their posterity; that the African race had no agency in their establishment; that they were rightfully held and regarded as an inferior and dependent race, and in that condition only could their existence in this country be rendered beneficial or tolerable." [68]

Apparently the framers of the Confederate Constitution assumed the existence of negro slavery; for, in the Montgomery Convention, D. F. Kenner from Louisana spoke of

[67] W. R. Smith, *Debates of the Alabama Convention of 1861*, 229.
[68] *Journal of the Texas Convention of 1861*, 64. For one of the strongest statements on this point, see W. L. Harris, commissioner from Mississippi, Address to the Georgia Legislature, December 17, 1860. *Journal of the Mississippi Convention of 1861*, 202-207.

"impairing the right of property in negro slaves"; Thomas N. Waul from Texas, of the "importation of negroes born in Africa"; and W. P. Miles from South Carolina, of "the right of property in slaves of the African race." [69] The terminology of the instrument which these men produced itself affirmed unquestionable recognition of the institution; for, whereas, the Federal Constitution had omitted the express term *slavery* entirely, the Confederate Constitution used the word repeatedly. Representation and direct taxes were based on three-fifths of all *slaves;* no *slave* or other person escaping might be discharged from service; citizens may go into other states with their *slaves* and other property. Nor was the fact that the slave was also a negro omitted from the terminology of the Confederate Constitution, for the institution of *negro* slavery was to be recognized in the territories; property in *negro* slaves was not to be impaired; and the importation of negroes of the African race was to be prohibited.[70]

The recognition of a racial problem in the South had also been brought to light in the discussions at Montgomery concerning the relation between suffrage and citizenship. In attempting to define citizenship in the Confederacy, one of the "fathers" during the debates suggested "every free white citizen of any one of the Confederate States"; another wished to limit the rights of citizenship to free white citizens; and a third would exclude from citizenship any "persons having one-eighth or more of African blood in their veins." [71] Though the question of determining citizenship in the Confederacy was left to the separate states, the Con-

---

[69] *Journal of the Confederate Congress,* Senate Document 234, 58 Cong., 2 sess., I, 874, 869, 883.

[70] Confederate Constitution: Art. I, sec. 9, cls. 1, 4, sec. 2, cl. 3; Art. IV, sec. 2, cl. 3, sec. 3, cl. 3. "Where the old Constitution by 'other persons' *meant* slaves, the new Constitution boldly called them slaves."

T. R. R. Cobb's Notes. A. H. Hull, "The Making of the Confederate Constitution," Southern Historical Association, *Publications,* IX, 291.

[71] Remarks of C. G. Memminger, T. R. R. Cobb, and B. H. Hill. *Journal of the Confederate Congress,* Senate Document 234, 58 Cong., 2 sess., I, 859, 860, 867.

stitution did provide that no person should exercise the right to vote for any officer, state or federal, who was not a citizen of the state in which he voted.[72] Robert H. Smith explained that "as the institutions we were about to establish were for our own citizens, it was wisely determined that none but such should exercise the highest political right ever given to a people." [73]

The place of the negro in the Southern Confederacy, as recognized in the Confederate Constitution, was most effectively described by Alexander H. Stephens in his famous "Cornerstone Speech" delivered at Savannah, Georgia, March 21, 1861: "The new constitution has put at rest, *forever,* all the agitating questions relating to our peculiar institution — African slavery as it exists amongst us — the proper *status* of the negro in our form of civilization." The old Constitution, he said, "rested upon the assumption of the equality of races. This was an error, it was a sandy foundation, and the government built upon it fell when the 'storm came and the wind blew.' Our new government is founded upon exactly the opposite idea; its foundations are laid, its corner-stone rests upon the great truth, that the negro is not equal to the white man; that slavery — subordination to the superior race — is his natural and normal condition." [74]

After elaborating this thesis, Stephens then continued: "May we not, therefore, look with confidence to the ultimate universal acknowledgement of the truths upon which our system rests? It is the first government ever instituted upon the principles in strict conformity to nature, and the ordination of Providence, in furnishing the materials of human society. Many governments have been founded upon the principle of the subordination and serfdom of certain classes

[72] Confederate Constitution: Art. I, sec. 2, cl. 1.
[73] R. H. Smith, *Address on the Constitution,* pamphlet, 15.

[74] Henry Cleveland, ed., *Stephens in Public and Private, with Letters and Speeches,* 721.

of the same race; such were and are in violation of the laws of nature. Our system commits no such violation of nature's laws. With us, all of the white race, however high or low, rich or poor, are equal in the eye of the law. Not so with the negro. Subordination is his place. . . . The architect, in the construction of buildings, lays the foundation with the proper material — the granite; then comes the brick or the marble. The substratum of our society is made of material fitted by nature for it, and by experience we know, that it is best, not only for the superior, but for the inferior race, that it should be so. . . . This stone which was rejected by the first builders 'is become the chief of the corner' — the real 'cornerstone' — in our new edifice." [75]

Having recognized openly the institution of negro slavery, the framers of the Confederate Constitution were confronted with the more puzzling problem of determining upon a definite policy of controlling the slave-trade with the outside world. Upon this issue, the South was divided into at least two schools of thought: the constitutional prohibitionists and the congressional restrictionists. For the first school, Henry L. Benning contended in the Virginia Convention that there was no danger of reopening the slave-trade, for Georgia, along with two or three other states, had already declared unanimously against it. [76] For the second school, the *Charleston Mercury* was quoted as contending that the slavetrade "is a matter of policy, and not of principle, to be decided now and hereafter, from sound views of the necessity and safety of our people. We think it a proper subject for legislation." [77]

In the Montgomery Convention these two views received further support. Thomas N. Waul of Texas introduced a constitutional amendment that the "importation of negroes

[75] *Ibid.*, 722-723.
[76] *Addresses of Hon. Fulton Anderson, Hon. Henry L. Benning and Hon. John S. Preston*, pamphlet, 40-41.

[77] As quoted in *Substance of Speech of S. McD. Moore in the Virginia Convention, February 24, 1861*, pamphlet, 24.

born in Africa is hereby forbidden; and Congress is required to pass such laws as shall effectually prevent the same." W. S. Barry of Mississippi would further extend this principle of restriction by incorporating a provision that the "importation of slaves from the slaveholding States of the United States of America is hereby forbidden." [78]

But James Chesnut, Jr., and R. B. Rhett, both of South Carolina, stood for congressional discretion. The former would allow Congress "to prohibit the importation of African negroes and slaves from any foreign country"; the latter would extend this application by permitting Congress to prohibit at its discretion "the importation of slaves, coolies, or persons held to service or labor into the Confederate States and their Territories, from any places beyond the limits thereof." [79]

During this division in the Convention upon the issue, T. R. R. Cobb wrote home to his wife: "Stephens and Toombs are both for leaving the door open. Wright goes with them and Hill also *we fear*. Kenan goes with us and this gives Howell, Bartow, Nisbet and myself a majority in our Delegation. . . . *Confidentially* and to be kept a secret *from the public*, Mr. Davis is opposed to us on this point also and wants to keep the door open. The Mississippi Delegation are wax in his hands. . . . I am much afraid of the result." [80]

The constitutional provisions finally adopted represented a compromise between the two views. The slave-trade with foreign countries was prohibited by the Constitution in these terms: "The importation of negroes of the African race, from any foreign country other than the slave-holding States or Territories of the United States of America, is hereby forbidden; and Congress is required to pass such laws as shall effectually prevent the same." But the slave-trade with

[78] *Journal of the Confederate Congress,* Senate Document 234, 58 Cong., 2 sess., I, 869.
[79] *Ibid.,* 868.

[80] A. H. Hull, "The Making of the Confederate Constitution," Southern Historical Association, *Publications,* IX, 284-285.

the states of the old Union was left to congressional discretion under the provision that "Congress shall also have power to prohibit the introduction of slaves from any State not a member of, or Territory not belonging to, this Confederacy." [81]

In justifying the first of these provisions, Robert H. Smith maintained that "whether regarded as an economical question, or one of merely political policy, or looked at in the light of duty to our own civilized negroes, the propriety of writing in the Constitution a prohibition against the trade, is to my mind clear." Since the late Union was dissolved "chiefly because of the negro quarrel," declared Smith, it is to be commended "that the strife has been put to rest forever" by a prohibition in the Constitution.[82]

The justification for the second of these measures was discussed at length in the Alabama Convention where it was thought that the greatest advantage to be derived from congressional discretion as applied to the states of the old Union lay in the pressure that might thus be exercised to force some of those states into the Confederacy.[83] Though in the ratifying conventions, exponents of both views objected to the compromise,[84] the provisions were generally accepted as a definite and satisfactory policy for controlling negro slavery in the Southern Confederacy.

More important than open recognition or certainty of control were the constitutional provisions protecting the institution of negro slavery. One such method of protection proposed was that of creating a Confederacy of slave-states only. Measures directed to this end had been introduced into several of the state conventions; and the idea was further considered at Montgomery, where it became a twofold issue: "Shall we admit only slave-states into the Union?"

[81] Confederate Constitution, Art. I, sec. 9, cls. 1, 2.
[82] R. H. Smith, *Address on the Constitution*, pamphlet, 18, 19.
[83] W. R. Smith, *Debates of the Alabama Convention of 1861*, 228, *et seq.*
[84] See *Journal of the South Carolina Convention of 1860-1-2*, 207, 214-215, 249.

and "Shall we require all states within the Confederacy to retain negro slavery?" On the first issue, the drafting committee of the permanent constitution had answered in the negative.[85] But to the contrary, W. P. Miles of South Carolina proposed in the Convention that "no State shall be admitted which, by its constitution or laws, denies the right of property in slaves of the African race, or does not fully protect such property by legal enactment."[86] This proposition was supported by John Perkins of Louisiana who moved "that no nonslaveholding State shall be admitted into the Confederacy," and by T. R. R. Cobb of Georgia, who offered as an amendment that "no State shall be admitted which, by its constitution or laws, denies the right of property in negro slaves, or the right of the master to recapture his slave."[87]

On the second of these issues, Duncan F. Kenner of Louisiana moved that no state shall "pass any law impairing the right of property in negro slaves"; whereupon R. B. Rhett offered as an additional proposal: "Nor shall any State remain in this Confederacy which does not authorize the institution of slavery within its limits."[88] Still others would meet this issue through the principle of unanimous consent. W. P. Harris of Mississippi moved that "no nonslaveholding State shall be admitted except by the consent of all the States expressed through their legislatures"; and W. S. Barry from the same state proposed that no "one of the Confederate States in which African slavery exists shall abolish it without the consent of all the slaveholding States."[89]

Despite this large number of proposed amendments looking to the formation of a Confederacy of slave-states only, the Montgomery Convention did not finally exclude free

[85] A. H. Hull, "The Making of the Confederate Constitution," Southern Historical Association, *Publications*, IX, 290.

[86] *Journal of the Confederate Congress*, Senate Document 234, 58 Cong., 2 sess.,

I, 883.

[87] *Ibid.*, 884, 885.

[88] *Ibid.*, 874.

[89] *Ibid.*, 883, 893.

states from membership by any provision of the adopted Constitution. Negro slavery was, nevertheless, adequately protected both in the states and in the territories, by specific constitutional provisions. Against the possibility of adverse congressional legislation, the Constitution provided that no "law denying or impa[i]ring the right of property in negro slaves shall be passed." [90] Under the Constitution, citizens of the several states possess "the right of transit and sojourn in any State of this Confederacy, with their slaves and other property; and the right of property in said slaves shall not be thereby impaired." [91]

On the protection of slavery in the territories of the Confederacy, the Constitution specifies that in "all such territory, the institution of negro slavery, as it now exists in the Confederate States, shall be recognized and protected by Congress and by the territorial government: and the inhabitants of the several Confederate States and Territories shall have the right to take to such territory any slaves lawfully held by them in any of the States or Territories of the Confederate States." [92]

And the institution of negro slavery was protected in both states and territories by a revised fugitive slave provision in the Constitution: "No slave or other person held to service or labor in any State or Territory of the Confederate States, under the laws thereof, escaping or lawfully carried into another, shall, in consequence of any law or regulation therein, be discharged from such service or labor: but shall be delivered up on claim of the party to whom such slave belongs, or to whom such service or labor may be due." [93]

Robert H. Smith, in reviewing the constitutional provi-

[90] Confederate Constitution, Art. I, sec. 9, cl. 4.
[91] *Ibid.*, Art. IV, sec. 2, cl. 1.
[92] Confederate Constitution, Art. IV, sec. 3, cl. 3. Since Congress was required by the Constitution to protect negro slavery in the territories, the framers were willing to give Congress the specific power "to legislate and provide governments for the inhabitants of all territory belonging to the Confederate States, lying without the limits of the several States." Art. IV, sec. 3, cl. 3.
[93] *Ibid.*, Art. IV, sec. 2, cl. 3.

sions concerning negro slavery, presented this brief summary: "We have now placed our domestic institution, and secured its rights unmistakably, in the Constitution; we have sought by no euphony to hide its name — we have called our negroes 'slaves,' and we have recognized and protected them as persons and our rights to them as property." [94]

REFORMS IN THE CENTRAL GOVERNMENT

The more constructive features of the Confederate Constitution lie in the attempted improvements in the work of the central government. The incorporation of these improvements, like that of other innovations in the new Constitution, grew directly out of the Southern attack upon conditions in the old Union. If the spoils of public office, the extravagance of national expenditures, or the injustice of sectional disbursements had precipitated the sectional conflict that led ultimately to a stroke for independence, then the innovations now to be considered are the most important in the Confederate Constitution; for in them the South would naturally be expected either to provide patronage and luxury for its own disappointed politicians at the risk of minority opposition within the Confederacy, or else, to prohibit the evils of public spoils and extravagant expenditures wherever possible, both for the protection of its own minorities and for the permanence of the Southern Confederacy.

It is easy to see to which alternative the fathers of the Constitution turned. The uses of the spoils of office developed in the old Union were restricted in the Southern Confederacy by seven distinct provisions in the Confederate Constitution. To the old congressional power of establish-

[94] Robert H, Smith, *Address on the Constitution*, pamphlet, 19. Perhaps sufficient evidence has already been introduced to question the importance, if not the sincerity, of these slavery sections of the Confederate Constitution. Further information may be found in B. B. Munford, *Virginia's Attitude towards Slavery and Secession*, Part II, pp. 15-237, entitled "Virginia Did not Secede in order to Extend Slavery into the Territories, or to Prevent Its Threatened Destruction within Her Own Borders."

ing "uniform Laws on the subject of Bankruptcies throughout the United States," the Confederate Constitution added: "but no law of Congress shall discharge any debt contracted before the passage of the same." [95] In order to prohibit the evils of riders attached to appropriation bills, the Constitution further required that "every law, or resolution having the force of law, shall relate to but one subject, and that shall be expressed in the title." [96] The President's power of appointment was curtailed by the constitutional requirement that "no person rejected by the Senate shall be re-appointed to the same office during their ensuing recess." [97] An indefinite tenure of office was granted to all administrative officials except heads of departments and diplomatic officers by granting the President the power of removing them only "when their services are unnecessary, or for dishonesty, incapacity, inefficiency, misconduct, or neglect of duty; and when so removed, the removal shall be reported to the Senate, together with the reasons therefor." [98] In the original draft of the permanent Constitution, the drafting committee had granted these officers a definite four-year term, unless otherwise provided by law; [99] but the Convention, as Henry D. Capers later explained, substituted such terms "as to secure the best of service from competent persons, and to inspire a sense of personal self-respect by investing the employe with such security in his tenure as would naturally provoke fidelity in the discharge of his duty, while at the same time the government had the benefit of his efficiency." [100]

The three remaining constitutional restrictions upon the

[95] Art. I, sec. 8, cl. 4.
[96] Art. I, sec. 9, cl. 20.
[97] Art. II, sec. 2, cl. 4.
[98] Art. II, sec. 2, cl. 3. The Constitution stated that the "principal officer in each of the executive departments, and all persons connected with the diplomatic service, may be removed from office at the pleas-ure of the President." *Ibid.*
[99] *Journal of the Confederate Congress,* Senate Document 234, 58 Cong., 2 sess., I, 856.
[100] H. D. Capers, *Life and Times of C. G. Memminger,* 320. Capers was chief clerk and disbursing officer in the Treasury Department of the Confederacy, 1861.

spoils of public office concern the elections of senators, the uses of the post office, and the term of the President. The new provision for the election of Senators specified that Senators shall be chosen by the state legislatures "at the regular session next immediately preceding the commencement of the term of service"; whereas, under the old Constitution, the *time* of choosing Senators was left to the discretion of Congress.[101] The constitutional provision that "the expenses of the Post-office Department, after the first day of March in the year of our Lord eighteen hundred and sixty-three, shall be paid out of its own revenues"[102] was inserted, so Robert H. Smith explained, not only for its economic advantages, but also for its political implications; "for it is manifest," said he, "that the much abused franking privilege is thus cut up and that our mails will not be loaded with the carriage, nor our treasury burdened with the printing of the political trash, tending more to mislead than to enlighten the public mind."[103] J. L. M. Curry of Alabama was another member of the Montgomery Convention who considered the political motive a primary one in the adoption of this provision; for, as he later explained in his *Civil History of the Confederate States*, "the franking privilege is greatly abused, and during a presidential campaign both parties send free tons of pamphlets under the flimsy and deceptive pretense that they are public documents." It was to correct these abuses, wrote Curry, that this provision was inserted.[104]

In place of the old Federal constitutional provision that the President "shall hold his Office during the Term of four Years," the Southern Constitution offered an important restriction on spoils in requiring that the President and Vice-President "shall hold their offices for the term of six years;

---

[101] Art. I, sec. 4, cl. 1, both Constitutions.
[102] Art. I, sec. 8, cl. 7.
[103] Robert H. Smith, *Address on the Con-stitution*, pamphlet, 16.
[104] J. L. M. Curry, *Civil History of the Confederate States*, 88.

but the President shall not be re-eligible." [105] The value of
this contribution was explained after the Convention had
completed its work both by Alexander H. Stephens and by
J. L. M. Curry. Stephens told the people of Georgia that
this provision would "remove from the incumbent all temp-
tation to use his office or exert the powers confided to him
for any objects of personal ambition." He further declared
that under the one-term plan for president, the "only incen-
tive to that higher ambition which should move and actuate
one holding such high trusts in his hands, will be the good
of the people, the advancement, prosperity, happiness,
safety, honor, and true glory of the confederacy." [106] Curry
wrote after the war that the purpose of this provision was
to eliminate the evils of the old system wherein "the President is practically an appointee of irresponsible bodies of
men, and the triumph of a party is of more consequence than
the public welfare, and the patronage of a President is used
as spoils of office for rewarding partisans or silencing free
thought." [107]

Extravagance in expenditures, like the spoils of public
office, was restricted in the Confederacy by specific constitutional provisions. Article One, section nine, of the Confederate Constitution required that "all bills appropriating
money shall specify in federal currency the exact amount of
each appropriation and the purposes for which it is made."
To this clause was added the further provision that "Congress shall grant no extra compensation to any public con-
tractor, officer, agent or servant, after such contract shall
have been made or such service rendered." [108] Payment of
claims against the Confederacy was constitutionally per-
missible only after the justice of these claims "shall have
been judicially declared by a tribunal for the investigation

---

[105] Art. II, sec. 1, cl. 1, both Constitutions.
[106] Address at Savannah, Georgia, March 21, 1861. Henry Cleveland, ed., *Stephens in Public and Private with Letters and*

Speeches, 720-721.
[107] J. L. M. Curry, *Civil History of the Confederate States,* 74-75.
[108] Art. I, sec. 9, cl. 10.

of claims against the government, which it is hereby made the duty of Congress to establish." [109] And through the omission of the words *general welfare* from the taxing clause, T. R. R. Cobb wrote that the power of Congress to tax "was by the Confederate Constitution clearly and definitely restricted to the payment of the public debt, the common defense and the expenses of the Government." [110]

Further checks upon profligacy in expenditures came through increased executive leadership in appropriations; for the Constitution required the President or the heads of the departments to submit estimates to Congress and to ask for appropriations there. Without this initiation from the executive department, Congress, except in certain contingencies, could appropriate money only by an extra-majority vote.[111] The President was also given the power to veto items in appropriation bills, and in such cases as shall arise from this power, "he shall, in signing the bill, designate the appropriations disapproved; and shall return a copy of such appropriations, with his objections, to the House in which the bill shall have originated; and the same proceeding shall then be had as in case of other bills disapproved by the President." [112] This extended executive control over expenditures, declared Stephens, was a part of the general plan of the new Constitution to guard "not only the pockets of the people, but also the public money, after it was taken from their pockets." [113]

Robert H. Smith explained the purpose of these provisions at greater length by a comparison of the old system with the new: "There is hardly a more flagrant abuse of it's power, by the Congress of the United States than the habitual practice of loading bills, which are necessary for

[109] Art. I, sec. 9, cl. 9.
[110] A. H. Hull, "The Making of the Confederate Constitution," Southern Historical Association, *Publications*, IX, 291-292.
[111] Art. I, sec. 9, cl. 9.

[112] Art. I, sec. 7, cl. 2.
[113] Speech at Savannah, Georgia, March 21, 1861. Henry Cleveland, ed., *Stephens in Public and Private with Letters and Speeches*, 728.

Governmental operations with reprehensible, not to say venal dispositions of the public money, and which only obtain favor by a system of combinations among members interested in similar abuses upon the treasury. Bills necessary for the support of the Government are loaded with items of the most exceptionable character, and are thrown upon the President at the close of the session, for his sanction, as the only alternative for keeping the Government in motion. . . . Hence the Convention of Confederate States wisely determined that the Executive was the proper department to know and call for the moneys necessary for the support of Government, and that here the responsibility should rest. . . . the chief Executive head of the country and his Cabinet should understand the pecuniary wants of the Confederacy, and should be answerable for an economical administration of public affairs, and at the same time should be enabled and required to call for whatever sums may be wanted to accomplish the purposes of Government." [114]

It was primarily in furtherance of this principle of checking extravagant expenditures through executive leadership that the provision was inserted in the Constitution specifying that "Congress may, by law, grant to the principal officer in each of the Executive Departments a seat upon the floor of either House, with the privilege of discussing any measures appertaining to his department." [115] In defending this provision, Alexander H. Stephens, who insisted upon its incorporation into the Constitution because he admired a similar feature in the British Government, spoke as follows: "Under the old constitution, a secretary of the treasury for instance, had no opportunity, save by his annual reports, of presenting any scheme or plan of finance or other matter. He had no opportunity of explaining, expounding, inforcing, or defending his views of policy; his only resort was through

---

[114] R. H. Smith, *Address on the Constitution*, pamphlet, 7-8.

[115] Art. I, sec. 6, cl. 2.

the medium of an organ. In the British parliament, the premier brings in his budget and stands before the nation responsible for its every item. If it is indefensible, he falls before the attacks upon it, as he ought to. This will now be the case to a limited extent under our system." [116]

How far the South succeeded in applying its political philosophy of the Ante-Bellum Period to the provisions of the Confederate Constitution, we had best leave to the words of three leaders in this work of application at the Montgomery Convention. Alexander H. Stephens declared that all the changes from the old Federal Constitution "were decidedly of a conservative character . . . such as in the judgment of a majority of these States, the experience of seventy years had shown were proper and necessary for the harmonious working of the system." [117] Speaking from the same approach, Howell Cobb maintained that the "departures from the provisions of that instrument have been suggested by the experience of the past, and are intended to guard against the evils and dangers which led to the dissolution of the late Union." [118] J. L. M. Curry, the third of the "fathers" to be quoted, wrote even more to the point: "The Constitution of the Confederate States, as the instrument of government, is the most certain and decisive expression of the views and principles of those who formed it, and is entitled to credence and acceptance as the most trustworthy and authoritative exposition of the principles and purposes of those who established the Confederate Government." [119]

[116] Speech at Savannah, Georgia, March 21, 1861. Henry Cleveland, ed., *Stephens in Public and Private with Letters and Speeches*, 720.
[117] A. H. Stephens, *War between the States*, II, 339.
[118] *Journal of the South Carolina Convention of 1860-1-2*, 186.
[119] J. L. M. Curry, *The Southern States of the American Union*, 194.

A SELECTION OF MATERIALS
CONSULTED

A SELECTION OF MATERIALS CONSULTED

ADAMS, JAMES TRUSLOW, editor:
> Jeffersonian principles. Extracts from the writings of Thomas Jefferson. 161 pp. cloth. 1928. Little, Brown. Boston, Mass.

" AGRICOLA ":
> *See* P. N. Nicholas.

ALABAMA:
> *See* W. R. Smith.

AMBLER, CHARLES HENRY:
> Sectionalism in Virginia from 1776 to 1861. 366 pp. cloth. 1910. University of Chicago Press. Chicago, Ill.

> Thomas Ritchie; a study in Virginia politics. 303 pp. cloth. 1913. Bell Book Co. Richmond, Va.

> Correspondence of Robert M. T. Hunter, 1826-1876. American Historical Association, Annual Report, 1916. Vol. II, 383 pp. cloth. 1918. Government Printing Office. Washington, D. C.

> Life of John Floyd, in The John P. Branch Historical Papers of Randolph-Macon College, June, 1918. Vol. V, nos. 1 & 2, pp. 5-117. Ashland, Va.

> Diary of John Floyd. *Ibid.,* pp. 119-233.

AMERICAN ANTI-SLAVERY SOCIETY:
> The constitution a pro-slavery compact: or selections from the Madison papers, etc. Second edition, enlarged. 131 pp. pamphlet. 1845. American Anti-Slavery Society, New York, N. Y.

AMES, HERMAN VANDERBURGH, editor:
> State documents on federal relations: the states and the United States. 320 pp. cloth. 1906. Also published as pamphlets in six numbers. University of Pennsylvania. Philadelphia, Pa.

> The proposed amendments to the Constitution of the United States during the first century of its history. American Historical Association, Annual Report, 1896. Vol. II, 442 pp. cloth. 1897. Government Printing Office, Washington, D. C.

ANDERSON, D. R.:
> *See* Richmond College.

THE SOUTH AS A CONSCIOUS MINORITY

ANDERSON, FULTON, AND OTHERS:

Addresses delivered before the Virginia state convention by Hon. Fulton Anderson, commissioner from Mississippi, Hon. Henry L. Benning, commissioner from Georgia, and Hon. John S. Preston, commissioner from South Carolina, February, 1861. 64 pp. pamphlet. 1861. Wyatt M. Elliott, printer. Richmond, Va.

ANNALS OF CONGRESS:

The debates and proceedings in the Congress of the United States: with an appendix, containing important state papers and public documents, and all the laws of a public nature; with a copious index. [First to] Eighteenth Congress.—first session: comprising the period from [March 3, 1789] to May 27, 1824, inclusive. Compiled from authentic materials. 42 volumes, cloth. 1834-1836. Gales & Seaton. Washington, D. C.

ANONYMOUS:

The northern man with southern principles, and the southern man with American principles: or a view of the comparative claims of Gen. William H. Harrison and Martin Van Buren, Esq., candidates for the presidency, to the support of the citizens of the southern states. 40 pp. pamphlet. 1840. Peter Force, printer. Washington, D. C.

Free Negroism. 32 pp. pamphlet. No date. No publisher.

Behind and before, or what is to be done? Tracts for the people no. 8. 16 pp. pamphlet. 1851. Edward C. Councell. Charleston, S. C.

" ARISTIDES ":

The prospect before us: or strictures on the late message of the president of the United States and the report of the secretary of the treasury in a series of letters by Aristides. To which is subjoined the late address of Governor Hamilton, before the State Rights and Free Trade Association. Published by the State Rights and Free Trade Association. 24 pp. pamphlet. 1832? E. J. Brunt. Charleston, S. C.

ATTORNEYS-GENERAL:

Official Opinions of the Attorneys-General of the United States, advising the President and heads of departments in relation to their official duties. 35 volumes published to 1930. Government Printing Office, Washington, D. C.

SELECT BIBLIOGRAPHY

AVARY, MYRTA LOCKETT, editor:
> Recollections of Alexander H. Stephens; his diary kept when a prisoner at Fort Warren, Boston harbor, 1865; giving incidents and reflections of his prison life with some letters and reminiscences. Edited with a biographical study. 572 pp. cloth. 1910. Doubleday Page. New York, N. Y.

BACON, GEORGE WASHINGTON:
> Life and speeches of President Andrew Johnson embracing his early history, political career, speeches, proclamation, etc., with a sketch of the secession movement, and his course in relation thereto; also his policy as president of the United States. 137 pp. cloth. 1865? Bacon and Co. London, Eng.

BANCROFT, FREDERIC:
> Calhoun and the South Carolina nullification movement. 199 pp. cloth. 1928. The Johns Hopkins Press. Baltimore, Md.

" BARBAROSSA ":
> *See* John Scott.

BASSETT, JOHN SPENCER, editor:
> Correspondence of Andrew Jackson. 4 volumes published to 1930. Approximately 500 pp. each; cloth. 1926-1929. Published by the Carnegie Institution of Washington, D. C.

BATTLE, KEMP PLUMMER:
> The legislation of the [North Carolina] convention of 1861. James Sprunt Historical Monographs. No. 1. pp. 98-144. University of North Carolina Publications. 1900. Chapel Hill, N. C.
>
> Letters of Nathaniel Macon, John Steele and William Barry Grove, with sketches and notes. 122 pp. paper. 1902. *Ibid.,* no. 3.

BAYARD, JAMES ASHETON; MACHENRY, GEORGE; and RALSTON, G.:
> The African race in America, north and south. Being a correspondence on that subject between two Pennsylvanians. With an appendix containing extracts in reference to the right of secession, from the writings of the late William Rawle . . . and the views of Senator Bayard . . . on the antagonism of the Caucasian and African races. 23 pp. pamphlet. 1861. Bradbury and Evans. London, Eng.

BELL, JOHN:
> *See* Edward Everett.

BENJAMIN, JUDAH PHILIP:
> *See* E. P. Oberholtzer, ed.

THE SOUTH AS A CONSCIOUS MINORITY

BENTON, THOMAS HART:

Thirty years' view; or, a history of the working of the American government for thirty years, from 1820 to 1850. Chiefly taken from the Congress debates, the private papers of General Jackson and the speeches of ex-Senator Benton, with his actual view of men and affairs: with historical notes and illustrations and some notes of eminent deceased contemporaries. Two volumes. I, 739 pp.; II, 799 pp. cloth. 1856. D. Appleton. New York, N. Y.

Abridgement of the debates of Congress, from 1789 to 1856. From Gales and Seaton's Annals of Congress; from their Register of Debates; and from the official reported debates by John C. Rives. 16 volumes, cloth. 1857-1860. D. Appleton. New York, N. Y.

See J. T. Morse, Jr., ed., E. P. Oberholtzer, ed.

[BERGUIN, H. K.]:

Considerations relative to a southern confederacy, with letters to the North, on the preservation of the union, and a note from the secret history of the emancipation in the English West Indies. By a citizen of North Carolina. 40 pp. pamphlet. 1860. " Standard Office." Raleigh, N. C.

BEVERIDGE, ALBERT JEREMIAH:

The fifth wheel in our government. The Century Magazine. December, 1909. Vol. 79, no. 2, pp. 208-214.

The life of John Marshall. 4 volumes. Approximately 600 pp. each; cloth. 1916-1919. Houghton Mifflin. Boston, Mass., and New York, N. Y.

BIGELOW, JOHN, editor:

The writings and speeches of Samuel J. Tilden. 2 volumes. I, 606 pp.; II, 601 pp. cloth. 1885. Harper. New York, N. Y.

BOUCHER, CHAUNCY SAMUEL:

The nullification controversy in South Carolina. 399 pp. cloth. 1916. University of Chicago Press. Chicago, Ill.

The secession and co-operation movements in South Carolina, 1848 to 1852. Washington University Studies. April, 1918. Series 4, Vol. V, pp. 67-138. Concord, N. H.

BOWERS, CLAUDE GERNADE:

The party battles of the Jackson period. 506 pp. cloth. 1922. Houghton Mifflin. Boston, Mass. and New York, N. Y.

Jefferson and Hamilton; the struggle for democracy in America. 531 pp. cloth. 1925. Houghton Mifflin. Boston, Mass. and New York, N. Y.

SELECT BIBLIOGRAPHY

BOYD, WILLIAM KENNETH:
> North Carolina on the eve of secession. American Historical Association, Annual Report, 1910. Pp. 167-197. Government Printing Office. Washington, D. C.

BRANCH, JOHN P.:
> For Branch Papers *see* Randolph-Macon College.

BROOKS, ROBERT PRESTON:
> Howell Cobb and the crisis of 1850. The Mississippi Valley Historical Review, December, 1917. Vol. IV, no. 3, pp. 279-298. Cedar Rapids, Iowa.
>
> Howell Cobb papers. Georgia Historical Quarterly. 1921. Vol. V, no. 1, pp. 50-61; no. 2, pp. 29-52; no. 3, pp. 35-55; no. 4, pp. 43-64. Published by the Georgia Historical Society. Savannah, Ga.
>
> The industrialization of the South. University of Georgia, School of Commerce, Bureau of Business Research, Study no. 1. April, 1929. Athens, Ga.

BROWN, EVERETT SOMERVILLE, editor:
> The Missouri compromises and presidential politics, 1820-1825. From the letters of William Plumer, Junior, representative from New Hampshire. 155 pp. cloth. 1926. Missouri Historical Society. St. Louis, Mo.

BROWN, JOSEPH EMERSON:
> *See* H. Fielder.

BROWNE, WILLIAM HAND:
> *See* Richard M. Johnston.

BRUCE, WILLIAM CABELL:
> John Randolph of Roanoke 1773-1833. A bibliography based on new material. 2 volumes. I, 661 pp.; II, 804 pp.; cloth. 1922. Putnam. New York, N. Y.

BRUMMER, SIDNEY D.:
> The judicial interpretation of the confederate constitution. In Studies in Southern History and Politics, pp. 107-133; cloth. 1914. Columbia University Press. New York, N. Y.

" BRUTUS ":
> *See* Robert James Turnbull.

BURGESS, JOHN WILLIAM:
> The middle period 1817-1858. 544 pp. cloth. 1897. Charles Scribner. New York, N. Y.

THE SOUTH AS A CONSCIOUS MINORITY

CAIRNES, JOHN ELLIOTT:

The slave power. Its character, career, & probable designs: being an attempt to explain the real issues involved in the American contest. 304 pp. cloth. 1862. No index. Parker, Son, and Bourn, London, Eng. Second edition, 1863, Carleton, New York, N. Y.

CALHOUN, JOHN CALDWELL:

Letters from John C. Calhoun to Charles Tait. The Gulf States Historical Magazine. September, 1902. Vol. I, no. 2, pp. 92-104. Montgomery, Ala.

See Frederick Bancroft, R. K. Crallé, ed., J. F. Jameson, ed., J. T. Morse, Jr., ed., C. E. Merriam, E. P. Oberholtzer, ed., N. W. Stephenson.

CALL, RICHARD K.:

Letter from Governor R. K. Call of Florida to John S. Littell, of Germantown, Pennsylvania. 31 pp. pamphlet. 1861. C. Sherman & Sons. Philadelphia, Pa.

CAMPBELL, JOHN ARCHIBALD:

See H. G. Connor, G. W. Duncan.

CANDLER, ALLEN DAVID, editor.

The confederate records of the state of Georgia. Compiled and published under the authority of the legislature. 6 volumes. Approximately 800 pp. each. Cloth. 1909-1911. C. P. Byrd, state printer. Atlanta, Ga.

CAPERS, HENRY D.:

The life and times of C. G. Memminger. 604 pp. cloth. 1893. Everett Waddey. Richmond, Va.

[CAREY, HENRY CHARLES]:

The North and the South. 48 pp. pamphlet. 1864. Reprinted from the New York Tribune. Published at the office of the Tribune. New York, N. Y.

CARPENTER, STEPHEN D.:

Logic of history. Five hundred political texts: being concentrated extracts of abolitionism; also, results of slavery agitation and emancipation; together with sundry chapters on despotism, usurpations and frauds. Second edition. 351 pp. cloth. 1864. S. D. Carpenter, publisher. Madison, Wisconsin.

CARPENTER, WILLIAM SEAL:

Development of American political thought. 190 pp. cloth. 1930. Princeton University Press, Princeton, N. J.

SELECT BIBLIOGRAPHY

CARSON, JAMES PETIGRU:
> Life, letters and speeches of James Louis Petigru. The union man of South Carolina. 497 pp. cloth. 1920. W. H. Lowdermilk. Washington, D. C.

CHANNING, EDWARD:
> A history of the United States. 7 volumes published to 1930. Approximately 600 pp. each. Cloth. 1905-1930. Macmillan. New York, N. Y.

CHEVES, LANGDON:
> Letter of the Hon. Langdon Cheves, to the editors of the Charleston Mercury, September 11, 1844. 15 pp. pamphlet. 1844. Walker & Burke. Charleston, S. C.

> Speech of the Hon. Langdon Cheves, in the Nashville Convention, November 15, 1850. 32 pp. pamphlet. 1850. A. S. Johnson, printer. Columbia, S. C.

CHITTENDEN, LUCIUS EUGENE:
> A report of the debates and proceedings in the secret sessions of the conference convention, for proposing amendments to the Constitution of the United States, held at Washington, D. C., in February, A. D. 1861. 626 pp. cloth. 1864. D. Appleton, New York, N. Y.

CLAIBORNE, JOHN FRANCIS HAMTRANCK:
> Life and correspondence of John A. Quitman, Major General, U. S. A., and governor of the state of Mississippi. 2 volumes. I, 400 pp.; II, 392 pp. Cloth. 1860. No index. Harper. New York, N. Y.

CLAY, HENRY:
> *See* Colvin Colton, ed., J. T. Morse, Jr., ed., E. P. Oberholtzer, ed.

CLEVELAND, HENRY, editor:
> Alexander H. Stephens in public and private with letters and speeches, before, during, and since the war. 833 pp. cloth. 1866. National Publishing Co. Philadelphia, Pa., and elsewhere.

CLINGMAN, THOMAS LANIER:
> Selections from the speeches and writings of Hon. Thomas L. Clingman, of North Carolina, with additions and explanatory notes. 623 pp. cloth. 1877. No index. John Nichols. Raleigh, N. C.

CLUSKEY, MICHAEL W., editor:
> The political text-book, or encyclopedia. Containing everything necessary for the reference of the politicians and statesmen of the United States. 12th edition. 794 pp. cloth. 1860. First edition 640 pp. 1857. C. Wendell. Washington, D. C.

COBB, HOWELL:

> Letter of Hon. Howell Cobb to the people of Georgia on the present condition of the country, December 6, 1860. 16 pp. pamphlet. 1860. McGill & Withrow. Washington, D. C.
>
> *See* R. P. Brooks, ed., U. B. Phillips, ed.

COLE, ARTHUR CHARLES:

> The Whig party in the South. 392 pp. cloth. 1913. American Historical Association. Washington, D. C., and Oxford University Press. London, Eng.
>
> The South and the right of secession in the early fifties. The Mississippi Valley Historical Review. December, 1914. Vol. I, no. 3, pp. 376-399. Cedar Rapids, Iowa.

COLEMAN, MRS. CHAPMAN:

> The life of John J. Crittenden with selections from his correspondence and speeches. 2 volumes. I, 389 pp.; II, 392 pp. Cloth. 1871. Lippincott. Philadelphia, Pa.

COLTON, COLVIN, editor:

> The works of Henry Clay. 6 volumes. Approximately 575 pp. each. Cloth. A. S. Barnes & Burr. New York, N. Y.

CONFEDERATE CONGRESS:

> Journal of the Congress of the Confederate States of America, 1861-1865. 7 volumes. Approximately 700 pp. each. Cloth. 1904. Senate Document no. 234. 58 Congress, 2 session. Government Printing Office, Washington, D. C.

CONGRESSIONAL GLOBE:

> [23rd Congress to the 42nd Congress, December 2, 1833 to March 3, 1873] 46 volumes. Cloth. 1834-1873. Printed at the Globe office for the editors. Washington, D. C.

CONGRESSIONAL RECORD:

> Congressional Record: containing the proceedings and debates of the Forty-third Congress [March 4, 1873—date]. Government Printing Office, Washington, D. C.

CONNOR, HENRY GROVES:

> John Archibald Campbell, Associate Justice of the United States Supreme Court, 1853-1861. 310 pp. cloth. 1920. Houghton Mifflin. Boston, Mass. and New York, N. Y.

COOPER, THOMAS:

> Political essays, originally inserted in the Northumberland gazette. Second edition with corrections and additions. 88 pp. cloth. 1800. First edition, 1799. R. Campbell. Philadelphia, Pa.

Two essays: 1. On the foundation of civil government: 2. On the Constitution of the United States. 71 pp. cloth. 1826. D. & J. M. Faust. Columbia, S. C.

Consolidation. An account of parties in the United States from the convention of 1787, to the present period. Second edition, 37 pp. pamphlet. 1830. First edition, 1824. Printed at the "Times and Gazette" office. Columbia, S. C.

Lectures on the elements of political economy. Second edition. 366 pp. cloth. 1829. First edition, 1826. Printed at "Times and Gazette" Office and by McMorris and Wilson, Columbia, S. C.

Letters of Dr. Thomas Cooper, 1825-1832. The American Historical Review, July, 1901. Vol. VI, no. 4, pp. 725-736. Macmillan. New York, N. Y.

See Dumas Malone.

COULTER, E. MORTON:
The nullification movement in Georgia. Georgia Historical Quarterly, March, 1921. Vol. V, no. 1, pp. 3-39. Georgia Historical Society, Savannah, Ga.

CRALLÉ, RICHARD K., editor:
The works of John C. Calhoun. 6 volumes. Approximately 550 pp. each. Cloth. 1854. D. Appleton, New York. Volume I consisting of Calhoun's Disquisition on Government and his Discourse on the Constitution of the United States was published in 1851 by A. S. Johnson. Charleston, S. C.

CRAWFORD, WILLIAM HARRIS:
See J. E. D. Shipp.

CRITTENDEN, JOHN JORDAN:
See Mrs. Chapman Coleman.

CURRY, JABEZ LAMAR MONROE:
Perils and duty of the South. Substance of a speech delivered by Jabez L. M. Curry, in Talladega, Alabama, November 26, 1860. 16 pp. pamphlet. 1860. L. Towers. Washington, D. C.

Legal justification of the South in secession. Volume I, pp. 1-58 of A library of Confederate States history in 12 volumes written by distinguished men of the South and edited by General Clements A. Evans of Georgia. Cloth. 1899. Confederate Publishing Co. Atlanta, Ga.

The Southern states of the American Union considered in their relations to the Constitution of the United States and to the resulting Union. 248 pp. cloth. 1895. B. F. Johnson. Richmond, Va., and Putman. New York, N. Y.

Civil history of the government of the Confederate States, with some personal reminiscences. 318 pp. cloth. 1901. B. F. Johnson. Richmond, Va.

" CURTIUS ":
See John Taylor.

DABNEY, ROBERT LEWIS:
A defence of Virginia and through her of the South, in recent and pending contests against the sectional party. 356 pp. cloth. 1867. No index. E. J. Hale & Sons. New York, N. Y.

DAVIS, JEFFERSON:
The rise and fall of the Confederate Government. 2 volumes. I, 707 pp.; II, 808 pp. cloth. 1881. D. Appleton. New York, N. Y.

A short history of the Confederate States of America. 505 pp. cloth. 1890. Belford Co. New York, N. Y.

See Dunbar Rowland, ed., E. P. Oberholtzer, ed., N. W. Stephenson.

DAVIS, WILLIAM WATSON:
Ante-bellum southern commercial conventions. Transactions of the Alabama Historical Society. 1904. Edited by Thomas McAdory Owen, secretary. Vol. V, pp. 153-202. Montgomery, Alabama.

DEBOW, JAMES DUNWOODY BROWNSON:
DeBow's Review. Volumes 1-29.

The interest in slavery of the southern non-slaveholder. The right of peaceful secession. The character and influence of abolitionism. 1860 Association Tracts no. 5. 30 pp. pamphlet. 1860. Evans & Cogswell. Charleston, S. C.

DODD, WILLIAM EDWARD:
The life of Nathaniel Macon. 443 pp. cloth. 1903. Edwards & Broughton. Raleigh, N. C.

Chief Justice Marshall and Virginia, 1813-1821. American Historical Review. July, 1907. Vol. XII, no. 4, pp. 776-787. Macmillan. New York, N. Y.

John Taylor of Caroline, prophet of secession. John P. Branch Historical Papers of Randolph-Macon College. June, 1908. Vol. II, nos. 3 & 4, pp. 214-252. Ashland, Va.

Statesmen of the old South; or from radicalism to conservative revolt. 242 pp. cloth. 1911. Macmillan. New York.

Expansion and conflict. 334 pp. cloth. 1915. Houghton Mifflin. New York, N. Y. and Boston, Mass.

Robert J. Walker, imperialist. Bulletin of Randolph-Macon Woman's College. January, 1915. Vol. I, no. 2, pp. 3-23. Lynchburg, Va.

DuBose, John Witherspoon:
The life and times of William Lowndes Yancey. A history of political parties in the United States from 1834-1864; especially as to the origin of the Confederate States. 752 pp. cloth. 1892. No index. Roberts & Son. Birmingham, Ala.

Yancey: a study. The Gulf States Historical Magazine. January and March, 1903. Vol. I, nos. 4 & 5, pp. 239-252; 311-324. Montgomery, Alabama.

Duncan, George W.:
John Archibald Campbell. Publications of the Alabama Historical Society. Transactions. 1904. Vol. V, pp. 107-151. Montgomery, Alabama.

Elliot, Jonathan, editor:
The debates in the several state conventions on the adoption of the Federal Constitution as recommended by the general convention at Philadelphia, in 1787, together with the journal of the federal convention, Luther Martin's letter, Yates's minutes, Congressional opinions, Virginia and Kentucky resolutions of '98-'99, and other illustrations of the constitution. Second edition with considerable additions. 5 volumes. Approximately 600 pp. each. Cloth. 1836. J. P. Lippincott. Philadelphia, Pa.

Everett, Edward:
The life, speeches, and public services of John Bell together with a sketch of the life of Edward Everett. Union candidates for the offices of president and vice-president of the United States. 118 pp. cloth. 1860. Rudd & Carleton. New York, N. Y.

Farrand, Max, editor:
The records of the federal convention of 1787. 3 volumes. Approximately 650 pp. each. Cloth. 1911. Yale University Press. New Haven, Conn., and Oxford University Press. London, Eng.

Fielder, Herbert:
A sketch of the life and times and speeches of Joseph E. Brown. 785 pp. cloth. 1883. Springfield Printing Co. Springfield, Mass.

FISHER, SIDNEY GEORGE:
>   The trial of the Constitution. 391 pp. cloth. 1862. No index. J. B.
>   Lippincott. Philadelphia, Pa.
>
>   The law of the territories. [Signed "Cecil"] 127 pp. cloth. 1859.
>   No index. Sherman & Sons. Philadelphia, Pa.

FITE, EMERSON DAVID:
>   The presidential campaign of 1860. 356 pp. cloth. 1911. Macmillan.
>   New York, N. Y.

FITZHUGH, GEORGE:
>   Sociology for the South or the failure of free society. 310 pp. cloth.
>   1854. A. Morris. Richmond, Va.

FLOYD, JOHN:
>   *See* C. H. Ambler.

FORD, PAUL LEICESTER, editor:
>   Pamphlets on the Constitution of the United States. Published during
>   its discussion by the people. 1787-1788. Edited with notes and a
>   bibliography. 451 pp. cloth. 1888. Brooklyn, N. Y.
>
>   Essays on the Constitution of the United States, published during its
>   discussion by the people 1787-1788. 424 pp. cloth. 1892. Historical
>   Printing Club. Brooklyn, N. Y.
>
>   The works of Thomas Jefferson. 10 volumes. Approximately 500
>   pp. each. Cloth. 1904-1905. Putnam. New York, N. Y., and London,
>   Eng.

FORD, WORTHINGTON CHAUNCEY, editor:
>   Letters of Joseph Jones to James Madison 1788-1802. 48 pp. pamphlet.
>   1901. Reprinted from the proceedings of the Massachusetts Historical
>   Society. June, 1901. J. Wilson & Son. Cambridge, Mass.

FOWLER, WILLIAM CHAUNCEY:
>   The sectional controversy; or, passages in the political history of
>   the United States, including the causes of the war between the
>   sections. 269 pp. cloth. 1862. No index. J. F. Trow. New York,
>   N. Y.

FRANKFURTER, FELIX, and LANDIS, JAMES M.:
>   The business of the Supreme Court. 249 pp. cloth. 1928. Macmillan.
>   New York, N. Y.

[GARNETT, MUSCOE RUSSELL HUNTER] "A Citizen of Virginia":
>   The Union, past and future: how it works and how to save it. 32
>   pp. pamphlet. 1850. J. T. Towers. Washington, D. C.

SELECT BIBLIOGRAPHY

GEORGIA:
>   Journal of the public and secret proceedings of the convention of the people of Georgia held in Milledgeville and Savannah in 1861, together with the ordinances adopted. 416 pp. cloth. 1861. Boughton, Nisbet & Barnes., state printers. Milledgeville, Ga.
>
>   *See* A. D. Candler, ed., E. M. Coulter, U. B. Phillips.

GEORGIA HISTORICAL SOCIETY:
>   Georgia Historical Quarterly. Vol. I. 1917—date. Savannah, Georgia.

GETTELL, RAYMOND GARFIELD:
>   History of American political thought. 633 pp. cloth. 1928. Century. New York, N. Y.

GRAYSON, WILLIAM JOHN:
>   Letter to his excellency Whitemarsh B. Seabrook, governor of the state of South Carolina. On the dissolution of the Union. Second edition. 24 pp. pamphlet. 1850. A. E. Miller. Charleston, S. C.

GULICK, CHARLES ADAMS, JR., editor:
>   The papers of Mirabeau Buonaparte Lamar. Edited from the original papers in the Texas State Library. 6 volumes. Approximately 550 pp. each. Cloth. 1920-1927. No index. Texas State Library. A. C. Baldwin and Sons. Austin, Texas.

HAMER, PHILLIP MAY:
>   The secession movement in South Carolina, 1847-1852. 152 pp. cloth. 1918. No index. University of Pennsylvania Thesis. H. Ray Haas. Allentown, Pa.

HAMILTON, ALEXANDER:
>   *See* Claude Bowers, A. M. Harvey, H. C. Lodge, ed., J. T. Morse, Jr., ed.

HAMILTON, JOSEPH GREGOIRE DE ROULHAC, editor:
>   The correspondence of Jonathan Worth. 2 Volumes, I, 656 pp.; II, 657-1313 pp. cloth. 1909. Publications of the North Carolina Historical Commission. Edwards and Broughton. Raleigh, N. C.
>
>   The papers of Thomas Ruffin. 4 volumes. Approximately 550 pp. each. Cloth. 1918. *Ibid.*
>
>   William Richardson Davie: A memoir followed by his letters with notes by Kemp P. Battle. James Sprunt Historical Monographs no. 7. 75 pp. paper. 1907. University of North Carolina Press. Chapel Hill, North Carolina.
>
>   Benjamin Sherwood Hedrick. *Ibid.,* Vol. X, no. 1, 42 pp. paper. 1910. Letters to Barlett Yancey, *Ibid.,* Vol. X, no. 2, pp. 25-76.

HAMILTON, STANISLAUS MURRAY, editor:
> The writings of James Monroe including a collection of his public and private papers and correspondence now for the first time printed. 7 volumes. Approximately 400 pp. each. Cloth. 1898-1903. Putnam. New York, N. Y.

HAMMOND, JAMES HENRY:
> Selections from the letters and speeches of the Hon. James H. Hammond of South Carolina. 368 pp. cloth. 1866. J. F. Trow. New York, N. Y.

> *See* William Harper, Elizabeth Merritt.

" HAMPDEN ":
> The genuine book of nullification: being a true—not an apochryphal—history, chapter and verse, of the several examples of the recognition and enforcement of that sovereign state remedy by the different states of this confederacy from 1798 down to the present day. [As originally published in the Charleston Mercury.] To which are added the opinions of distinguished statesmen on state rights doctrines. Published at the request of the State Rights Association. 155 pp. paper. 1831. E. J. Van Brunt. Charleston, S. C.

HARPER, WILLIAM:
> The remedy by state interposition or nullification; explained and advocated by Chancellor Harper in his speech at Columbia (S. C.) on the twentieth September, 1830. 24 pp. pamphlet. 1832. E. J. Van Brunt. Charleston, S. C.

> The proslavery argument as maintained by the most distinguished writers of the southern states containing the several essays, on the subject, of Chancellor Harper, Governor Hammond, Dr. Sims, and Professor Dew. 490 pp. cloth. 1853. Lippincott, Grambo & Co. Philadelphia, Pa.

HART, ALBERT BUSHNELL, editor:
> The American nation. A history from original sources by associated scholars. . . . 28 volumes. Approximately 350 pp. each. 1904. Harper. New York, N. Y.

HARVEY, ALEXANDER MILLER:
> Hamilton and Jefferson and the American Constitution. Collections of the Kansas State Historical Society, 1926-1928. Vol. XVIII, pp. 744-787. Topeka, Kansas.

HAY, JOHN:
> *See* John G. Nicolay.

SELECT BIBLIOGRAPHY

HAYNE, ROBERT YOUNG:

An oration, delivered . . . before the state rights and free trade party . . . on the 4th of July, 1831. . . . 47 pp. pamphlet. 1831. A. E. Miller. Charleston, S. C.

See T. D. Jervey.

HEARON, CLEO CARSON:

Mississippi and the compromise of 1850. 229 pp. cloth. 1913. Reprinted from the publications of the Mississippi Historical Society. Vol. XIV. 1913. Ph.D. Thesis at the University of Chicago, Oxford, Miss.

HELPER, HINTON ROWAN:

The impending crisis of the South: how to meet it. 420 pp. cloth. 1857-1860 (many editions). A. B. Burdick Brothers. New York, N. Y.

Nojoque; a question for a continent. 479 pp. cloth. 1867. G. W. Carleton. New York.

The negroes in negroland; the negroes in America; and the negroes generally, also, the several races of white men considered as the involuntary and predestined supplanters of the black races. 254 pp. cloth. 1868. G. W. Carleton, New York, N. Y. S. Low & Son, London, Eng.

See S. M. Wolfe.

HENRY, PATRICK:

See J. T. Morse, Jr., ed.

HERNDON, DALLAS TABOR:

The Nashville convention of 1850. Alabama Historical Society. Transactions. 1904. Vol. V, pp. 203-237. Montgomery, Alabama.

HILL, BENJAMIN HARVEY:

See B. H. Hill Jr., H. J. Pearce.

HILL, BENJAMIN HARVEY, JR.:

Senator Benjamin H. Hill of Georgia. His life, speeches and writings, written and compiled by his son . . . Also memorial addresses, etc. Illustrated. 823 pp. cloth. 1891. No index. H. C. Hudgins & Co. Atlanta, Ga.

HILLIARD, HENRY WASHINGTON:

Speeches and addresses. 497 pp. cloth. 1855. No index. Harper. New York, N. Y.

THE SOUTH AS A CONSCIOUS MINORITY

HOSMER, WILLIAM:

The higher law, in its relations to civil government with particular reference to slavery, and the fugitive slave law. 204 pp. cloth. 1852. No index. Derby & Miller. Auburn, N. Y.

HOUSTON, DAVID FRANKLIN:

A critical study of nullification in South Carolina. 169 pp. cloth. 1896. Harvard Historical Studies. Vol. III. Longmans Green. New York, N. Y.

HOYT, WILLIAM HENRY, editor:

The papers of Archibald D. Murphy. 2 volumes. I, 399 pp.; II, 508 pp. cloth. 1914. Publications of the North Carolina Historical Commission. E. M. Uzzel and Co., state printer. Raleigh, N. C.

HUGER, DANIEL E.:

Speech . . . in the House of Representatives of South Carolina, December, 1830, on the resolutions reported by the committee on federal relations. 41 pp. pamphlet. 1831. W. Riley. Charleston, S. C.

HULL, AUGUSTUS LONGSTREET:

The making of the Confederate Constitution. Southern History Association. Publications. September, 1905. Vol. IX, no. 5, pp. 272-292. Washington, D. C.

HUNT, GAILLARD, editor:

Disunion sentiment in Congress in 1794; a confidential memorandum hitherto unpublished written by John Taylor of Caroline, senator from Virginia, for James Madison. 23 pp. pamphlet. 1905. W. H. Lowdermilk & Co. Washington, D. C.

The writings of James Madison, comprising his public papers and his private correspondence, including numerous letters and documents now for the first time printed. 9 volumes. Approximately 450 pp. each. Cloth. 1900-1910. Putnam. New York, N. Y.

HUNTER, ROBERT MERCER TALIAFERRO:
See C. H. Ambler, ed.

IREDELL, JAMES:
See G. J. McRee.

JACKSON, ANDREW:
See J. S. Bassett, ed., J. T. Morse, Jr., ed.

JAMESON, JOHN FRANKLIN, editor:

Correspondence of John C. Calhoun. American Historical Association. Annual Report, 1899. Vol. II, 1218 pp. cloth. 1900. Government printing office. Washington, D. C.

SELECT BIBLIOGRAPHY

JAY, WILLIAM:
> A letter to the right Rev. L. Silliman Ives, bishop of the protestant episcopal church in the state of North Carolina; occasioned by his' late address to the convention of his diocese. Third edition. 32 pp. cloth. 1848. William Harned. New York, N. Y.

JEFFERSON, THOMAS:
> *See* J. T. Adams, ed., Claude Bowers, P. L. Ford, ed., A. M. Harvey, J. T. Morse, Jr., ed.

JERVEY, THEODORE DEHON:
> Robert Y. Hayne and his times. A historical sketch of the state of South Carolina in the first five decades of the Constitution and the political influence of the state on the Union of that period. 555 pp. cloth. 1909. Macmillan. New York, N. Y.

JOHNSON, ALLEN, editor:
> Chronicles of America series. 50 volumes. Approximately 250 pp. each. Cloth. 1921. Yale University Press. New Haven, Conn.

> The nationalizing influence of party. Yale Review. November, 1906. Vol. XV, 282-292. New Haven, Conn.

JOHNSON, ANDREW:
> *See* G. W. Bacon.

JOHNSTON, RICHARD MALCOMBE, and BROWNE, WILLIAM HAND:
> Life of Alexander H. Stephens. New and revised edition. 709 pp. cloth. 1884. J. P. Lippincott. Philadelphia, Pa.

KENNEDY, JOHN PENDLETON:
> The border states: their power and duty in the present disordered condition of the country. 46 pp. pamphlet. 1861. J. P. Lippincott. Philadelphia, Pa.

LAMAR, LUCIUS QUINTUS CINCINNATUS:
> *See* Edward Mayes.

LAMAR, MIRABEAU BUONAPARTE:
> Letter of Gen. Mirabeau B. Lamar, ex-President of Texas, on the subject of annexation, addressed to the several citizens of Macon, Geo. 48 pp. pamphlet. 1844. Thomas Purse. Savannah, Ga.

> *See* C. A. Gulick, Jr., ed.

LANDIS, JAMES M.:
> *See* Felix Frankfurter.

THE SOUTH AS A CONSCIOUS MINORITY

LEARNED, HENRY BARRETT:
> Casting votes of the vice-presidents, 1789-1915. American Historical Review. April, 1915. Vol. XX, pp. 571-576. Macmillan. New York, N. Y.

LIEBER, FRANCIS:
> An address on secession. Delivered in South Carolina in the year 1851. 12 pp. pamphlet. No. 77. 1865. Loyal Publication Society. New York, N. Y.

LINCOLN, ABRAHAM:
> *See* J. G. Nicolay and John Hay, ed., E. P. Oberholtzer, ed., J. T. Morse, Jr., ed.

LODGE, HENRY CABOT, editor:
> The works of Alexander Hamilton. Constitutional edition. 12 volumes. Approximately 450 pp. each. Cloth. 1904. Putnam. New York, N. Y.

> The federalist. A commentary on the Constitution of the United States being a collection of essays written in support of the Constitution agreed upon September 17, 1787, by the Federal Convention reprinted from the original text of Alexander Hamilton, John Jay, and James Madison. With an introduction by Charles W. Pierson of the New York bar, 586 pp. cloth. 1888. Putnam. New York, N. Y.

LOUISIANA:
> Official journal of the proceedings of the convention of the state of Louisiana. By authority. 330 pp. cloth. 1861. J. O. Nixon, printer to the state convention. New Orleans, La.

LOWNDES, WILLIAM:
> *See* H. H. (Mrs. St. Julien) Revenel.

LUNT, GEORGE:
> The origin of the late war: traced from the beginning of the Constitution to the revolt of the southern states. 491 pp. cloth. 1866. D. Appleton. New York, N. Y.

MACDONALD, WILLIAM, editor:
> Documentary source book of American history. 1606-1926. Third edition. 713 pp. cloth. 1926. First edition. 1908. Macmillan. New York, N. Y.

MACHENRY, GEORGE:
> *See* James A. Bayard.

SELECT BIBLIOGRAPHY

McDOUGAL, (Mrs.) MARION GLEASON:
Fugitive slaves 1619-1865. Prepared under the direction of Albert Bushnell Hart. 150 pp. cloth. 1891. Fay House Monographs no. 3. Ginn & Co. Boston, Mass.

MACON, NATHANIEL:
Nathaniel Macon correspondence. The John P. Branch Historical Papers of Randolph-Macon College. June, 1909. Vol. III, no. 1, pp. 27-93 Ashland, Va.

See K. P. Battle, ed., W. E. Dodd.

McREE, GRIFFITH JOHN:
Life and correspondence of James Iredell, one of the associate justices of the supreme court of the United States. 2 volumes. I, 570 pp.; II, 605 pp. cloth. 1857-1858. No index. D. Appleton. New York, N. Y .

MADISON, JAMES:
See Gaillard Hunt, ed., J. T. Morse, Jr., ed.

MALONE, DUMAS:
The public life of Thomas Cooper, 1783-1839. 432 pp. cloth. 1926. Yale University Press. New Haven, Conn. Oxford University Press. London, Eng.

MARSHALL, JOHN:
See A. J. Beveridge, W. E. Dodd, J. T. Morse, Jr., ed.

MASON, EDWARD CAMPBELL:
The veto power. Its origin, development and function in the government of the United States (1789-1889). Harvard Historical Monographs no. 1. edited by Albert Bushnell Hart. 232 pp. cloth. 1890. Ginn & Co. Boston, Mass.

MASON, GEORGE:
See K. M. Rowland.

MASON, JAMES MURRAY:
See Virginia Mason.

MASON, VIRGINIA:
The public life and diplomatic correspondence of James M. Mason with some personal history. 603 pp. cloth. 1906. The Neale Publishing Co. New York, N. Y., and Washington, D. C. Also published at Roanoke, Virginia, by the Stone Printing and Manufacturing Co. in 1903, and signed " by his daughter."

MAYES, EDWARD:
>   Lucius Q. C. Lamar: his life, times, and speeches 1825-1893. 820 pp. cloth. 1896. Methodist Publishing House. Barbee and Smith, agents. Nashville, Tenn.

MEIGS, WILLIAM MONTGOMERY:
>   The growth of the Constitution in the Federal Convention of 1787. An effort to trace the origin and development of each separate clause from its first suggestion in that body to the form finally approved. Containing also a fac-simile of a heretofore unpublished manuscript of the first draft of the instrument made for use in the committee of detail. 374 pp. cloth. 1900. J. B. Lippincott. Philadelphia, Pa.

MEMMINGER, CHRISTOPHER GUSTAVUS:
>   *See* H. D. Capers.

MERRIAM, CHARLES EDWARD:
>   History of the theory of sovereignty since Rousseau. 232 pp. cloth. 1900. Studies in History, Economics and Public Law by the Faculty of Political Science of Columbia University. Vol. XII, no. 4. Columbia University Press. New York, N. Y.

>   The political philosophy of John C. Calhoun. In Studies in Southern History and Politics. Pp. 319-338. Cloth. 1914. Columbia University Press. New York, N. Y.

>   A history of American political theories. 364 pp. cloth. 1920. Macmillan. New York, N. Y.

MERRITT, ELIZABETH:
>   James Henry Hammond 1807-1864. Johns Hopkins University Studies in Historical and Political Science. Series XLI, no. 4, 151 pp. cloth. 1923. Johns Hopkins Press. Baltimore, Md.

MISSISSIPPI:
>   Journal of the state convention and ordinances and resolutions adopted in January, 1861, with an appendix published by order of the convention. 256 pp. paper. 1861. No index. E. Barksdale, state printer. Jackson, Miss.

>   *See* C. C. Hearon, T. H. Woods.

MONROE, JAMES:
>   *See* S. M. Hamilton, ed., J. L. Morse, Jr., ed.

MOORE, S. McD.:
>   Substance of a speech delivered by S. McD. Moore of Rockbridge in the Convention of Virginia, on his resolutions on federal relations, on the 24th of February, 1861. 24 pp. pamphlet. 1861. Whig Book & Job Office. Richmond, Va.

SELECT BIBLIOGRAPHY

MORSE, JOHN TORREY, JR., editor:
> American Statesmen Series. By various authors. 31 volumes. Approximately 325 pp. each. Cloth. 1898. Houghton Mifflin. Boston, Mass., and New York, N. Y.

MUNFORD, BEVERLEY BLAND:
> Virginia's attitude towards slavery and secession. 329 pp. cloth. 1909. Longmans Green. New York, N. Y.

MURPHY, ARCHIBALD DeBOW:
> *See* W. H. Hoyt, ed.

NATIONAL DEMOCRATIC EXECUTIVE COMMITTEE:
> Address to the democracy and the people of the United States, . . . 16 pp. pamphlet. 1860. M'Gill & Withrow. Washington, D. C.

[NICHOLAS, P. N.] " Agricola ":
> Virginia doctrines not nullification. 52 pp. pamphlet. 1832. Material first published in the Richmond Enquirer between the 17th of August and the 15th of September, 1832. Samuel Shepherd. Richmond, Va.

NICOLAY, JOHN GEORGE, and HAY, JOHN:
> Abraham Lincoln complete works, comprising his speeches, letters, state papers, and miscellaneous writings. 2 volumes. I, 695 pp.; II, 770 pp. cloth. 1894. Century. New York, N. Y.

NILES, HEZEKIAH:
> Things as they are, or federalism turned inside out!! Being a collection of extracts from federal papers, etc., and remarks upon them, originally written for and published in the Evening Post. 75 pp. pamphlet. 1809. Evening Post. Baltimore, Md.

> Niles' Weekly Register.

NORTH CAROLINA:
> Debate on Mr. Fisher's resolutions against caucuses in the House of Commons of North-Carolina in December, 1823. 83 pp. buckram. 1824. J. Gales & Sons. Raleigh, N. C.

> Proceedings and debates of the convention of North-Carolina called to amend the constitution of the state . . . which assembled at Raleigh, June 4, 1835 . . . 424 pp. cloth. 1836. J. Gales & Son. Raleigh, N. C.

> Journal of the convention of the people of North Carolina . . . [1861-1862]. 4 volumes bound in one; approximately 25 pp. each. Cloth. 1862. J. W. Syme, printer to the convention. Raleigh, N. C. *See* K. P. Battle, W. K. Boyd, R. H. Taylor, H. M. Wagstaff, C C. Weaver.

THE SOUTH AS A CONSCIOUS MINORITY

NORTH CAROLINA UNIVERSITY:

>The James Sprunt Historical Publications, nos. 1-11, edited by J. G. de Roulhac Hamilton and Henry McGilbert Wagstaff. First eight volumes bear the title of James Sprunt Historical Monographs. Approximately 100 pp. each. Paper. 1900-1910. Published by the University of North Carolina Press. Chapel Hill, N. C.

OBERHOLTZER, ELLIS PAXON, editor:

>American Crisis Biographies. By various authors. 20 volumes. Approximately 350 pp. each. Cloth. About 1908. George W. Jacobs. Philadelphia, Pa.

OWSLEY, FRANK LAWRENCE:

>State rights in the confederacy. 290 pp. cloth. 1925. University of Chicago Press. Chicago, Ill.

PALMER, BENJAMIN MORGAN:

>A vindication of secession and the South from the strictures of Rev. R. J. Breckinridge, D.D. LL.D., in the Danville Quarterly Review. 46 pp. pamphlet. 1861. (From the Southern Presbyterian Review for April, 1861.) Southern Guardian Steam-power Press. Charleston, S. C.

>The life and letters of James Henley Thornwell, D.D. LL.D., ex-president of the South Carolina college . . . 614 pp. cloth. 1875. Whittet & Shepperson. Richmond, Va.

PEARCE, HAYWOOD JEFFERSON, JR.:

>Benjamin H. Hill, secession and reconstruction. 330 pp. cloth. 1928. University of Chicago Press. Chicago, Ill.

PEARCE, JAMES ALFORD, and PRATT, THOMAS G.:

>An appeal for the Union. Letter of the Hon. Thomas G. Pratt and Hon. James Alford Pearce United States Senators, to their constituents, the people of Maryland. Pamphlet.

PERRY, BENJAMIN FRANKLIN:

>Speech . . . delivered in the House of Representatives of South-Carolina on the 11th December, 1850, on a number of propositions referred to the committee of the whole on the state and federal affairs. 40 pp. pamphlet. 1851. J. B. Nixon. Charleston, S. C.

PETIGRU, JAMES LOUIS:

>*See* J. P. Carson.

SELECT BIBLIOGRAPHY

PHILLIPS, ULRICH BONNELL:

Georgia and state rights. A study of the political history of Georgia from the revolution to the Civil War, with particular regard to federal relations. American Historical Association. Annual Report, 1901. Vol. II, 360 pp. cloth. 1902. Government Printing Office. Washington, D. C.

The southern Whigs 1834-1854. In Turner Essays in American History. Pp. 203-229. Cloth. 1910. Henry Holt. New York, N. Y.

The correspondence of Robert Toombs, Alexander H. Stephens and Howell Cobb. American Historical Association. Annual Report, 1911. Vol. II, 759 pp. cloth. 1913. Government Printing Office. Washington, D. C.

The life of Robert Toombs. 281 pp. cloth. 1913. Macmillan. New York, N. Y.

The literary movement for secession. In Studies in History and Politics, pp. 26-60. Also printed separately as a pamphlet, 1914. Columbia University Press. New York, N. Y.

American negro slavery. A survey of the supply, employment and control of negro labor as determined by the plantation régime. 529 pp. cloth. 1918. D. Appleton. New York, N. Y.

PIKE, ALBERT:

State or province? Bond or free? Addressed particularly to the people of Arkansas. 40 pp. pamphlet. 1861.

PINCKNEY, MARIA:

The quintessence of long speeches, arranged as a political catechism: by a lady for her god-daughter. 24 pp. pamphlet. 1830. A. E. Miller. Charleston, S. C.

POLK, JAMES KNOX:
See M. M. Quaife, ed.

POLLARD, EDWARD ALBERT:

The lost cause. A new southern history of the war of the confederates. Comprising a full and authentic account of the rise and progress of the late southern Confederacy—the campaigns, battles, incidents, and adventures of the most gigantic struggle of the world's history. . . . 752 pp. cloth. 1866. E. B. Treat. New York, N. Y.

PORTER, KIRK HAROLD, editor:

National party platforms. 522 pp. cloth. 1924. Macmillan, New York, N. Y.

THE SOUTH AS A CONSCIOUS MINORITY

PORTER, WILLIAM DENNISON:
> State sovereignty and the doctrine of coercion, . . . together with a letter from Hon. J. K. Paulding, former sec. of navy. The right to secede by "States." 36 pp. pamphlet. 1860. Ivans & Cogswell. Charleston, S. C. Also published under pseud. "Rutledge" with the title: Mr. Douglas and the doctrine of coercion . . .

POWELL, EDWARD PAYSON:
> Nullification and secession in the United States. A history of the six attempts during the first century of the Republic. 461 pp. cloth. 1897. Putnam. New York, N. Y.

[POWELL, SAMUEL]:
> Notes on Thomas Prentice Kettell's southern wealth and northern profits. 31 pp. pamphlet. 1861. C. Sherman & Son. Philadelphia, Pa.

PRATT, THOMAS G.:
> *See* J. A. Pearce.

QUAIFE, MILO MILTON, editor:
> The diary of James K. Polk during his presidency, 1845 to 1849. Now first printed from the original manuscript in the collections of the Chicago Historical Society . . . with an introduction by Andrew Cunningham McLaughlin. 4 volumes. Approximately 500 pp. each. Cloth. 1910. A. C. McClurg. Chicago, Ill.

QUITMAN, JOHN ANTHONY:
> *See* J. F. H. Claiborne.

RALSTON, G.:
> *See* James A. Bayard.

RANDOLPH, JOHN:
> *See* W. C. Bruce, J. T. Morse, Jr., ed.

RANDOLPH-MACON COLLEGE:
> The John P. Branch Historical Papers of Randolph-Macon College. Bound in five volumes. Approximately 350 pp. each. 1901-1918. Published annually by the Department of History of Randolph-Macon College. Ashland, Va. Printed by the Richmond Press and others in Richmond, Va. William E. Dodd edited the first two volumes; Charles H. Ambler the last three.

RAVENEL, HARRIOTT HARRY (RUTLEDGE): Mrs. St. Julien Ravenel:
> Life and times of William Lowndes of South Carolina. 1782-1822. 257 pp. cloth. 1901. Houghton Mifflin. Boston, Mass., and New York, N. Y.

SELECT BIBLIOGRAPHY

REED, JOHN CALVIN:
>The brothers war. 456 pp. cloth. 1905. Little Brown. Boston, Mass.

REGISTER of debates in Congress, comprising the leading debates and incidents of the second session of the eighteenth Congress (Dec. 6, 1824 to the first session of the twenty-fifth Congress, Oct. 16, 1837) together with an appendix containing the most important state papers and public documents . . . 14 volumes. Cloth. 1825-1837. Gales & Seaton. Washington, D. C.

RHETT, ROBERT BARNWELL:
>Oration . . . before the legislature of South Carolina, November 28, 1850. The death and funeral ceremonies of John Caldwell Calhoun . . . Pp. 119-168. Pamphlet. 1850. A. S. Johnston. Columbia, S. C.

RICHARDSON, JAMES DANIEL, editor:
>A compilation of the messages and papers of the presidents, 1789-1907. 11 volumes. Approximately 700 pp. each. Cloth. 1897-1911. Bureau of National Literature and Art. New York, N. Y.

RICHMOND COLLEGE:
>Richmond College Historical Papers. Edited by D. R. Anderson and published annually since 1915 at Richmond, Va.

RICHMOND ENQUIRER.

RITCHIE, THOMAS:
>Unpublished letters of Thomas Ritchie. John P. Branch Historical Papers of Randolph-Macon College. June, 1911. Vol. III, no. 3, pp. 199-252.

>Address of the Democratic Central Committee to the voters of Virginia, October 24, 1840. *Ibid.,* pp. 263-270.

>Ritchie Letters. *Ibid.,* June, 1916. IV, no. 4, pp. 372-418.

>Thomas Ritchie's letter containing reminiscences of Henry Clay and the compromise. 12 pp. pamphlet. (From the Richmond Enquirer of September 10, 1852.) This was a letter to the editors of the Richmond Enquirer, dated September 6, 1852.

>*See* C. H. Ambler.

ROANE, SPENCER:
>Roane Correspondence 1799-1821. The John P. Branch Historical Papers of Randolph-Macon College. June, 1905. Vol. II, no. 1, pp. 123-142. Ashland, Va.

Interesting case. Hunter v. Martin. On a special mandate from the Supreme Court of the United States. Judge Spencer Roane's opinion. *Ibid.*, June, 1904. Vol. I, no. 4, pp. 326-357. Reprinted from the Richmond Enquirer for February 1, 1816.

Roane on the national Constitution. *Ibid.*, June, 1905. Vol. II, no. 1, pp. 47-121. Reprints from the Richmond Enquirer and Richmond Chronicle, March 30 to June 22, 1819, comprising Roane's "Hampden" and "Amphictyon" letters.

Virginia Opposition to Chief Justice Marshall. *Ibid.*, June, 1906. Vol. II, no. 2, pp. 78-183. Reprints from the Richmond Enquirer, May 5 to June 8, 1821, comprising Roane's "Algernon Sidney" letters.

Letters of Spencer Roane, 1788-1822. Bulletin of the New York Public Library. March, 1906. Vol. X, no. 3, pp. 167-180. Printed from the original manuscripts.

ROWLAND, DUNBAR, editor:
Jefferson Davis, constitutionalist. His letters, papers and speeches. 10 volumes. Approximately 600 pp. each. Cloth. 1923. Mississippi Department of Archives and History. Jackson, Miss.

ROWLAND, KATE MASON:
The life of George Mason, 1725-1792. . . . including his speeches, public papers, and correspondence; with an introduction by General Fitzhugh Lee. 2 volumes. I, 454 pp.; II, 527 pp. cloth. 1892. Putnam. New York, N. Y.

RUFFIN, EDMUND:
The political economy of slavery; or, the institution considered in regard to its influence on public wealth and the general welfare. 31 pp. pamphlet. 1857? L. Towers. Washington, D. C.

RUFFIN, THOMAS:
See J. G. de R. Hamilton.

RUSSEL, ROBERT ROYAL:
Economic aspects of southern sectionalism, 1840-1861. 325 pp. cloth. 1924. University of Illinois Studies in the Social Sciences. 1923. Vol. IX, nos. 1 & 2. University of Illinois Press. Urbana, Illinois.

RUSSELL, JOHN HENDERSON:
The free negro in Virginia, 1619-1865. 194 pp. cloth. 1913. Johns Hopkins University Studies in Historical and Political Science. Vol. XXXI, no. 3. Johns Hopkins Press. Baltimore, Md.

SELECT BIBLIOGRAPHY

Scott, Charles L.:
Address of the Hon. Charles L. Scott of California, to his constituents on the constitutional right of secession. 16 pp. pamphlet.

[Scott, John] " Barbarossa ":
The lost principle; or the sectional equilibrium: How it was created—How destroyed—How it may be restored. 266 pp. cloth. 1860. No index. James Woodhouse. Richmond, Va.

Segar, Joseph:
Speech of Joseph Segar, Esq., of the York District delivered in the House of Delegates of Virginia, March the 30th, 1861, on the resolutions of the Senate, directing the governor of Virginia to seize, by military force, the U. S. guns at Bellona Arsenal, and on the secession of Virginia. 23 pp. pamphlet.

Seward, William Henry:
The irrepressible conflict. A speech . . . delivered at Rochester, Monday, October 25, 1858. 15 pp. pamphlet. 1858. New York Tribune Office. New York, N. Y.

Shipp, John Edgar Dawson:
Giant Days; or, the life and times of William H. Crawford, embracing also excerpts from his diary, letters and speeches, together with a copious index to the whole. 266 pp. cloth. 1909. Southern Printers. Americus, Ga.

Shryock, Richard Harrison:
Georgia and the Union in 1850. 406 pp. cloth. 1926. Duke University Press. Durham, N. C.

" Sidney, Edward William ":
See N. B. Tucker.

Sioussat, St. George Leakin:
Tennessee and national political parties, 1850-1860. American Historical Association. Annual Report, 1914. Vol. I, pp. 243-258. Cloth. 1916. Washington, D. C.

Smith, Edward Conrad:
The borderland in the Civil War. 412 pp. cloth. 1927. Macmillan. New York.

Smith, Robert Hardy:
An address to the citizens of Alabama on the Constitution and laws of the Confederate States of America. . . . at Temperance Hall on the 30th of March, 1861. 24 pp. pamphlet. 1861. Mobile Daily Register. Mobile, Alabama.

THE SOUTH AS A CONSCIOUS MINORITY

SMITH, WILLIAM RUSSELL:

The history and debates of the convention of the people of Alabama, begun and held in the city of Montgomery, on the seventh day of January, 1861; in which are preserved the speeches of the secret sessions and many valuable state papers. 464 pp. cloth. 1861. Wood, Hanleiter, Rice and Co. Atlanta, Ga.

SOUTH CAROLINA:

Journal of the conventions of the people of South Carolina held in 1832, 1833 and 1852. 173 pp. cloth. 1860. R. B. Gibbes, state printer. Columbia, S. C. Also separately published.

Journal of the convention of the people of South Carolina in 1860, 1861 and 1862. Together with the ordinances, reports, resolutions, etc. 873 pp. cloth. 1862. R. W. Gibbes, state printer. Columbia, S. C.

Letters on the nullification movement in South Carolina, 1830-1834. The American Historical Review, July, 1901, and October, 1901. Vol. VI, no. 4, pp. 736-765; Vol. VII, no. 1, pp. 92-119. Macmillan. New York, N. Y.

See Frederic Bancroft, C. S. Boucher, P. M. Hamer, D. F. Houston.

SOUTHERN Review (1828-1834). Published quarterly and bound in 8 volumes of apparently 500 pp. each. Printed and published by A. E. Miller for the proprietors. Charleston, S. C.

SPENCE, JAMES:

The American Union; its effect on national character and policy, with an inquiry into secession as a constitutional right, and the causes of the disruption. 366 pp. cloth. 1861. No index. Richard Bentley, London, Eng.

SPRUNT, JAMES:

See North Carolina University for James Sprunt Publications.

STATE RIGHTS ASSOCIATION:

Proceedings of the state rights celebration at Charleston, S. C., July 1, 1830, containing the speeches of Hon. Wm. Drayton & Hon. R. Y. Hayne, who were invited guests; also of Langdon Cheves, James Hamilton, Jr., and Robert J. Turnbull, esqurs. And the remarks of his honor the intendant, H. L. Pinckney, to which is added the volunteer toasts given on the occasion. 56 pp. pamphlet. 1830. A. E. Miller. Charleston, S. C.

Proceedings of the state rights and free trade convention held in Charleston, (S. C.) on the 22nd and 25th February, 1832. Political Tract no. 7. 16 pp. pamphlet. 1832. Published by the State Rights and Free Trade Association. Charleston, S. C.

SELECT BIBLIOGRAPHY

STEPHENS, ALEXANDER HAMILTON:

Extract from a speech by Alexander H. Stephens, vice-president of the Confederate States, delivered in the secession convention of Georgia, January, 1861. 4 pp. pamphlet.

A constitutional view of the late war between the states; its causes, character, conduct and results. Presented in a series of colloquies at Liberty Hall. 2 volumes. I, 654 pp.; II, 827 pp. cloth. First published, 1867. National Publshing Co. Philadelphia, Pa., and elsewhere.

The reviewers reviewed; a supplement to the "War between the States" etc., with an appendix in review of "reconstruction" so called. 273 pp. cloth. 1872. D. Appleton. New York, N. Y.

A comprehensive and popular history of the United States, embracing a full account of the discovery and settlement of the country . . . and events down to the present time. 1048 pp. cloth. 1882. Strong. Dallas, Texas, and Vicksburg, Miss.

See M. L. Avary, ed., Henry Cleveland, ed., R. M. Johnston, E. P. Oberholtzer, ed.

STEPHENSON, NATHANIEL WRIGHT:

A theory of Jefferson Davis. American Historical Review. October, 1915. Vol. XXI, no. 1, pp. 73-90. Also separately published. Macmillan. New York, N. Y.

Calhoun, 1812 and after. American Historical Review. July, 1926. Vol. XXV, no. 4, pp. 701-707. .

TAYLOR, JOHN:

Definition of parties; or the political effects of the paper system considered. 16 pp. pamphlet. 1794. Francis Bailey. Philadelphia, Pa.

An Enquiry into the principles and tendency of certain public measures. 92 pp. pamphlet. 1794. Thomas Dobson. Philadelphia, Pa.

A defence of the measures of the administration of Thomas Jefferson. 88 pp. pamphlet. 1805. The pamphlet was signed "Curtius," supposedly, John Taylor. William Olney. Providence, R. I.

An Inquiry into the principles and policy of the government of the United States. 656 pp. cloth. 1814. No index. Green & Cady. Fredericksburg, Va.

Construction construed and constituents vindicated. 344 pp. cloth. 1820. No index. Shepherd and Pollard. Richmond, Va.

Tyranny Unmasked. 349 pp. cloth. 1822. No index. Davis and Force. Washington, D. C.

New Views of the Constitution of the United States. 316 pp. cloth. 1823. No index. Way and Gideon. Washington, D. C.

Letters of John Taylor of Caroline County, Virginia. The John P. Branch Historical Papers of Randolph-Macon College. June, 1908. Vol. II, nos. 3 & 4, pp. 252-353. Ashland, Va.

See also W. E. Dodd, Gaillard Hunt, ed., B. F. Wright, Jr.

TAYLOR, ROSSER HOWARD:

The Free Negro in North Carolina. The James Sprunt Historical Publications. Vol. XVII, no. 1, pp. 1-26. Paper. 1920. North Carolina Historical Society. Chapel Hill, N. C.

TEXAS:

Journal of the secession convention of Texas 1861. 469 pp. cloth. 1912. Austin Printing Co. Austin, Texas. Printed for the Texas Library and Historical Commission.

THORNWELL, JAMES HENLEY:

The state of the country: an article republished from the Southern Presbyterian Review. 32 pp. pamphlet. 1861. Southern Guardian Steam Power Press. Columbia, S. C.

See B. M. Palmer.

TILDEN, SAMUEL JONES:
See John Bigelow.

TOOMBS, ROBERT:
See U. B. Phillips.

TORRE, D.:

Is southern civilization worth preserving? 39 pp. pamphlet. 1851. Reprinted from the Southern Presbyterian Review for January, 1851. Southern Rights Association. Charleston, S. C.

TOWNSEND, JOHN:

The South alone, should govern the South. And African slavery should be controlled by those only, who are friendly to it. Originally published in the Charleston Mercury. Fourth edition. 62 pp. pamphlet. 1860. First edition, 1860. Evans and Cogswell. Charleston, S. C.

The doom of slavery in the union: its safety out of it. 39 pp. pamphlet. 1860. Evans and Cogswell. Charleston, S. C. This pamphlet consisted of the address of the Hon. John Townsend delivered before the Edisto Island vigilant association, October 29, 1860.

SELECT BIBLIOGRAPHY

TUCKER, HENRY ST. GEORGE:
> Lectures on constitutional law, for the use of the law class at the University of Virginia. 242 pp. cloth. 1843. No index. Shepherd & Colin. Richmond, Va.

TUCKER, HENRY ST. GEORGE (1853-   ):
> Judge Story's position on the so-called general welfare clause. American Law Association Journal, July and August, 1927. Vol. XIII, pp. 363-370; 465-469. Reprinted as Senate Document 17, 70 Congress, 1 session; and again in the Constitutional Review for January, 1929. Vol. XIII, pp. 13-35.

TUCKER, NATHANIEL BEVERLEY:
> The partisan leader; a tale of the future. 2 volumes bound in one. 201 pp. cloth. 1836. Published under the pen-name Edward William Sidney and republished in 1863.
>
> Correspondence of Judge N. B. Tucker. William and Mary College Quarterly Historical Magazine. October, 1903, and January, 1904. Vol. XII, pp. 84-95, 142-155. Williamsburg, Va.
>
> *See* M. H. Woodfin.

TUCKER, ST. GEORGE:
> View of the Constitution of the United States. Vol. I, appendix, note D, pp. 140-377 of Tucker's Blackstone's Commentaries. (1803.) Birch and Small. Philadelphia, Pa.

TURNBULL, ROBERT J.:
> Observations on state sovereignty, federal usurpations, and state interposition. 144 pp. paper. 1850. Published by Cornish, Lamport, and Co. New York, N. Y.

[TURNBULL, ROBERT JAMES] " Brutus ":
> The crisis: or, essays on the usurpations of the federal government. 166 pp. cloth. 1827. No index. A. E. Miller. Charleston, S. C.

TYLER, LYON G.:
> The letters and times of the Tylers. 2 volumes. I, 633 pp.; II, 736 pp. cloth. 1884-1885. Whittet & Shepperson. Richmond, Va.

UNITED STATES:
> United States Supreme Court Reports.
>
> Negro population in the United States. 1790-1915. 844 pp. cloth. 1918. Bureau of the Census. Government Printing Office. Washington, D. C.

Documents illustrative of the formation of the Union of the American states. 1115 pp. cloth. 1927. House Document no. 398. 69 Congress, 1 session. Edited by Charles C. Tansill. Government Printing Office. Washington, D. C.

Biographical directory of the American Congress 1774-1927. . . . compiled under the direction of the joint committee on printing. Ansel Wold, clerk. 1740 pp. cloth. 1928. House Document 783. 69 Congress, 2 session. Government Printing Office. Washington, D. C.

UPSHUR, ABEL PARKER:

A brief enquiry into the true nature and character of our federal government being a review of Judge Story's commentaries on the Constitution of the United States. 131 pp. cloth. 1840. Edmund and Julian C. Ruffin. Petersburg, Va. Republished in 1863 from the original Petersburg edition by John Campbell. Philadelphia, Pa.

VIRGINIA:

Proceedings and debates of the Virginia state convention of 1829-1830. To which are subjoined, the new constitution of Virginia, and the votes of the people. 919 pp. cloth. 1830. No index. Printed by S. Shepherd & Co. for Ritchie & Cook. Richmond, Va.

Alien and sedition laws: debates in the House of Delegates of Virginia in December, 1798, on resolutions before the House on the acts of Congress called the Alien and Sedition Laws. 187 pp. paper. 1912. Senate Document 873. 62 Congress, 2 sessions. Government Printing Office. Washington, D. C.

The Virginia Report of 1799-1800, touching the Alien and Sedition Laws; together with the Virginia resolutions of December 21, 1798, the debate and proceedings thereon in the House of Delegates of Virginia, and several other documents illustrative of the report and resolutions. 264 pp. cloth. 1850. J. W. Randolph. Richmond, Va.

Preamble and resolutions adopted by the General Assembly of Virginia on the subject of the right of the state legislatures to instruct their senators in Congress. 28 pp. pamphlet. 1812.

Virginia and Texas, 1844. Letters reprinted in The John P. Branch Historical Papers of Randolph-Macon College. June, 1913. IV, no. 1, pp. 116-137. Ashland, Va.

Journal, acts and proceedings of a general convention of state of Virginia, assembled at Richmond on Monday the fourteenth day of October, eighteen hundred and fifty. 424 pp. cloth. 1850. William Culley. Richmond, Va.

Journal of the acts and proceedings of a general convention of the state of Virginia, assembled at Richmond on Wednesday, the thirteenth day of February, eighteen hundred and sixty-one. 459 pp. cloth. 1861. W. M. Elliott. Richmond, Va. The Appendix contains the Journal of the Committee of the Whole, and numerous other ordinances and reports.

The change of secession sentiment in Virgina in 1861. [Letters of Judge Edward Calohill Burks and of Bishop James Harvey Otis.] The American Historical Review. October, 1925. Vol. XXX, no. 1, pp. 82-101. Macmillan. New York, N. Y.

See C. H. Ambler, B. B. Munford, R. L. Dabney, J. H. Russell.

" VIRGINIUS ":

Four essays on the right and propriety of secession by southern states, by a member of the bar of Richmond. 56 pp. pamphlet. 1861. Ritchie & Dunnavant. Richmond, Va.

WAGSTAFF, HENRY MCGILBERT:

State rights and political parties in North Carolina 1776-1861. 155 pp. cloth. 1906. The Johns Hopkins University Studies in Historical and Political Science. Series 24, nos. 7-8. The Johns Hopkins Press. Baltimore, Md.

WALKER, ROBERT JAMES:

Letters of Mr. Walker, of Mississippi, relative to the reannexation of Texas: in reply to the call of the people of Carroll County, Kentucky, to communicate his views on that subject. 32 pp. pamphlet. 1844. Printed at the Globe Office. Washington, D. C.

An appeal for the Union. Letter . . . September 30, 1856, to Hon. Charles Shaler and others, Democratic Committee, Pittsburgh, Pennsylvania. 15 pp. pamphlet.

See W. E. Dodd.

WARREN, CHARLES:

New light on the history of the federal judiciary act of 1789. Harvard Law Review. November, 1923. Vol. 37, pp. 49-132. Cambridge, Mass.

The Supreme Court in United States History. Revised edition. 2 volumes. I, 814 pp.; II, 812 pp. cloth. 1926. First published in 3 volumes in 1922. Little Brown. Boston, Mass.

The making of the Constitution. 832 pp. cloth. 1929. Little Brown. Boston, Mass.

WEAVER, CHARLES CLINTON:
>   Internal Improvements in North Carolina previous to 1860. 94 pp.
>   cloth. 1903. Johns Hopkins University Studies in History and Politi-
>   cal Science. 1903. Series 21, nos. 3-4. The Johns Hopkins University
>   Press. Baltimore, Md.

WHITE, MELVIN JOHNSON:
>   The secession movement in the United States 1847-1852. 122 pp.
>   cloth. 1916. Tulane University Press. New Orleans, La.

WIGFALL, LOUIS TRESVANT:
>   Speech . . . on the pending political issues; delivered at Tyler,
>   Smith County, Texas on September 3, 1860. 32 pp. pamphlet. Pub-
>   lished by request of the Breckinridge and Lane Club of Smith
>   County.

WILLOUGHBY, WESTEL WOODBURY:
>   The constitutional law of the United States. Second edition. 3
>   volumes. 2022 pp. numbered consecutively. Cloth. 1929. First
>   edition, 2 volumes, 1910. Baker, Voorhis. New York, N. Y.

WISE, BENTON HAXALL:
>   The life of Henry A. Wise of Virginia. 1806-1876. 434 pp. cloth.
>   1899. Macmillan Co. New York, N. Y.

WISE, HENRY ALEXANDER:
>   Seven decades of the Union. The humanities and materialism, illus-
>   trated by a memoir of John Tyler, with reminiscences of some of his
>   great contemporaries. The transition state of this nation—its dangers
>   and their remedy. 320 pp. cloth. 1876. No index. J. B. Lippincott.
>   Philadelphia, Pa.

>   *See* B. H. Wise.

WOLFE, SAML. M.:
>   Helper's Impending Crisis dissected. 223 pp. paper. 1860. J. T.
>   Lloyd, agt. New York, N. Y.

WOODFIN, MAUDE HOWLETT:
>   Nathanial Beverley Tucker: His writings and political theories, with
>   a sketch of his life. Richmond College Historical Papers. June, 1917.
>   Vol. I, no. 1, pp. 9-42. Published annually at Richmond, Va.

WOODS, THOMAS H.:
>   A sketch of the Mississippi Secession Convention of 1861,—its mem-
>   bership and work. Publications of the Mississippi Historical Society.
>   Vol. VI, pp. 91-104.

SELECT BIBLIOGRAPHY

WRIGHT, BENJAMIN FLETCHER, JR., editor:

A source book of American political theory. Edited with introductory notes. 644 pp. cloth. 1929. Macmillan. New York, N. Y.

The philosopher of Jeffersonian democracy. American Political Science Review, November, 1928. Vol. XXII, pp. 870-892.

YANCEY, WILLIAM LOWNDES:

See J. W. DuBose.

INDEX

INDEX

INDEX

gress, 195; non-coercion, 214-215, 217, 218.

Burley, James: right of revolution, 199 note.

Butler, Pierce: sectionalism, 8; judiciary, 62-63.

Byrdsall, Fitzwilliam: slavery in the territories, 154-155.

Cabell, Judge: Fairfax Case, 69.

Cabinet: seats in Congress, 259-260.

Calhoun, John C.: separation of churches, 16 note; slavery, 19, 148-149, 150, 155; control of central government, 21; biographical sketch, 28; the South as a minority, 28-29; sectionalism in appointments, revenues, and disbursements, 33 and note; cases in law and equity, 67; concurrent voice, 77-79; numerical majority rule, 81; dual executive plan, 94-95; bicameralism in South Carolina, 102; sectional equilibrium, 108 note, 110 note; nationalism, 116; parties, 112-113, 121, 122, 189; constitutionalism, 76, 128, 129, 147, 150; a logic chopper, 136 and note; the amending clause, 131-140, 168, 237; nullification, 137-141 note, 236, 237; territories, 148-149, 150, 155; retaliation, 164, 165; Missouri, 178 note; Southern coöperation, 184-185 and note; dissolution of the Union, 185 note; state sovereignty, 203; references, 9 note, 16 note, 75 note.

California: 107-111.

Call, Richard K.: 17.

Campbell, John A.: sectionalism, 18; acquisition of Mexico, 180 note.

Capers, Henry D.: 255.

Carey, Henry C.: 32 note.

Carpenter, S. D.: 173 note.

Carson, Hampton L.: judiciary, 145-146 note.

Cass, Lewis: 118, 119.

Caucus, Congressional: 85-86.

"Cecil": See Fisher, S. J.

Charleston Mercury: 185, 249.

Checks and balances: 82-89; See concurrent voice.

Chesnut, James, Jr.: secession in the Confederacy, 230; slave trade in the Confederacy, 250.

Cheves, Langdon: internal improvements, 19; executive department, 93 note; sectional equilibrium, 110-111; Southern coöperation, 185-186.

Chisholm v. *Georgia:* 65.

Churches, separation of: 16 and note.

Citizenship in the Confederacy: 247-248.

Clay, C. C.: territorial growth, 24; federal disbursements, 32.

Clay, Henry: 89 note; 118.

Clingman, Thomas L.: negro, 15; sectionalism, 16; South as a minority, 27; sectional disbursements, 31; parties, 113, 114, 115, 120; references, 10 note, 13 note, 30 note, 37 note, 150 note.

Cobb, Howell: parties, 114, 122, 123 note; Southern independence, 194; right of revolution, 198; compact theory, 209-210; state sovereignty, 228-229; Confederate Constitution, 223, 260; reference, 158 note.

Cobb, T. R. R.: secession, 167; on President of the Provisional Government of the Confederacy, 223 note; Confederate Constitution, 229; Confederacy: slavery in, 247 note, citizenship in, 247, slave trade in, 250, slave states only, 252.

Coercion: See non-coercion.

Cohens v. *Virginia:* 70, 72.

Commerce, regulation of: 100.

Committee on the territories: report on sectional equilibrium, 106.

INDEX

Committees of public safety: 187-188.

Common law: 57-58, 66 and note.

Compact theory of the Union: *See* Union, nature of the; state sovereignty.

Concurrent voice: explained and defended, 77-82; checks and balances, 82-89; applied in the executive department, 89-97, in the judicial department, 97-99, in the legislative department, 99-112, in political parties, 112-126, in the Confederacy, 239-240.

Confederacy, formation of: 221; *See* Constitution, Confederate.

Confederate Constitution: *See* Constitution, Confederate.

Congress, Confederate: *See* Constitution, Confederate.

Congress, national: *See* legislative department; House of Representatives; Senate; territories; fugitive slaves.

Conner, H. W.: Southern coöperation, 186.

Consolidated republic: in the Union, 73-76; in the South, 226.

Constitution: functions of, 127-130. *See* Constitution, United States; Constitution, Confederate.

Constitution, Confederate: formation of, 221; model of, 221-225; similarity with national, 224; ratification of, 225, 229-230; terminology, 228; state sovereignty, 228-229; preamble, 233; supremacy of national law, 233, 234; amending clause, 237-239; concurrent voice, 239; admission of new states, 239; export taxes, 239; appropriations, 239, 257-260; legislative power, 242; welfare clauses, 240; internal improvements and bounties, 240-242; judiciary, 243-244; tonnage duties, 244; interstate contracts, 244; impeachment, 244-245; slavery provisions, 245-254; spoils of office, 254-257; riders, 255; tenure of office, 255; election of senators, 256; post office, 256; President, 256-257; item-veto, 258; Cabinet in Congress, 259-260.

Constitution, United States: reasons for adoption, 35-36; preamble, 42; taxing clause, 42; sweeping clauses discussed, 41-54; necessary and proper clause, 48-54; Amendment X, 41, 213; Amendment XI, 65; Amendment XII, 86 note; protection to minorities, 129 and note, 130; amending clause discussed, 130-141; slavery, 142 and note; territories, 148-155; possible amendments, 166, 167-169; model of Confederate Constitution, 221-225; comparison with Confederate Constitution, *see* Constitution, Confederate; development of, *see* Federal Convention, various state ratifying conventions, constitutional guarantees.

Constitutional Guarantees: 127-170; Southern reliance upon, 141-148, 160-164; enforcement of constitutional limitations, 130-141; the swing to constitutionalism: an explanation, 141-148; the territories, 148-155; the irrepressible conflict, 155-157; the higher law, 158-160; new schemes for enforcing, 164-167; failure as a protection, 167-170; in the Confederacy, 234-239. *See* Constitution.

Constitutional Union Party: 123.

Cooper, Thomas: welfare clauses, 47 note; parties, 113; references, 66 note, 76 note, 82 note.

Coöperationists: 184-190.

Cornerstone speech: 248. *See* A. H. Stephens.

Council of state: 94.

INDEX

INDEX

INDEX

Irrepressible conflict: 155-157.

Item-veto: 258.

Iverson, Alfred: sectionalism, 17; right of revolution, 195, 198; consolidated republic, 226.

Jackson, Andrew: presidential policies, 86-87; non-coercion, 217 note; reference, 189 note.

Jackson, James: judiciary, 63-64.

Jay, William: 14 note.

Jefferson, Thomas: the negro, 15-16; sectionalism, 18; division of powers, 34, 35, 39; local self-government, 34, 58 and note; individualism, 38 and note; internal improvements, 38, 61; amendment X, 41; general welfare clauses, 45, 46-47; necessary and proper clause, 49; judiciary, 51-52, 61-62, 72, 74 and note, 85; reduction of public offices, 60; Louisiana Purchase, 61 note; national consolidation, 75-76; parties, 114, 177; declaration of independence, 196; Kentucky Resolutions, 140, 201; slavery, 15-16, 245; references, 37 note, 73 note, 83 note, 113 note; 132 note; 140.

Jenkins, Albert G.: reorganization of executive, 96.

Johnson, Andrew: reorganization of executive, 96; reorganization of judiciary, 99.

Johnson, Cave: parties, 120 note.

Johnson, G. W.: secession and revolution, 196.

Johnson, H. V.: new amendments, 166; reference, 13 note.

Johnson, Robert W.: slavery, 194.

Johnson, William: appointed to Supreme Court, 62.

Johnston, Samuel: instruction of senators, 57.

Jones, Joseph: constitutional ambiguities, 42 note.

Judge, H. M.: slavery in territories, 155.

Judiciary, confederate: 236-237, 243-244.

Judiciary, national: structure of, 23; sectional control, 61-62, 97; inferior courts, 62-65; law and equity, 67 and note; appellate power over state courts, 68-71, 163; relation to other departments, 85; reorganization of, 98-99; applications of concurrent voice in, 97-99; position on slavery, 145; Southern reliance upon, 162; changes in sectional attitude, 162-163.

Judiciary Act of 1789: 64-65; 68-69; 163.

Kanawha Valley Star: 17.

Kennedy, John P.: Southern independence, 171-172.

Kenner, Duncan F.: slavery in the Confederacy, 246-247, 252.

Kent, Joseph: veto power, 88.

Kentucky and the judiciary: 72.

Kentucky Legislature: Alien and Sedition Acts, 55-56, 140, 201.

Kentucky Resolutions: First, 201: Second, 140.

Kettell, Thomas P.: 32 note.

Kimball, A.: secession in the Confederacy, 232.

Lamar, Lucius Q. C.: John Brown's raid, 18 note; concurrent voice, 80 note; slavery in the territories, 154; constitutionalism, 161 note; Southern independence, 193 note, 225 note; reference, 230 note.

Lamar, Mirabeau B.: 183.

"Langdon": secession, 208 note.

"Law and equity": See judiciary, national.

League of United Southerners: 188, 189.

Lee, Henry: 26.

INDEX

Legislative department: relation to executive, 85-86; applications of the concurrent voice, 99-112; extra-majority vote, 99-101; bi-cameralism, 101-102; sectional equilibrium, 104-112.

Legislatures, state: *See* state legislatures by states.

Liberty Party: 124.

Lieber, Francis: secessionists *per se,* 182 note.

Lincoln, Abraham: 12 note, 156-157, 192.

Local self-government: division of powers, 34-41; sweeping clauses, 41-54; strict construction, 54-76; in the Confederacy, 240-245.

Longstreet, A. B.: sectionalism, 8-9; South as a minority, 27; the concurrent voice, 80-81; party, 112; Texas, 183 note; Southern independence, 192-193.

Louisiana Convention of 1861: 222, 223 note, 227, 231-232.

Louisiana Purchase: 61 note, 178.

Lowndes, Rawlins: South as a minority, 26 note, 175-176.

Lumpkin, John H.: secessionist *per se,* 182; parties, 190 note.

Lumpkin, Wilson: Southern coöperation, 186.

McCulloch v. *Maryland:* 49, 51, 71, 72.

McDuffie, George: 27 note, 37.

Mackay, Charles: 173 note.

McLean, Justice: Prigg Case, 145.

McQueens, Hugh: the negro, 12 note.

Macon, Nathaniel: constitutionalism, 76; parties, 114 note.

Madison, James: South as a minority, 26; division of powers, 36; Amendment X, 41; welfare clauses, 43, 44, 45, 47; necessary and proper clause, 50-51; executive patronage, 59-60; internal improvements, 61;

judiciary, 63; concurrent voice, 79 and note; checks and balances, 88; bi-cameralism, 101-102; parties, 114; amending clause, 131; nullification, 138; charters of incorporation, 174; sweeping clauses, 177 note; compact theory, 209; non-coercion, 216; references, 58 note, 83 note, 94, 113 note. *See* Madison's Report of 1800.

Madison's Report of 1800 on the Resolutions: preamble, 44; welfare clauses, 43, 45, 47; common law, 66; implied powers, 134 note; reference, 54 note.

Marbury v. *Madison:* 62.

Marcy, William L.: parties, 119 note.

Marshall, John: necessary and proper clause, 51; cases in law and equity, 67 note; opinion in *Cohens* v. *Virginia,* 70; reference, 97.

Martin v. *Hunter's Lessee:* 69.

Mason, George: South as a minority, 26; judiciary, 63; council of state, 94; commerce clause, 26, 100; sumptuary laws, 174; growth of population, 175; non-coercion, 216; references, 11 note, 26 note, 44.

Mason, James M.: South as a minority, 25; Free Soil Convention, 121-122; slavery, 142, 193-194; Missouri question, 178; Southern independence, 193 note; right of secession, 200; references, 58 note, 150 note.

Memminger, C. G.: Model of the Confederacy, 223 note; non-coercion, 233; Confederate judiciary, 243-244; citizenship, 247; reference, 25 note.

Mercer, Charles F.: 168 note.

Mexico: acquisition of, 180 note.

Middleton, J. I.: secession in the Confederacy, 232.

INDEX

INDEX

INDEX

Segar, Joseph: 153 note.

Self-government: *See* local self-government.

Senate, United States: resolutions on slavery, 143; resolutions on state sovereignty, 202-203; reference, 40 note. *See* sectional equilibrium.

Senators: instruction of, 56-57.

Sentinel, Columbus, Georgia: Southern independence, 191.

Separation of powers: 83-84. *See* checks and balances, concurrent voice.

Seward, William H.: sectional equilibrium, 109 note; irrepressible conflict, 156; higher law, 158, 159.

Slave labor: a factor in sectionalism, 9-11.

Slavery: sectionalism, 19, 171-181; parties, 121-122; constitutional provisions, 142 and note; resolutions of the House on, 142-143; resolutions of the Senate on, 143; in the District of Columbia, 144; in the territories, 148-155; of early opinions on, 216 note; in the Confederacy, 245-254. *See* fugitive slaves, slave labor, slave trade, the negro, free negroes.

Slave trade: regulation, 25, 142 note; in the Confederacy, 249-251.

Smith, Robert H.: explanations of the Confederate Constitution: the amending clause, 238-239; bounties and internal improvements, 241-242; impeachment, 244-245; suffrage, 248; slave trade, 251; slavery, 253-254; post office, 256; presidential leadership in appropriations, 258-259.

Smith, William L.: sectionalism, 10 note; the judiciary, 64.

South. As a section, 7-21; occupation, 7-9, slave labor, 9-11, the negro, 11-16, Southern consciousness, 17-21. As a minority, 21-29; in population, 21-22; states, 22-23. Recognition of minority rôle, 24-29, 108, 109-111, 129, 130, 161, 168-170, 174-176. Control of the government, 90 and note, 93 and note, 97, 173-175, 180-181 and note.

South Carolina Convention of 1832: 30 note, 47 note, 204 note.

South Carolina Convention of 1852: on state sovereignty, 204.

South Carolina Convention of 1860-1-2: irrepressible conflict, 157; declaration of the causes of secession, 198, 206-207, 210; the Confederacy, 222, 224-225, 227, 232, 251 note.

South Carolina Declaration of the causes of secession: right of revolution, 198; state sovereignty, 206-207; compact theory of Union, 210.

South Carolina House of Representatives: manifesto on tariff, 56.

South Carolina Senate: 185 note.

Southern Address: of 1849, 12-13, 186; of 1850, 187; of 1860, 193.

Southern commercial convention: reopening the slave trade, 24-25.

Southern Confederacy: organization of, 221, 223 note; nature of the Union, 226-234. *See* Constitution, Confederate.

Southern independence: secessionists *per se,* 171-184; coöperationists, 184-190; the appeal for independence, 190-194; justifications for independence, 194-220. *See* revolution, secession, non-coercion.

Southern Literary Messenger: 20.

Southern newspaper: proposal for one at Washington, 187.

Southern Presbyterian Review: 183, 191.

Southern Quarterly Review: sectional equilibrium, 111.

Southern Review: on the judiciary, 71, 97-98.